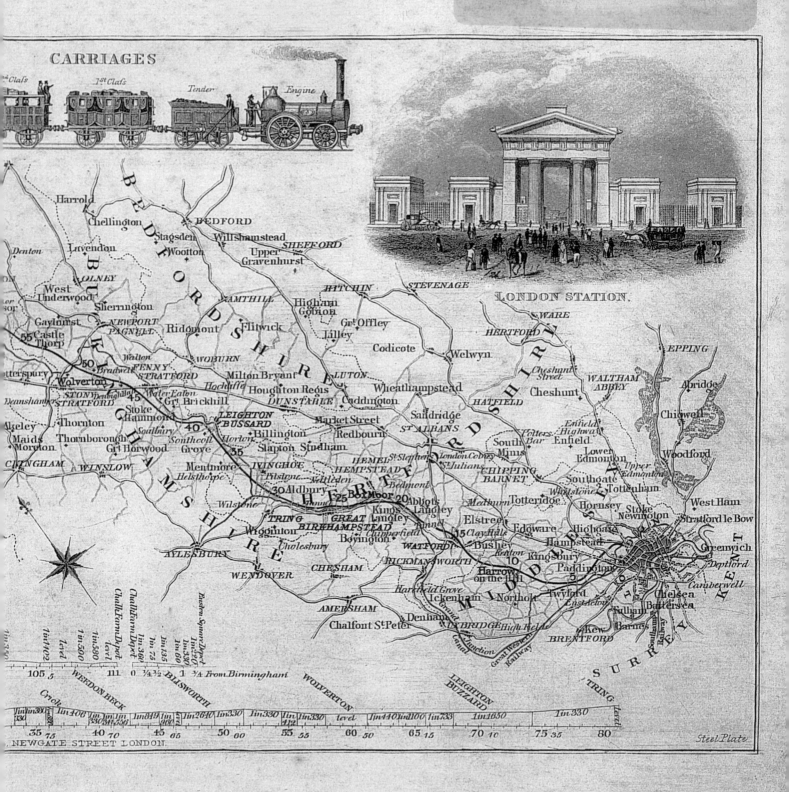

CARRIAGES

3rd Class   1st Class   Tender   Engine

LONDON STATION.

NEWGATE STREET LONDON.

Steel Plate.

RAILWAYS
and the
VICTORIAN IMAGINATION

MICHAEL FREEMAN

RAILWAYS

and the VICTORIAN IMAGINATION

MICHAEL FREEMAN

YALE UNIVERSITY PRESS
NEW HAVEN AND LONDON

'To live over other people's lives is nothing unless we
live over their perceptions, live over their growth, the
varying intensity of the same – since it is by these
they themselves lived.'
Henry James

Copyright © 1999 Michael Freeman

Published by Yale University Press, New Haven and London

Edited and designed by Jane Havell
Printed in Singapore

Library of Congress Cataloging-in-Publication Data

Freeman, Michael J., 1950–
  Railways and the Victorian imagination / Michael Freeman.
     p.   cm.
  Includes bibliographical references and index.
  ISBN 0-300-07970-2 (cloth : alk. paper)
    1. Railroads—History.   2. Railroads—Social aspects—History.
  3. Technology and civilization—History.   I. Title.
HE1041.F74 1999
385'.09—dc21   99-20495
                                                       CIP

First endpaper: Map of the London and Birmingham Railway, c. 1840.
(Bodleian Library, Oxford, John Johnson Collection, Railways Box 7)

Last endpaper: W. Humber, *The Welwyn Viaduct*, pencil and watercolour, 1850.
(Ironbridge Gorge Museum Trust, Elton Collection)

Title pages: T. T. Bury, *The Moorish Arch*, aquatint, 1831. The arch at
Liverpool on the Liverpool and Manchester Railway was almost as potent
a symbol of the early railway age as the Euston Arch in London.
It was modelled on the Gate of Grand Cairo.
(Yale Center for British Art, Paul Mellon Collection)

Contents

Preface and Acknowledgements

THE MAKING OF THIS BOOK goes back many years. I think its origins may come from afternoons spent as a young child on the platform of a suburban station on the old southern region of British Railways. While loathing the soot and smell of the passing steam trains, an indulgent mother appeared to sense the fascination that these contraptions held for her four-year-old son. My father, too, had a role in the process. As a child, he had acquired a whole variety of model trains, including a garden railway, and these were soon removed from his old home for his son's use, to be supplemented in turn by a whole sequence of new train sets as juvenile birthdays came and went. I think that, like most fathers, he derived as much pleasure from setting up and working the different trains as did his son.

As a young teenager in the mid 1960s, I might have expected that a fascination with trains would quickly fade amid the rebellious youth culture represented by groups like the Beatles and the Rolling Stones. Somewhat curiously in hindsight, it did nothing of the sort. It was translated into a craze for trainspotting, but one that appeared to sit quite comfortably alongside a fascination with all the familiar cultural icons of the period. Thus many hours of the school holidays were whiled away on the ends of station platforms, busily engaged in 'copping', to use the familiar trainspotting jargon. In between trains, though, we would argue about the hit parade.

I was, of course, greatly fortunate to be pursuing such a hobby in the final days of the steam locomotive on Britain's railways. And as well as the memory of taking down engine names and numbers, I cannot fail to recall the exhilaration of seeing, hearing and smelling a crack steam-hauled express in full motion. This I used to do from a position high up on one of the massive embankments of Joseph Locke's dramatically engineered London and Southampton line, as it cut through the chalk downs north of Winchester. Here, even today, one can still see mile after mile of straight double track, merging at a point on the horizon. Approaching trains began first as tiny specks which grew gradually in size until all of a sudden one was overcome by the rush of air, the whirls of smoke and all the sounds of rapid steam locomotion. Each passing train was an event to recall. And when writing this book, I did not find it hard to imagine how the population of the 1840s must have reacted to the same sights, unfamiliar as they were with inanimate propulsion.

As an undergraduate reading geography my fascination with the railway continued, and was much affected by the vogue for quantitative social science that dominated the early 1970s. After this date, my interest in the railway age was forsaken in favour of the turnpike and canal eras that preceded it. For more than a decade, the transport agencies of the industrial revolution seemed to offer more fertile realms for research. However, as the tides of academic fashion shifted to embrace such fields as structuralism and postmodernism, a slow realization came that there was yet intellectual life in the railway age. However, it was not the railway *per se* that was the focus; instead, it was its cultural connections. This book tells the story.

Many people have helped in the preparation and writing of this book. Many institutions have also supported it. My first acknowledgement must go to the Marc Fitch Fund for providing a substantial grant to aid the reproduction of the pictures. The Yale Center for British Art, the Ironbridge Gorge Museum Trust, the Science and Society Picture Library in London, the Bodleian Library, Oxford, the Birmingham Central Library, along with a host of other institutions and individuals, also made generous concessions in the matter of picture fees. The research and writing for chapter eight was undertaken while I was a Visiting Fellow at the Yale Center for British Art and I must thank Patrick McCaughey, the Center's Director, for making my stay there so profitable. My time at Yale was made easier by the Governing Body of Mansfield College, Oxford, agreeing to grant me remission from my teaching duties there.

It would have been very difficult to write this book without the amazing resources of the Bodleian Library in Oxford. Researching and writing in Oxford for over twenty years now, I never cease to wonder at the range of its holdings, particularly if one can find the time and the patience to comb the catalogue resources. In this process, I have been greatly helped by Helen Rogers and her staff in the Upper Reading Room, and by the staff in Room 132, which houses the John Johnson Collection of modern papers. I must also single out the assistance given to me by Clive Hurst, Head of Special Collections, and Julie Anne Lambert, Superintendent of the John Johnson Collection, as well as that by Sylvia Gardiner, who looks after the Opie collection of children's literature.

The library of the Oxford School of Geography has also often come to my rescue on the rare occasions when the Bodleian proved unable to answer my requirements. Sue Bird, in particular, has obtained inter-library loans for me with remarkable speed and Linda Atkinson has answered many queries on more general references.

Among individuals who have read all or parts of the draft text, I must first of all thank John Nicoll, my publisher at Yale University Press's London office, for taking such a close interest in the project throughout the entire period of its creation. Professor Christy Anderson, of the Art History Department at Yale University, was a constant source of inspiration and encouragement, particularly in the writing of chapter eight. Finally, I must thank the Press's anonymous referee who several times read and commented on the entire book.

At different times, I have presented parts of my research work to audiences in Oxford and in Yale. Their comments, critical and otherwise, have all helped to fashion the final book. One audience member, Warder Cadbury, subsequently proved a mine of information on picture material and I must thank him for his generosity and his unflagging interest.

The prolific illustrative content of the book would have been impossible without the help of a whole array of highly skilled photographers. But I must single out especially the staff of the photographic studio of the Bodleian Library in Oxford who probably wondered when my requests were ever going to end.

MICHAEL FREEMAN
Mansfield College, Oxford
February 1999

Prologue

By the establishment of a general iron rail-way in a
direct line, the distance, between the capital and the
manufacturing towns, and principal cities, might be
reduced one quarter, and in many cases one third,
instead of the ridiculously winding course the stage
and mail coaches now daily run.[1]

IN 1830, THERE WERE just under 100 miles of railway open in Britain. By 1852, there were some 6,600.[2] Had all the railways authorized up to that time been constructed, the figure would have been a staggering 12,000.[3] Within less than two decades, the main body of Britain's railway system was in place – a basic network of trunk routes, together with most of the subsidiary lines that the country was likely ever to require. This was undeniably a startling achievement. As Michael Robbins has memorably remarked, 'the Victorians who created the railway look like a race imbued with some daemonic energy'.[4] Robbins has further described these formative years as 'heroic' – heroic in the enormous faith and will-power of the capitalists and constructors; heroic in terms of the phenomenal organizing skills that each of these groups displayed.[5] The period effectively saw three investment booms: one in 1824–5, one in 1836–7, and one in 1845–7, the last being far and away the greatest.[6] The physical outcome is clearly visible in the maps shown in this chapter.

By 1845, the country had some semblance of a national railway system. Comprising some 2,200 miles of line, most had been added in just the five preceding years. As both a construction and a capital enterprise, this dwarfs the road-building programme of the third quarter of the twentieth century. It is difficult to conceive how progress could have been faster. Brunel's great broad-gauge project had by then linked London and Bristol. Most of the Channel ports could be reached by railway from London. Robert Stephenson's London and Birmingham line offered the capital access to a growing spider's web of routes centred upon the Midlands and the North. As yet, Wales remained largely a blank on the map. There were no trunk routes joining England and Scotland. And in the south-west, travellers hit the buffers at Exeter. Even so, the scale of the system completed by that time was breathtaking. In the very early days, the array of lines appeared positively disjointed and haphazard. As more were opened, though, and as prospectors and surveyors pored over their maps, grander spatial strategies began to form.

By 1852, the Great Northern line had struck its way along the path of the old Great North Road from London to Doncaster. There were two cross-border routes between England and Scotland. Central and northern England had become criss-crossed with a veritable mass of lines. A continuous band of rails now extended

1. Francis Whishaw, plan of the railways of Great Britain and Ireland, 1840.

west to Plymouth in the south-west and to Carmarthen in South Wales. In short, the country had a mature railway system.[7]

It was above all the power of the free market that underscored the apparently boundless energy of railway building over the 1840s. By 1844, Britain had no fewer than 104 separate railway companies. Within six years this number had doubled. Together they formed an intense competitive realm. A few of these companies were led by men with quite exceptional vision. They saw their task as one of carrying railway communication to the far corners of the land. Ultimately, their object became to form trunk lines which would confer an unassailable route monopoly. It was 'a species of imperialism, no less'.[8] Directors did not call their railway companies 'Great' for nothing. The inexorable logic was amalgamation. By 1848, the main railway companies that were to dominate the Victorian age were in place: the London and North Western, the Great Western and the Midland. Between them, in 1848, they accounted for slightly more than half the route

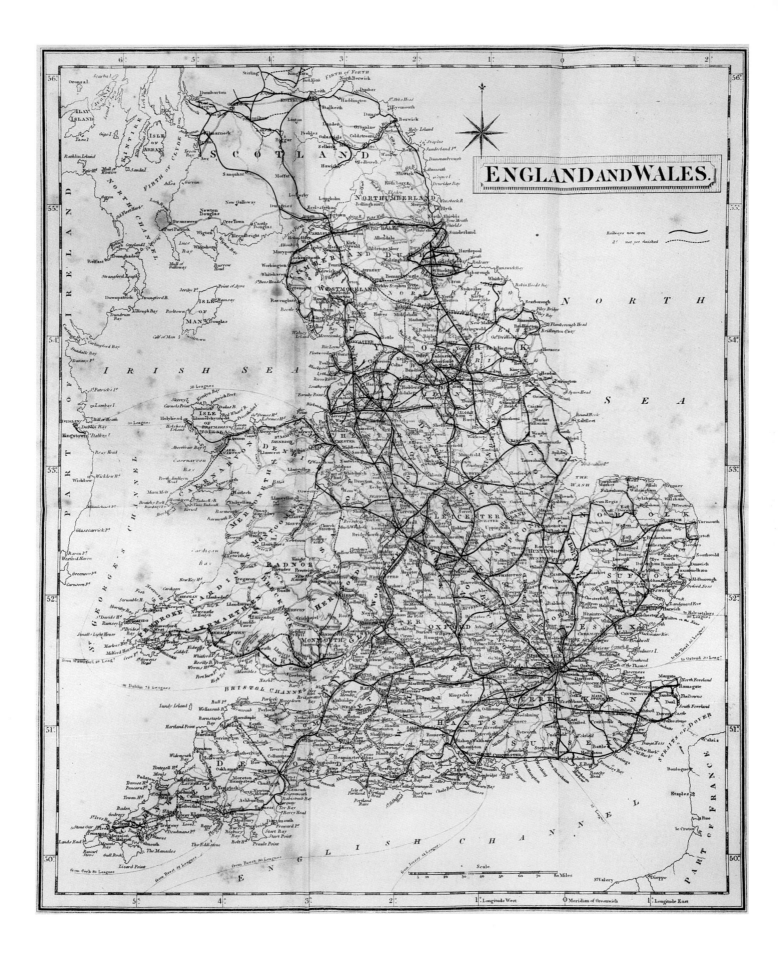

4. J. C. Bourne, lithograph, 1839, showing the London and Birmingham railway under construction near Hampstead, September 1836.

5 (opposite). The *Illustrated London News*, first issued in 1842, gave fulsome coverage to the railway age. Pictorial images became a regular feature when new lines of railway were inaugurated. The Trent Valley Railway, depicted here, was opened in 1847.

mileage then open.[9] The wholesale absorption of companies by others raised the spectre of monopoly. Thus in 1844 there was an initial move towards some sort of state control over the burgeoning railway system. The eventual provisions of Gladstone's Railway Act of 1844, though, proved a dead letter as far as any sort of nationalization was concerned. This was partly because there were by then too many vested interests among parliamentarians in maintaining the status quo. The Act was also in tune with the deregulatory spirit of the age. There was not a little antipathy in the country at large for centralist measures of the kind that had given birth to the Factory Act (1833) and the New Poor Law (1834).[10]

The second half of the nineteenth century saw copious further additions to Britain's railway network.[11] By the death of Queen Victoria in 1901, the total route mileage had grown to almost 19,000, nearly three times the figure of 1852.[12] Indeed, during the last decade of the Victorian age, the network grew by a further 1,500 miles. There were even a few new trunk lines: the Great Central's London extension to Marylebone being one, and the spectacular Settle–Carlisle route of the Midland Railway another. There were also some startling engineering efforts, among them the bridging of the Firth of Forth in Scotland, the tunnelling beneath the River Severn and the first underground railways.[13] The 1860s witnessed a burst of railway promotion and building which vied in some ways with the manias of the formative years. It collapsed almost equally spectacularly in 1866. Among its legacies were a whole series of bold but highly costly metropolitan railway extensions, notably into the centre of London. Main-line and engineering projects aside, though, the bulk of subsequent railway additions comprised suburban and rural lines. A railway station soon became a kind of *sine qua non* for every responsible and self-respecting town council. The wayside station became 'the place where

THE TRENT VALLEY RAILWAY.

VIADUCT OVER THE RIVER AVON, BELOW NEWBOLD.—(SEE PRECEDING PAGE).

THE RUGELEY STATION.

THE TUNNEL IN SHUGBOROUGH-PARK.

THE TAMWORTH STATION.

6. The great cantilever bridge across the Firth of Forth, from a photograph taken not long after its completion in 1890.

every invention of the Victorian age could first be seen'.[14] Much of the time, Victorian railway companies were only too eager to extend their rural domains, for they often saw this as an opportunity to close yet another potential gap in their territory in the face of possible hostile competitors. Hilaire Belloc, in 1908, defied anyone to come up with anything more quintessentially English than the country station.[15] W. G. Hoskins, in his appreciation of the English landscape some fifty years on, picked up a similar theme in an account of the experience of travelling by stopping train through the Rutland countryside on a fine summer morning:

> the barley fields shaking in the wind, the slow sedgy streams with their willows shading meditative cattle, the elegant limestone spires across the meadows, the early Victorian stations built of sheep-grey Ketton stone and still unaltered, the warm brown roofs of the villages half buried in the trees, and the summer light flashing everywhere.[16]

The railway, Hoskins observed, did not create much of this beauty. But it gave new vistas of it. Thus the new-fangled absurdity that was steam locomotion in the 1830s had a century later found its way deep into the national consciousness. The pages that follow explore this cultural journey.

CHARLBURY STATION.

7 (above). A line of the North British Railway skirting the Spean Gorge near Fort William. The extension into the Scottish Highlands in the closing decades of the Victorian era accorded travellers some spectacular scenic panorama.

8 (left). Charlbury station in the Cotswolds: the country railway station in Edwardian times was the quintessence of Englishness.

THE
GREAT WESTERN RAILWAY.
BY
J.C.BOURNE.

Introduction

THE DEVIL'S MANTLE

> . . . they would assuredly not pay the slightest attention
> to our fine-spun theory of steam, or believe that any
> thing less than some supernatural, probably infernal,
> power could contrive to send us, by a smoking,
> grumbling, little inanimate machine, at a pace so very
> different to the old plans of human motion on the
> surface of this our strange antiquated earth.[1]

THE COUNTRY into which the railways were born is not easily apprehended or understood. The British industrial revolution has been conventionally viewed as marking a clear break with former traditions of economic life, in turn involving changes in almost every aspect of the country's history and institutions.[2] Now, one prevailing view of the period seems to be that less happened, less dramatically, than was once supposed.[3] A gradualist perspective has progressively colonized much historical interpretation. It has also been claimed that Britain was, in any case, never fundamentally an industrial economy.[4] Nor did the industrial bourgeoisie ever usurp the power and social position of the aristocracy and the landed élites.[5] For others, however, there remains a need to step back from this gradualist perspective to reassess the features of radical change and historical discontinuity recognized by earlier historians and contemporary commentators.[6] The industrial revolution was not a phase of economic history in the form of a curve.[7] It may indeed have disappeared from some statistical series, but in some sectors it is still dazzlingly bright.[8]

For the authors of a new biography of Darwin, radical change and historical discontinuity form key features of the social context within which Darwin's ideas about biological evolution emerged – and which, even more significantly, made them possible. England, by 1839, was 'tumbling towards anarchy, with country-wide unrest and riots.' The gutter presses were fizzing, fire-bombs flying and the shouts on the street were for revolution. 'A million socialists', it was claimed, 'were castigating marriage, capitalism, and the fat, corrupt Established Church'. Spirits and souls were a delusion, just 'parts of the gentry's cruel deceit to subjugate working people'. Biology, the science of life, lay ruined within the clergy's 'Creationist Citadel'.[9] It was not necessarily true that England was actually on the brink of social collapse, but it *seemed* so to many of the gentry and the socially privileged, Darwin among them.

In the pages of the *Illustrated London News*, first published in June 1842, it is not hard to find echoes of this perceived social tumult. In Accrington, Lancashire,

9. J. C. Bourne, frontispiece to *The History and Description of the Great Western Railway*, lithograph, 1846.

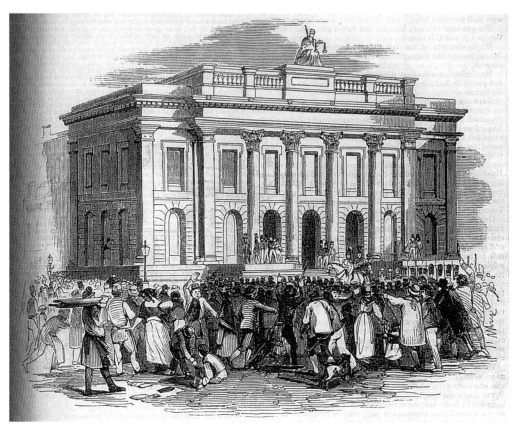

10. *Town Hall, Manchester – Reading the Riot Act, Illustrated London News,* August 1842.

11. *Messrs. Wilson's Mill, Salford, Illustrated London News,* August 1842, showing rioters outside a Salford print works.

the paper claimed, only a hundred people out of a population of nine thousand were fully employed. In Manchester, traders had seen their income fall by a third.[10] July of that year witnessed an attempt on the life of Queen Victoria.[11] In mid August, there were signs of systematic insurrection in the northern manufacturing towns.[12] Preston was descended upon by immense bodies of rioters from Wigan, Chorley and other colliery districts, armed with axes, spades and bludgeons. The authorities in Manchester reputedly appointed 2,500 special constables as rioters attacked mills there.[13] The paper went on to launch into a long and detailed account of the factory system and all its distresses.[14] Parts of this account anticipated with uncanny similarity some of the commentary that Friedrich Engels was to offer just two years later in his *Condition of the Working Class in England.*

One highly respected study has described the six years from 1837 to 1842 as 'the grimmest period in the history of the nineteenth century'.[15] Much of early Victorian society reacted with deep concern, and at times panic, over the quite unprecedented hordes that seemed to be everywhere around them. The Malthusian spectre of overpopulation was becoming daily more real.[16] Moreover, it was not just fear about numbers that was overwhelming, but fear of radical social change.[17] Darwin's bleak imaginings of the warring natural world thus found a disturbing counterpoint in the equally bleak war that appeared to be going on in the social world.[18] Another commentator has described how 'for two or three generations the English mind was vitally affected by the idea of revolution, by the prevalence of a revolutionary *mystique*'. What was important above all was the attitude of men who were 'themselves unlikely to take part in physical violence'.[19]

Such stirring, almost cataclysmic, accounts of Britain at the dawn of the Railway Age do not, however, find a place within the perspectives of other historians. For example, the period has also been characterized as 'neatly demonstrating the twin forces of continuity and change that are always at work in society'. The opening of the Liverpool and Manchester Railway in 1830 ushered in the new – 'an unknown territory of urbanized and industrialized society' – while the almost exactly contemporary Reform Act of 1832 'glanced backward with an approving eye on the traditional order which it sought to buttress'.[20] While technological innovation was revolutionizing industrial production, the corresponding extent and pace of social transformation was quite another matter.[21] In 1830, typical men and women were neither town dwellers nor factory workers; indeed, 'the most representative working man was the agricultural labourer'.[22] Many Manichaean images of the industrial revolution of the kind broadly rehearsed in Desmond and Moore's biography of Darwin are thus erroneous, if pardonable.[23] However, it is perhaps these very images that offer a key to understanding the sympathies and reactions of contemporary society. It may be possible to cite statistic after statistic showing that there were more non-factory workers in 1830 than there were factory workers, that children had always earned their keep in the era before the factory,

12. *Entrance to the Tunnel of the Liverpool and Manchester Rail-Way, Edge-Hill*, steel engraving, *Lancashire Illustrated*, 1831. This rarely reproduced image shows construction work in progress on the Edge Hill tunnel.

13. *Cotton Factories, Union Street, Manchester*, steel engraving, *Lancashire Illustrated*, 1831, depicting what was perhaps among the defining images of the industrial revolution.

14. Thomas Malthus, whose famous *Essay on the Principle of Population* of 1798 was viewed by some commentators as a scourge on the poor.

and that farm employment was growing right up until 1851.[24] But such knowledge carries with it all the familiar perils of hindsight, not to mention the problems that statistical reductionism typically imposes. The cure for excess metaphor, as Hudson has remarked, is not always counting.[25] Curiosity and anxiety about factory production existed because it was a portent of what might be in the future.[26] The restricted nature of the reform of the political franchise in 1832, described as 'driving a wedge between the middle and the working classes, buying off the one with votes and representation and leaving the other . . . outside the pale', in many respects reinforced such anxiety.[27]

One potentially vital clue to the further understanding of this debate is located in the evolving language of class. The social conflict which figured in the clash of emerging class interests was not a new feature in itself. It was more that the nature and intensity of that conflict was changing, including the manner in which people thought about it.[28] For the working classes, or for the proletariat, voluntary organizations, pressure groups and trades unions accelerated the pace of class formation and action.[29] This, in turn, produced a sense of disruptive social change among the population at large and especially among privileged society. Existing social hegemony, meanwhile, was being enhanced by the introduction of an organized police force, a move that was bitterly resisted in many working-class communities.[30] In parallel, there was an 'intensification of religious and educational activity by the middle and ruling classes', to try to deliver a more consensual acquiescence among working people to the authority that was being exercised over them.[31]

The New Poor Law offered the most powerful symbol of the evolving sense of class consciousness of the 1830s and 1840s.[32] Malthus had brought to the discourse on poverty exactly the same norms that were central to the emerging political economy of the day. Charity towards the able-bodied poor undermined the pursuit of national wealth. They had to be shaken from their indolence into self-help. Thus the centuries-old tradition of parish relief was swept away in favour of the much harsher and far more restricted regime of the Union Workhouse. To the middle-class industrialists and traders, Malthus was a saviour. His theory that poverty was an inevitable and recurring feature of society gave moral legitimacy to a policy of *laissez-faire*. The New Poor Law proved 'the one big success of the century for the transmission of middle class standards . . . to the working classes'.[33] Its implementation, though, provoked serious social unrest, especially in northern industrial areas. On the longer time-scale, it cast a shadow of deprivation over many working-class families. The *Illustrated London News*, echoing Carlyle, was vituperative in its attack on the New Poor Law. It was 'tyrannical in complexion', 'brutal in spirit' and 'remorseless in operation', putting humanity and Christianity to shame.[34] As the Victorian era unfolded, the sanctions of the law became less harsh, but its moral imperative persisted. The labouring poor had to conform to new standards of social and economic rectitude.

If there were godlessness and a lack of Christian sensitivity in the provisions of the New Poor Law, the revelations emerging about the history of the earth, part of the new-found and increasingly popular science of geology, did nothing to diminish them.[35] Lyell's *Principles of Geology* (1830–33) had already dispensed with the Flood, so that geological time was indisputably extended; Darwin's researches on his *Beagle* voyage had daily added to this thesis.[36] Soon Darwin was also toying with the idea of life as nothing but a set of self-organizing atoms. Clerical society was understandably 'petrified'. The 'chain of command from God down through the priesthood into nature' was being everywhere contested.[37] Worse, even some members of the Church were beginning to accommodate the end of Creation.[38] Geology appeared to be suggesting that there was neither end nor beginning. The subject revealed to man the immensities of time and space and the 'seeming insignificance of his being'.[39] Nature had been reduced to an inexplicable puzzle, according to Emily Brontë – one in which life appeared to exist on the principle of destruction.[40]

As one surveys and ponders the mass of contemporary documentation that records the dawn of the railway age in Britain, it is hard to avoid being drawn towards the more cataclysmic perspectives. John Milton's *Pandaemonium* has been cited as the image that best represents or captures the impact that the industrial revolution and the coming of the machine age had upon people's minds.[41] The sight of a moving cylindrical contraption on wheels, belching smoke and fumes, but without any visible means of animate propulsion, brought desperate fears and anxieties, as well as awe and admiration. Many thought that there was something supernatural about steam locomotion. Why else did engineers give their contraptions names like 'Wildfire', 'Dragon' and 'Centaur'? For Thomas Carlyle, journeying on the Grand Junction Railway in September 1839, the steam railway was the devil's mantle; Lord Shaftesbury, journeying from Manchester to Liverpool a month earlier, remarked that the devil, if he travelled, would have gone by train.[42] The speed of even the earliest railway engines outstripped anything that could be observed in nature. To travel at rates of thirty miles an hour was sensational. Travelling in a carriage that was open to the air intensified the shock and exhilaration, as did passing through deep cuttings or tunnels.[43] And when one reads contemporary accounts of the convulsions that the physical construction of railways brought, not to mention the equivalent convulsions in contemporary social thought and policy, it is easy to appreciate the potential interpretative force of Milton's famous image of Hell. Mary Shelley's *Frankenstein* (1818) had already articulated the fear that science might destroy man. Moreover, the identification of

15. Title page of Charles Lyell's geological treatise of 1835, complete with a quotation from John Playfair's *Illustrations of the Huttonian Theory of the Earth* (1802): 'Amid all the revolutions of the globe, the economy of Nature has been uniform, and her laws are the only things that have resisted the general movement. The rivers and the rocks, the seas and the continents, have been changed in all their parts; but the laws which direct those changes, and the rules to which they are subject, have remained invariably the same.'

16, 17. John Martin, *The Palace of Pandemonium* and *Satan arousing the Fallen Angels*, illustrations to nineteenth-century editions of Milton's *Paradise Lost*.

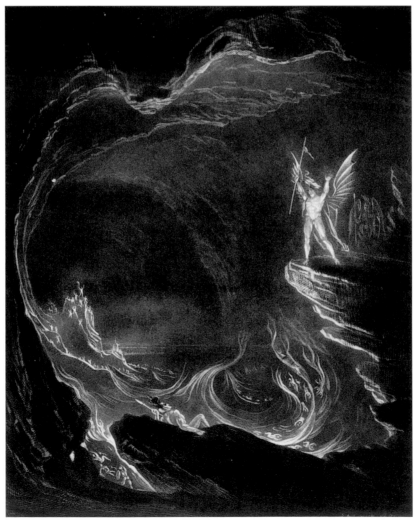

the power of industry with Satan was already well established by the painter John Martin in his famous renditions of scenes from *Paradise Lost*.[44] So Carlyle and Shaftesbury, along with many other observers, were doing nothing more than echoing deeply seated contemporary emotions when they attached to the railway images from Hell.

If the first railways clearly added to the turbulence of the age, they were also deeply founded within it. As the navvies laboured to make the cuttings of Robert Stephenson's famous London and Birmingham trunk line, they were simultaneously striking out at the Creation story. For the cuttings laid bare to view the Uniformitarianism of Lyell's new geology, particularly the co-relation of stratigraphic formations by their fossil content.[45] Amateur geologists flocked to view the new rock exposures, often endangering life and limb in the process.[46] This seemingly accidental relationship between railroad construction works and the extension of geological knowledge had an earlier pedigree in the person of William Smith, the father of British geological mapping. Smith had been a 'navigator' of a sort himself. A canal surveyor in the late eighteenth century, he had become convinced of the uniformity of the stratigraphic record from observing fossils in the exposed sections of canal trenches in Somerset. He went on to produce the first geological maps of the British Isles.[47] Where railway works differed from those of canals was in the vastly greater scale of the declivities they forged, and their far wider occurrence. Some of the cuttings on the London and Birmingham line were sixty or seventy feet deep, so adding enormously to the profile of geological history.

Contemporaries, including many artists, saw the magnitude of railway earth and masonry works as comparable to the constructions of ancient Egypt. But whether or not this analogy was valid, the great gashes struck in the landscape applied a hammer blow to Creation. On the London and Birmingham line, the massive embankment at Wolverton appeared to re-write nature's signature. The even more dramatic tunnel works at Kilsby were contemptuous of it altogether. On the line from Liverpool to Manchester, the gaping chasm at Olive Mount and the

18. J. C. Bourne, lithograph, 1839, showing Blisworth Cutting on the London and Birmingham Railway.

19. A. B. Clayton, lithograph, 1831, showing the Moorish Arch on the Liverpool and Manchester Railway.

floating embankment that traversed with such acute linearity the boggy fen of Chat Moss repeated the pattern. To many it appeared to be the 'Death of Nature'.[48]

The railways were no less involved in political turmoil. The authorizing Acts of railway companies gave them the altogether novel right of compulsory purchase of land. The traditional and largely Tory landowning classes saw this as an inexcusable affront to their amenities and their social status.[49] 'There is nobody so violent against railroads as George,' observed Lady Marney of her husband in Disraeli's novel *Sybil*.[50] Many landowners fought tooth and nail to block or frustrate the courses of individual lines. Their labourers and hired bullies engaged in pitched battles with teams of surveyors who searched for level paths for the railroads' permanent way. Matters were made worse by the fact that the bulk of early railway enterprise was financed by the accumulated wealth of the new manufacturing and urban élites of the north. There was unease about the growth of a society represented by Lancashire, whose industrial capital underpinned nearly all the early trunk railroads, including many of those into London.[51] In a sense, the railroads marched upon London and took it by storm. The great Doric portico fronting the entrance to Euston station was a monument to such conquest. Critics of the time derided the vast scale of the entrance front, contrasting it with the meagre train sheds behind. But they were missing the point. The portico was a 'triumphal arch, bestriding the processional way of the first railway to march on London'. It also celebrated 'the victory of the engineers over the subterranean waters and quicksands of Kilsby and their passage through the great hewn defiles of Tring and Roade'.[52] As the Tory political establishment crumbled in the face of popular dissent and rising political pressure from the Whigs, the northern urban and industrial classes were busily underwriting the wholesale extension of the steam railway southward to the metropolis. Coupled with the extended voting franchise and the new constituency base of the Great Reform Act whereby many

new industrial towns got political representation for the first time, the traditional landed classes appeared in some eyes to be under attack from all sides.

As Charles Darwin grappled with the competitive struggle among organisms in the study of his country rectory at Downe in Kent, he was to witness around him one of the most frenetic episodes of social or, more precisely, economic competition ever seen. Steam railway capitalism first took Britain by storm in the late 1830s. It returned to scale even greater heights of capital formation and speculation in the middle 1840s and continued to ferment intermittently for the rest of the century. Wordsworth thought of the railway capitalists as a kind of new informal power: 'the Thirst of Gold, that rules o'er Britain like a baneful star'.[53] The railway manias transformed the English stock market, made millions for a few and ruined many more. Darwin himself became a railway capitalist. By the early 1850s, the Darwin family portfolio ran to some £14,000 of railway stock. It originated from his wife's inheritance, but Charles took up the overseeing of the investment, extending the portfolio when values were low and selling when he thought the market in railway stock was over-heating. Darwinism, 'the survival of the fittest', was always intended to explain human society. Steam railway capitalism became one of its most powerful exemplars.[54]

The social turmoil of the 1830s, with its threats to property and to persons, had brought forth the creation of a professional police force. The early railways, interestingly, echoed this trend, with companies forming their own police establishments, in some cases modelled on the metropolitan force founded by Peel in 1829.[55] Their primary purpose was the safety of railway operation, but it is clear that their role also shaded into questions of public order at a time when political agitation and social grievance were features of everyday existence. The association of railways with public order was reinforced, too, in their early use by the government for carrying troops to sites of political demonstrations.[56] In August 1842, the

20. J. C. Bourne, lithograph, 1839, showing Philip Hardwick's massive Doric portico fronting the station at Euston Grove, the London terminus of the London and Birmingham Railway.

21. 'Police signals' on the railway, *Illustrated London News*, 1844.

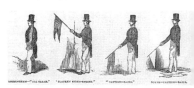

22. Troops departing from Euston by the London and Birmingham Railway, *Illustrated London News*, 1842.

Illustrated London News carried an engraving of troops marching under the Euston Arch prior to embarking on trains of the London and Birmingham Railway for destinations in the northern manufacturing districts.[57] Roughly a month later, Charles Darwin was noting the barristers bustling into Euston to catch trains northward to deal with the 1,500 strikers who by then awaited government prosecution.[58] Railway companies appear to have been readily disposed to assist the authorities in maintaining the peace. In part this was a basic matter of protecting their property; more widely, it was a function of the dominance of the new middle classes in railway enterprise. Again, one is reminded of the way railways were embedded in the emergent class relations of the age.

THE RAILWAY AS CULTURAL METAPHOR

The history of the English railway is probably among the most prolifically researched of all facets of the nineteenth century.[59] Library shelves bow under the weight of railway company histories, detailed narratives of individual lines and encyclopaedic offerings on motive power and rolling stock.[60] In parallel, there exists an astonishing photographic record of the railway era which has helped to fashion a nostalgia industry perhaps second to none. Indeed, publishing houses have been built upon it.[61] Within the more confined realms of academic study, the railway has provided a central focus in debate about Victorian economic growth and business performance.[62] Under the revisionist gaze of social scientific analysis in the 1960s, however, the railway lost its pride of place in the cavalcade of Victorian economic progress. Amid flights of statistical ingenuity and manipulation, its role was reduced to a few percentage points of GNP, a catalyst for particular regional industrial economies within particular spans of years, but not the kind of *sine qua non* that many commentators had traditionally suggested for it.[63] However, as the scientific vogue waned in the humanities and in social studies over the 1970s, to be succeeded by such widely divergent discourses as structuralism and post-modernism, there has been no corresponding reconsideration of the railway age.[64] As the interpretative focus shifted from composition to context – in fields as far apart as art history and the history of science – and as cultural materialism and the sociology of knowledge came to figure as prominent frames of reference in many branches of the humanities, the railway age appeared to remain a foreign field. Save for Wolfgang Schivelbusch's brilliant pioneering study, *The Railway Journey* (1977), the formula for railway history has, with a few other isolated and not always successful exceptions, remained largely institutional in mould.[65]

The central ambition of this book is to re-engage the railway with the age of which it was part. It is a study not of railways *per se*, but of their cultural relations. It is an examination of the railway as cultural metaphor. The familiar litany of lines opened, tons of coal moved and financial performance can never provide more than a partial view. The railway was deeply embedded in the evolving structures of Victorian society. It both echoed those structures and interacted with them. It had educational, intellectual, emotional and psychological dimensions. It was enmeshed in the spirit of the age, an undiminishing zest for bigger and better, for an all-pervasive machine technology and, in concert, a perpetual fascination with a sense of becoming, of living in an age of transition, in anxious and sometimes fearful contemplation of what the future held. The high drama of the Victorian railway is laid bare for all to see in contemporary texts in periodicals and newspapers, in art, literature, poetry and all manner of other forms of representation. It is even apparent in the first railway histories, which were being penned long before much of the system was complete. Here, railways were cast not as institutional undertakings but as social phenomena. So breathtaking were the changes they brought that history was being written in the present.[66] This book tries to present the 'imaginative history' of the railway, addressing the railway as 'human experience'.[67] There are 'moments' in history when historical processes suddenly show themselves with extraordinary clearness – 'and which through that clearness can stand for the whole inexpressible uncapturable process'.[68] Nineteenth-century geology also functions as a powerful cultural metaphor.[69] Writing on its history in the nineteenth century has recently undergone a remarkably parallel kind of transformation. Evidence is no longer just sought in the geological treatise or in the field notebook, but in painting, map-making, poetry, religious discourse and a host of other forms.

The time is therefore long overdue for a new portrait of the railway at a critical turning-point in the history of society. With such a goal in mind, this book is structured in eight chapters. All are concerned with different aspects of the railway as cultural metaphor, and with what have been called 'Illuminations' or 'Moments of Vision'.[70] Apart from the brief commentary offered in the Prologue, no attempt has been made to give a full-scale narrative of the growth of the railway system; material of this kind is readily available in a wealth of different forms elsewhere.[71] To try to include such an account would be to undermine the book's central claim that the railway cannot be disengaged from the wider economic, social and political fabric.

23. Guardsmen leaving London for Canada by the London and South Western Railway, *Illustrated London News*, 1861.

Chapter One has as its central focus the 'death of the old order'. It explores the discontinuities between the railway and preceding modes of transport and connects these to debates about the decline of the *ancien régime* in society. Certain aspects of this theme have an explicitly geographical dimension in the decay of the traditional bonds between community and territory. The 'death of the old order' is also manifest in altered experiences of nature. Thus the third part of the chapter begins by addressing the metaphor of flight which was used with such unremitting frequency in commentary on the sensation of railway travel in the 1830s and 1840s. It also looks at railroads and the idea of a 'produced' nature,[72] together with popular anxieties about the changing experience of nature that they wrought. Here the book takes up more fully the Darwinian connection.

Chapter Two explores the railway's intellectual context more explicitly. The Victorian age saw a wholesale application of science to everyday life. The inexorable progress of machine technology in industry was matched by a desire to introduce the machine idea right across the range of ordinary existence. Victorians were fascinated by mechanical contraptions of every sort. They produced kitchen appliances of almost unending ingenuity. Children played with all manner of clockwork toys and what, a century later, would be styled techno-games. The catalogue of the Great Exhibition (1851) bears staggering witness to the pervasive presence of the machine in Victorian lives.[73] Steam locomotion was at the centre of this experience. The effects of the earlier decades of the industrial revolution had been directly seen by only a minority of the population, those who laboured in mines, mills and foundries. But the application of steam to locomotion changed all that. Nearly all classes and all groups within society had witnessed first-hand the power of the new industrialism by the close of the 1840s. In town and countryside alike, the hissing, clanking spectacle of steam locomotion touched the lives of the most ordinary of men and women, even more so when cheap excursion fares gave them the opportunity to ride the railway. One of the critical features of the machine was that it speeded up the rate of doing things and multiplied the scale of

24. The fantasy of steam locomotion, as it apppeared on the front cover of a song performed around 1830 at Vauxhall Gardens and Margate.

output. The machine age thus also became an age of statistics. What had really begun with the first census of 1801 became a nationwide preoccupation. Charles Dickens lampooned the trend in the character of Gradgrind in *Hard Times* (1854). Matthew Arnold was deeply suspicious of it as a measure of cultural attainment.[74] But the statistics kept on coming. Moreover, the early railways afforded no end of copy. Not only did they enlarge enormously the size of the travelling public, but their construction works assumed greater and greater orders of magnitude. There was hardly a railway commentary of the 1830s and 1840s that was not awash in a sea of statistical superlatives. The 'march of intellect' also embraced a novel geographical awareness. The railway became associated with a new sense of relativism as regards place (i.e. space). The experience of place, or space, was greatly enlarged by the facility that railway travel brought. Commentators soon coined the now memorable phrase 'the annihilation of space by time',[75] later to be taken up by Marx in connection with the circulation of capital. The new speed of travel inevitably brought about a new speed of living. Punctuality and time-keeping were transplanted from railway operation directly into people's lives.[76] The frenetic pressure to be 'on time' was born out of the early railway age.

Chapter Three has capital as its central focus. This is not in order to offer a determinedly Marxist account, but rather a recognition of the way 'capital' and 'capitalists' were terms of common currency in the mid Victorian period. The chapter is concerned above all with the railway as a capital enterprise, as a project of private business. However, following the mould of cultural materialism,[77] it also explores the relationship between what is typically called the material base and the over-arching superstructure. This was most powerfully demonstrated in the emergence of a railway press, but it also embraced many other fields, the wider world of reading among them. Nor can the railway as a capital enterprise be examined outside its class affiliations. Class distinctions were an early and manifest feature of all

25. J. Osborn Brown, watercolour, 1868, showing an unidentified station. The scene has an almost palpable domesticity, not least by virtue of the style and orientation of the station house. By 1868, the railway had long since passed its novelty; it had been assimiliated into a wide range of the cultural spectrum.

railway experience. Later in the century, the railway became a central agency in the segregation of classes in urban space and in their politicization.

The urban realm forms the subject of Chapter Four. Railways were potent influences upon nineteenth-century urbanization. They revolutionized, for example, urban food supply, both from foreign and domestic sources. In their absence, the pathway towards large-scale urbanization of the Victorian populace would have been very different. Within towns and cities, the railway combined both creative and destructive force. It tore its way through inner working-class districts to make new central terminals. In turn, these sites became templates for the re-organization of urban space and their often dramatic architectural treatments elevated the railway station into a quasi-religious emblem, a shrine to the circulatory ferment that became such a hallmark of the age. The railway also forged a role in the geographical extension of the built-up area, permitting a sharper and more extended separation of home and workplace than did omnibuses and trams. The monotony of suburbia, with all its various social gradations and identities, was unmistakably interwoven with suburban railway extension and station building. Arnold Bennett explored this theme in fiction.[78] John Betjeman was later to explore it in poetry.[79] By the twentieth century, one word came to symbolize the phenomenon: Metroland.

Chapter Five examines the relationship between railways and territory. Although railways acted towards the annihilation of space, they simultaneously differentiated it. In part, this was a function of the comparative advantage and, in its wake, the geographic specialization that they enabled. But it was also a function

26. John Gordon Thomson, pencil, pen and ink, 1852. The scene on Christmas Eve at the newly opened King's Cross station is a dramatic testament to the 'circulatory ferment' of the railway age.

27. A. F. Tait, lithograph, 1848, showing Victoria Street, Manchester, with the new railway bridge leading to Victoria station in the middle distance.

of the division of railway operation among private, competing companies, each with discrete territorial identities and, sometimes, too, with distinctive bases in pre-existing regional economic systems. As individual companies consolidated their power and influence, especially in alliance with local enterprise, they acquired the nature of regional development agencies, almost quasi-states. One such institution was the North Eastern Railway Company, which became a remarkable model for corporate management by the close of the Victorian era.[80]

A startling feature of the Victorian railway as a large-scale capital project of the machine age was its dependence on old-fashioned muscle power for its construction (Chapter Six). The brute strength of the navvy became a social as much as an economic phenomenon. Navvy encampments came to be cast by some observers as a species of hell on earth, such was the depravity of their society and day-to-day living. Certainly they formed 'armies' the like of which had not been seen since the Civil War. In the context of evolutionary theory, they appeared to give credence to the 'savagery' of human ancestry. The operation of the railway also required 'armies' of men, but of a significantly different social order. They had to demonstrate a certain standard of literacy. Some needed to have mechanical and technical knowledge. All had to subscribe to an organizational model based around hierarchy, duty and discipline.

Chapter Seven considers the railways in relation to the continuation and reproduction of social life and, more particularly, to education. Children's literature, for instance, was quick to encompass the technology of the railway, using its example to teach the alphabet and as a means of addressing the altered perceptions that railway travel invited. Houses, trees and fields looked as if they were moving; they looked like items in a toy-shop.[81] These were novel sensations, about the experience of rapid motion and about visual perspective. Board-games, jig-saw puzzles and sheet music were increasingly adapted and developed to record the railway phenomenon. Predictably, the railway was also very soon being repre-

28. J. C. Bourne, lithograph, 1839, of work on the masonry of Watford tunnel portal on the London and Birmingham Railway, June 1837.

sented in toy and in model form. German and French toy-makers were quick to explore the potential of the British market and, by the close of the Victorian era, dominated it (the commonly assumed synonymity between toy trains and the English firm of Hornby was not realized until well into the twentieth century). One of the earliest model railways, at the Baker Street Bazaar in London in 1834, featured a working, miniaturized version of the Liverpool and Manchester line.[82]

The final chapter of the book focuses specifically on artistic interpretations of the railway. The 1830s and 1840s brought forth a plethora of engravings of the first operational lines. In part this was a response to the remarkable novelty of the steam railway – the striking linearity of its permanent way, its sometimes overpowering topographical impact, and then the strange sight of the self-propelling locomotive engine with its string of carriages and wagons. But artistic representation was also a deliberate ploy on the part of some companies to quell public fears and anxieties about the railway phenomenon, and to counter-balance the vigorous resistance that came from landed and other vested interests. A number of companies were responsible for commissioning artists directly; others lent their support to such projects. The outcome was an enormous range of engravings, documenting almost every aspect of the railway's progress in the decades immediately before photography. This chapter examines in detail the production, format and subject of these engravings as an integral part of the railway's cultural production. In turn, it considers the contribution of painting, including, inevitably, J. M. W. Turner's remarkable *Rain, Steam and Speed* (1845) and extending to the extraordinary station scenes of painters like W. P. Frith.

When, in 1851, John Francis published his *History of the English Railway*, covering the years 1820 to 1845, he used the sub-title: 'its social relations and revelations'. Francis was acutely aware of the manner in which the railway had implicated the entire fabric of society. In the eyes of many in the 1840s, it had become 'the wonder of the world', the mightiest moral and social revolution', 'the great iron revolution of science'.[83] It is the task of this book to recover not only material features of the railway age, but the way in which it was apprehended by a society with very different sympathies and outlooks from those of our own. The idea that corn might soon be made to 'grow at railway speed' was certainly no more than a jest.[84] But it betokened a belief in progress for which the railway became probably the most powerful of embodiments.

Some readers of this book may wonder about its rather uneven temporal and geographical coverage. There is, for example, a clear emphasis on the early to mid Victorian era; there is also a concentration on England – at the expense of Wales, Scotland and, even more especially, Ireland. It is vital to remind readers that this book seeks to capture the *experience* of the railway. This is not achieved by geographical inclusiveness *per se*. Discussion of railways and territory inevitably focuses on the later decades of the nineteenth century, for this was the time it took for company bases in territory fully to crystallize. By contrast, study of the railway as a mechanical and scientific sensation must inevitably focus on the middle period of the century, for by the closing decades of the Victorian age such novelty was long spent. The book's emphasis, in other words, rests on the spatio-temporality of experience, rather than the more conventional bounds of traditional frames of geography and history.

29. A. F. Tait, lithograph, 1848, showing an unusually animated view of the station at Liverpool Edge Hill.

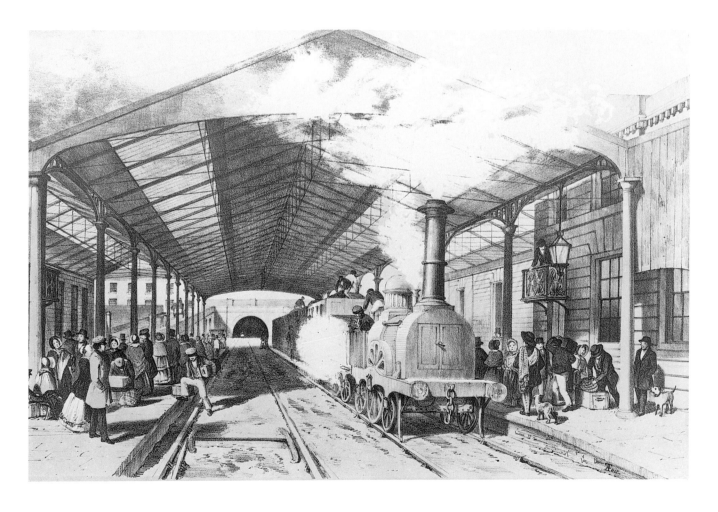

DEATH OF THE OLD ORDER?

> . . . the men who made the railways were not merely creating a revolutionary means of transport. They were helping to create a new society and a new world. They were, as they themselves were aware, men ahead of their time, visionary, energetic, self-reliant individuals, scornful of difficulties, ruthless with rivals and opponents, moving what they considered prejudice and reaction as they moved mountains of earth and rock to smooth the road into the future. They were typical representatives of the bustling, go-getting, self-confident, Victorian capitalist middle-class.[1]

RAILWAYS AND REFORM

THE STEAM LOCOMOTIVE or 'iron monster', as it was so often labelled, brought to a close an era of transport improvement that had as one of its most central distinctions a continued reliance on the muscle power of the horse.[2] It is thus only with considerable licence that commentators have talked of a transport revolution in the eighteenth century.[3] Little was revolutionary, for instance, about the turn-pike and its traffic. And while, in technical terms, canals were certainly a sophisticated extension of the river system, they were peculiarly prone to frost stoppage in sub-zero weather and water shortage in dry. At sea, wind remained a critical arbiter of the direction and tempo of maritime trade. And port facilities were still unsophisticated, almost primitive, outside such places as London and Liverpool.[4]

It might appear foolish to suggest that the opening of the Liverpool and Manchester Railway in 1830 marked the end of the *ancien régime* in transport, rather in the way that one historian has controversially claimed that the Reform Act of 1832 did the same for society generally.[5] But it does help to focus attention on the era after 1830 as the one that saw a radical transformation in the dynamics of the transport sector. Until then, transport improvement had amounted to little more than a process of refining and adjusting pre-existing systems.[6] The pace of change was certainly quicker in some decades than in others – witness the canal mania of the 1790s and its aftermath – but there was nothing really to compare with the age of steam.

Part of the thesis about the general survival of the *ancien régime* in society revolves around the continuing significance of the family unit in the first stages of industrialisation, whether in terms of 'masters and men' in leading industries like metal-working, or in the various dimensions of domestic manufacture.[7] The joint stock company, by comparison, was a much later phenomenon. What distinguished the family unit was the way it presented economic and political continuity.

30 (opposite). T. T. Bury, aquatint, 1831, of the chasm of Olive Mount cutting on the Liverpool and Manchester Railway.

31. *The Hour and the Man*, cartoon from *Punch*, 1848, with the railway as a symbol of reform. 'Cobden: "Now, Sir, are you going by us?" Russell: "No, thank you; you're too fast for me; I shall go by the Parliamentary Train."'

32. Steel engraving (anonymous, n.d.), of the Trent and Mersey Canal on the outskirts of the Potteries.

Certainly, much transport organisation before 1830 focused on the family unit. Road carriage of goods, for instance, was almost exclusively a family-based enterprise well into the nineteenth century.[8] Where the family was not the critical element, it was the local community, as exemplified in the coasting trade where almost eighty per cent of vessel owners in 1825 resided within twenty miles of the port of registration, half of them within the port itself.[9] Canals, likewise, were predominantly financed by local enterprise, in cases by leading industrial families like the Wedgwoods, or by members of the landed élite with economic interests who stood to make immediate gain from waterway extension or improvement.[10] Pioneer railway ventures, by contrast, presented an increasingly different organisational form. The complex enabling legislation of the Liverpool and Manchester Railway demonstrated something of the phenomenon. It broke with the business practices of turnpikes and canals by owning outright and operating the whole installation within a single undertaking. Further, it employed a regular staff to run it, not permitting the sub-contracting of any of its operations, nor allowing others to use the line on payment of toll.[11] Above all, it raised the level of transport investment to a whole new pitch: by the middle decades of the Victorian age, railways had become the flagship of managerial capitalism, the system whereby ownership and control were made clearly separate.[12] Railway companies began to attain a scale of market capitalisation that vied with business corporations of the twentieth century.[13] When Parliament legislated the first public railways into existence, it had not done so with the intention of creating private monopolies, but within a few years it became plain that the claims of public safety and efficient running rendered any clauses that sought to guarantee against private monopoly a 'dead letter'.[14]

Another feature concerning the survival of the *ancien régime* that finds common ground with the railways is that of urbanization. The contention is that 'no homogeneous urban phenomenon' could be discerned before 1830, 'whether defined in terms of *mentalité* or mere numbers'.[15] Culture remained heavily influenced by the values of rural society even as late as 1800.[16] The fully urbanised society of great cities and conurbations did not became manifest until the late nineteenth century. Whereas in 1831 there were just seven towns outside London with populations of more than 100,000, in 1901 there were forty.[17] It would be foolish to claim that railways forged or facilitated a homogeneous urban condition: the urban process was too complex and its outcomes too varied to adduce from it single causative or contributory agents. But it is impossible to ignore the way that railways contributed to the large-scale urbanization of capital in the second half of the nineteenth century, whether we conceive of this in terms of commodity circulation, the built environment of towns and cities, or of the city as a focus of conspicuous consumption.[18] London's Great Exhibition of 1851 and the array of resort towns that sprang up around the coastline were illustrative of the last-named. The relative ubiquity of particular building materials, combined with the growing ease of their carriage, enabled a scale and anonymity of the urban environment unexperienced in earlier decades. Meanwhile, entrepôt cities like Cardiff bore testament to the circulatory ferment of capital that railways underpinned – in this case, mile upon mile of coal on its way down the valley branch lines as part of a vibrant export economy. For at least one writer, though, the railway did become the embodiment of the new egalitarian civilisation of the towns. By its medium, 'the great social forces let loose by the Reform Bills of 1832 and 1867 were made concrete and visible'.[19]

The idea that the railways coincided with and marked out the defeat of the old social order is echoed in much contemporary commentary. Thomas Arnold, when seeing the first train pass through the Rugby countryside, remarked that feudality had gone for ever.[20] For the headmaster of Rugby's prestigious school, the railway signalled the downfall of the aristocracy. An article in the *Economist* for 1851 described the railways as the *Magna Carta* of the poor's motive freedom.[21] In William Pickering's *Railroad Eclogues* of 1846, the juxtaposition of the railroads and reform is made plain in celebratory verse:

33. Edward Duncan (attrib.), watercolour, c. 1850, of the Eastern Counties Railway at Ely: the old order looks down upon the new.

The wine's with you: a bumper, fill your glass,
Fill to the brim, and then the bottle pass.
'Repeal, free trade, and railroads by the score.
Hurrah-hurrah-hurra-a-a- one cheer more!'[22]

Richard Trevithick, one of the railroad's founding fathers, saw the deep symbolism of the Reform Bill in his plans for a conical cast-iron monument one thousand feet high to commemorate its passage.[23] When the Liverpool and Manchester Railway was opened, the event was turned into a festival, a kind of jubilee, with a reported 400,000 spectators lining the route.[24] At Liverpool, 'in a sort of area surrounded by offices and high walls, were drawn up two ranges of carriages of every shape and quality, from the gorgeous car of triumph, decorated with gold and crimson, to plain homely unadorned butter-and-egg sort of market carts.' Further, 'to every carriage, or set of carriages, a trumpeter was appointed, in addition to which a full military band was stationed at the head of the procession'.[25] For some later commentators, the festive character of the railways's opening celebrated the triumph of the new – the technology and enterprise of capital.[26] But for Marxist and other critical analysts, the celebration was part of a more sinister process of distracting attention from the appalling social consequences of contemporary capitalist development.[27] Edward Stanley, author of the report in *Blackwood's*

34. Richard Trevithick's planned monument to the Reform Bill.

35. Isaac Shaw, *The Opening of the Liverpool and Manchester Railway*, pencil, sepia and brown wash, 1831, portrays the magnificent opening in September 1830.

Magazine, noted how at Liverpool the sentiment of the crowd was predominantly one of honest, loyal feeling, whereas the Manchester crowds watched the procession 'with looks of sullen or insolent indifference'.[28] According to Fanny Kemble, in another eye-witness account, those at Manchester were of the lowest order of mechanics and artisans, among whom a dangerous spirit of discontent with the government prevailed: groans and hisses greeted the influential personages, among them the Duke of Wellington, while 'high among the grim and grimy crowd of scowling faces a loom had been erected, at which sat a tattered, starved-looking weaver, evidently set there as a *representative man*, to protest against [the] triumph of machinery'.[29] Behind the façade of celebration, in other words, was a society in a state of convulsion. Moreover, according to one historian, it was fast becoming no society at all: 'men and classes were no longer parts of a Christian-feudal organism where everyone had his recognized place and function and was united to Church and State by established rights and duties.' It was being replaced by a society that was simply 'a collection of individuals, each motivated – naturally and rightly – by self-interest'.[30] Here was Darwinism applied to the social world.

36. Edward Bury, *The 'Liverpool' Locomotive*: steam traction on the Liverpool and Manchester Railway, 1831.

The remarkable struggle to bring the Liverpool and Manchester Railway project to fruition was arguably 'the final battle between two economic systems and two ways of living'.[31] The Earl of Sefton and the Earl of Derby, across whose estates the new line was to run, vigorously opposed it. Their tenants threw stones at the survey teams. Their agents were instructed to place guards on the lands to be surveyed.[32] The Squire in William Pickering's *Railroad Eclogues* of 1846 offered an admirable representation of their attitude:

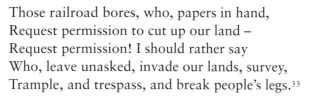

> Those railroad bores, who, papers in hand,
> Request permission to cut up our land –
> Request permission! I should rather say
> Who, leave unasked, invade our lands, survey,
> Trample, and trespass, and break people's legs.[33]

In *Middlemarch* (1871–2), George Eliot drew on her memories of the time when the London and Birmingham Railway's surveyors arrived in rural Warwickshire. In the hundred to which Middlemarch belonged, railways were 'as exciting a topic as the Reform Bill'. Landowners there were unanimous in their view that such 'pernicious agencies' as railway companies should be made to pay a very high price.[34] Their field labourers, meanwhile, turned on the railway agents with hay-forks and had to be persuaded of the futility of their opposition by the farm agent, Caleb Garth: 'Now, my lads, you can't hinder the railroad: it will be made whether you like it or not.'[35]

According to one recent writer, 'the railway movement brought about the most dramatic infringement of private property rights in England since the Civil war'. Virtually no stretch of land was immune from the grasp of railway promoters. Social rank and wealth meant comparatively little in the face of what became known as 'the railway invasion of the land'.[36] Railway companies were entitled under their private Acts 'to take a man's land without any conveyance at all'. The Acts gave companies the authority 'to enter, survey and even to excavate private land situated on a prescribed route'. Notices of intention to purchase were then issued and, failing a response from the landowner, the railway company was entitled to have the matter settled by a sheriff's jury.[37] The railways,

37. *The Great 'Land' Serpent!*, a contemporary view of the railway's invasion of the land.

38. A. F. Tait, lithograph, 1848, of the railway viaduct over the Sankey Valley.

in other words, inaugurated the era of compulsory land purchase. This was legislative appropriation on a grand scale. The *Illustrated London News* of September 1845 described the powers of the Acts as being nearly as absolute as the Russian Ukase. And so pervasive was the railway's land invasion to become that it prompted a bitter controversy about the concept of 'property in land'.[38] In response, the landowning interests used their wealth to instruct lawyers vigorously to defend their property interests and, in parallel, employed their still powerful political influence in Parliament to press for concessions. Railway companies reacted to this onslaught by trying to buy off opposition. They were often successful, but the inevitable outcome was the gross inflation of land costs. And these rose in the wake of the passing of the Land Clauses Bill in 1845 which gave landowners greater protection in the face of the railway juggernaut.[39] The struggle over land expropriation in some ways stood proxy for wider political tensions between the two parties. Many within the railway interest, for example, were enthusiastic supporters of the Anti-Corn Law League, a movement fiercely opposed by many of the landed élite. The railway interest saw the fight to allow cheap imports of grain as akin to the fight against abusive practices in the sale of land for railway schemes. The railway press certainly had no doubts about the coalition of landed interests which was set against it. As late as 1855 the *Railway Gazette* was commenting on 'the extortionate sums demanded and obtained by landlords' in the making of new lines.[40] Ultimately, though, within society at large and the legal profession more particularly, there emerged a view that the railway invasion of land could be justified in part on the basis of public benefit, the so-called 'public weal'. Hence a utilitarian theory of property in land emerged, which could be said to have had its origin in the railway interest.[41]

In the first survey of the Liverpool–Manchester line (1822), the antagonism of the landed interest was such that the railway venturers resorted to hiring a prize-fighter to carry the theodolite.[42] In subsequent surveys, much of the levelling was done by moonlight and by torchlight to try to evade the worst vigour of the opposition.[43] In Stephenson's orginal scheme, the line was to run on a level, skirting the sandstone ridges to the north. Blank rejections from landowners, however, forced him to drive a tunnel through Edge Hill, to cut a ravine through Olive Mount and to swing a viaduct, seventy feet high, across the Sankey valley.[44] Nor was the Liverpool–Manchester project peculiar in this regard. The survey for the London and Birmingham Railway had to be completed 'at night by means of dark lanterns', such was the scale of the opposition from the so-called 'Lords of the soil'.[45] In this case, the resistant peers were Clarendon and Essex,[46] but the clergy were not exempt from the appellation. In one case the survey team for the London and Birmingham had to resort to the extraordinary expedient of performing their work during the hour of divine service, when the reverend gentleman concerned was otherwise disposed.[47]

Aside from issues of land expropriation, the great landowners also saw railroads as potentially damaging to the amenity of their parks and gardens and invasive of their farming routines.[48] It was claimed with great boldness and bitterness of spirit that the railways would be a 'drug on the country' and that bridges and culverts would become 'antiquarian ruins'.[49] Perhaps more critically in the context of emerging class relations, the landowners saw railroads as potentially destructive of what E. P. Thompson has described as the 'societal field-of-force': the complex web of reciprocal social attitudes that had for centuries defined patrician–pleb relations.[50] And when estate tenants or labourers and others of the common populace stoned the survey teams, they were defending this traditional social order as much as they were doing the bidding of their lordships.

Alongside opposition from the great landed estates, railway projects also had to contend with powerful antagonism from existing transport interests. The lucrative business enjoyed by many road and waterway proprietors along the route between Liverpool and Manchester, for example, meant that they fought bitterly against the railroad scheme.[51] The landed interest was once more behind some of these enterprises but, in other cases, they were family-based concerns or closed groups of merchant-proprietors founded a century before. Their supporters, such as Edward Alderson, denied that they enjoyed any monopoly over trade and argued that the relative speed of railroad carriage would have little significance for the Manchester cotton merchants since they regularly kept five to six weeks' supply of cotton on hand in their warehouses.[52] Alderson's view was that the railroad was a speculation on the Liverpool Exchange and his scathing demolition of George Stephenson in Parliament led to the defeat of the first Bill.[53] Within the increasing tempo of capitalist economy, of course, cotton bales stockpiled in Manchester for weeks at a time were unnecessary and potentially disastrous impediments to the circulatory scheme of capital. But, perhaps predictably, it was the prospect of inflated pecuniary gain that persuaded some of the leading oppositional forces eventually to support the railroad project. The Marquess of Stafford, for example, in the end provided roughly a fifth of its capital.[54]

As the Victorian era unfolded, Stafford's example was followed by other

39. J. C. Bourne, *Bath Hampton*, lithograph, 1846. Cattle graze peacefully alongside the Great Western Railway; such compositions were common among early artists of the railway – perhaps deliberately, in order to counter the propaganda of the railway opposition.

members of his class. Indeed, such was the eventual force of the railway as a focus of investment that few Peers were altogether immune from its allure.[55] As the century wore on, moreover, the landed élites began to see the potential value to their agricultural estates of local branch railways – that is, quite aside from the often highly favourable financial compensation that the railway's invasion of land brought. Thus did the Earls of Leicester invest in lines in Norfolk and the Earls of Yarborough encourage lines in Lincolnshire.[56] By the close of the Victorian era, it has been argued that 'the relationship between the landowners and the railways [had] changed fundamentally'.[57] The aristocracy began to see the great Victorian railway companies as a highly appropriate outlet for large-scale investment. By this time, companies like the London and North Western were among the largest and most secure businesses in the land. It was thus almost inevitable that they should be targets for landed investors. In parallel, the grandees of the land also began to join the railway companies' boards. By 1900, titled directors of railway companies were commonplace. On this evidence, then, there is clearly a measure of justice in the claim made by some historians that the old social order never actually faded, and certainly not in the wake of the 1832 Reform Act.[58] There was a sense in which, in Schumpeter's words, 'the aristocratic element continued to rule the roost'.[59] The traditional élites retained some of their political, social and cultural primacy throughout the Victorian era.[60] In this respect, the railways ultimately helped to cement the persistence of the old order. But this was hardly the prevailing perspective in mid-century.

A man born in 1800 would have grown up in a
pre-railway world that was nearer to medieval England
than it is to our own. He would have seen the railway
invade it and suck its life away into the growing
manufacturing towns.[61]

The argument about the defeat of the old order also has a geographical dimension, and it is possible to claim that railways were no less implicated in this. The feudal nexus of society was grounded in territory, familiarly in the manor and its appendages.[62] When manorialism began to decline, the vestiges of its spatial power were assumed by the parish and the parish vestry.[63] This became most acutely expressed in the administration of the Old Poor Law with its myriad variations in the pattern of relief, not to mention the related issue of 'settlement'.[64]

Feudal society, as well as its later vestiges, was heavily agricultural. Underlying the concepts of territory represented by the manor and the parish was a kaleidoscope of what have been called 'natural economies' or, to use the French term, 'pays'.[65] Some historians have talked of the 'chalk and cheese' of English farming in the seventeenth century – that is, arable versus pastoral.[66] The argument is that different natural systems gave rise to different livelihood systems, displaying often very distinctive cultural traits and social organisation. In the cultural ecology

40. A. F. Tait, oil on canvas, 1848. The pastoral landscape of north Cheshire, as viewed from Alderley Edge.

of political allegiance during the English Civil War, it is claimed that arable regions were more communal, more traditionalist and more deferential and hence, it is argued, more supportive of the royalist cause; whereas pastoral regions were more individualist and non-conforming, and supported Cromwell. It has further been suggested that these differences also extended to sports and pastimes.[67] For a whole range of reasons, then, social life was rooted in territory, and this was a feature that persisted into the nineteenth century (the Old Poor Law, for example, based on the parish unit, survived until 1834). After the 1830s, however, railways helped progressively to undermine such roots. Most 'natural economies' faded as the spreading web of railways overturned their equilibria of economic and social self-sufficiency and as operating companies pursued the food import trades for the more profitable business that they afforded.[68]

Thomas Hardy captured features of the old order (and of its passing) in some of his Wessex novels. For Tess in *Tess of the d'Urbervilles* (1891), the Vale of Blackmoor 'was to her the world, and its inhabitants the races thereof'.[69] Only a small tract even of the Vale and its environs was known to her by close inspection.[70] In Little Hintock, in *The Woodlanders* (1887), 'there were hardly two houses . . . unrelated by some matrimonial tie or other'; 'intermarriages were of Hapsburgian frequency'.[71] In many of Hardy's novels, however, the railway was already providing intermittent contact between this secluded world and modern life. In *Tess*, the little railway station proffered only a feeble, smoky lamp to Angel Clare and Tess as they arrived to load the milk cans.[72] Yet this 'poor terrestrial star . . . was in one sense of more importance to Talbothays Dairy and mankind than the celestial ones to which it stood in such humiliating contrast'; this was the point of contact with the 'whirl of material progress'.[73] In *Tom Brown's Schooldays* (1856), we learn how, before the railroad era, young boys found their own amusements 'within a walk or a ride home'. They got to know all the country folk, including their ways, their songs and their stories. It was Berkshire boys, or Gloucestershire boys, or Yorkshire boys then – not 'young cosmopolites, belonging to all counties and no countries'.[74] All this was a product of being born into 'these racing railroad times'. No longer did people know much about their own birthplaces. They were 'all in the ends of the earth'.[75]

Social commentators of the later nineteenth century deplored this loss of a sense of community in urban industrial society. Social relations, to quote Beatrice Webb, had 'no roots in neighbourhood, in vocation, in creed'.[76] The *Economist* remarked how in 1850, in one week of holiday time, over 200,000 people left Manchester by cheap excursion trains.[77] Whereas the older generations had often never stirred from their native villages in a lifetime, the new became rapidly accustomed to a vast extension in their spatial horizons. A very early commentary on the social influences of the railway remarked that

> men who but a few years since scarcely crossed the precincts of the county in which they were born, and knew as little of the general features of the land of their birth as they did the topography of the moon, now unhesitatingly avail themselves of the means of communication that are afforded . . .[78]

A treatise on nineteenth-century migration trends remarked how women were more migratory than men.[79] This was attributed to the growing army of female domestic servants within urban industrial society. In England, it was compounded by a gender imbalance in the population: there were roughly 108 females to every

41. An early excursion poster for the Newcastle and Carlisle Railway.

42. The railway was the means by which many a young girl left the family home for a life in domestic service.

100 males.[80] Railways were critical to the valorisation and mobilisation of this division of labour, as encapsulated in Marian Gardiner's portrait of a sad young woman, seated in a third-class railway compartment, off to a life in service.

In one area, however, railways did *not* manage to triumph over localism – the matter of parochial taxation. The great problem that railway companies faced was that their legislated invasion of the land was not accompanied by any displacement of the fiscal and political prerogatives of the gentry over the local governments.[81] Canals had been subjected to parish taxation, but in a manner that had brought no cries of unfairness from their proprietors. Initially this was also true of railways, but as the country élites began to appreciate the scale of profits that leading railway companies enjoyed, they saw an opportunity to expand their local tax base. The land occupied by the London and North Western Railway, for example, was, prior to its company utilisation, assessed at £2,445 annually. In turn, this constituted a 150th part of the total rates of the parishes within which the land was situated. By 1848, though, the same land was charged at £128,000, a full third of the total assessable value of all the parishes concerned.[82] What rural government officials had begun to do was to assess companies on 'the full rental value of their property as commercially developed or improved land'.[83] The railway interest naturally sought remedy in law to tackle this perceived iniquity. However, appeals at Quarter Sessions and applications to the Court of Queen's Bench largely fell on deaf ears. In effect, parish authorities were being permitted to levy a *de facto* income tax on railway companies.[84] The companies eventually responded by negotiating long-term deals with parish vestries.[85] But it remained true that, for all its many revolutionary features, the railway failed to transform the centuries-old system of local government. And to the extent that local government remained the province of the old social élites, this was another instance where the relationship between the railway and reform was ambiguous.

THE DEATH OF NATURE

Flight

> We feel ourselves as powerful as the sorcerers of old!
> We put our magic-horse to the carriage and space
> disappears; we fly like the clouds in a storm, as the bird
> of passage flies . . .[86]

The image of flight is a pervasive one among early railway commentaries. The rail-road locomotive defied all existing conventions of land speed, tied as these were to horse-power. So the Victorian imagination resorted to flight as the most credible way of representing railroad speed:

> You'll go four hundred miles per day, –
> Aye, faster than an eagle flies,
> For steam all other things outvies.[87]

In one of William Pickering's *Railroad Eclogues* of 1846, a railway stoker seeks to persuade a respectable young lady to elope with him, and flight is once again the image chosen to try to represent the speed of travel:

> Quit, quit with me this antiquated scene,
> And fly on railroad wings to Gretna Green.[88]

References to sorcery and magic (see quotation above) formed another very common image. Anderson argued that the railroad rendered a potency in flight that those in the Middle Ages thought only the devil could attain.[89] Robert Louis Stevenson echoed the sentiments in a line of his famous verses 'From a Railway Carriage': 'Faster than fairies, faster than witches'.[90] The frequent perception of the locomotive as an iron monster extended such reactions. Thomas Roscoe, describing an early journey on the Grand Junction Railway in the late 1830s, claimed how the 'Fire Fly' engine thundered along the line 'like a huge monster in mortal agony, whose entrails are like burning coals'.[91] At almost precisely the same date, Thomas Carlyle wrote of a railway journey from the north-west of England to London as if it was a Faustian flight:

> The whirl through the confused darkness on those steam wings, was one of the strangest things I have experienced – hissing and dashing on, one knew not whither. We saw the gleam of towns in the distance – unknown towns. We went over the tops of houses – one town or village I saw clearly, with its chimney heads vainly stretching up towards us – *under* the stars; not under the clouds, but among them. Out of one vehicle into another, snorting, roaring we flew: likest thing to a Faust's flight on the Devil's mantle; or as if some huge steam night-bird had flung you on its back, and was sweeping through unknown space with you . . .[92]

Nor did the imagery fade with the passage of the years. William Cosmo Monkhouse, for example, offered the following personified acount of the departure of a night express in 1865:

> With three great snorts of strength,
> Stretching my mighty length,
> Like some dragon stirring in his sleep,
> Out from the glare of gas
> Into the night I pass,
> And plunge alone into the silence deep.

Such potentially frightening images were the more powerful because the 'monstrosity' was a Victorian creation, as Monkhouse's verses subsequently made plain:

> Little I know or care
> What be the load I bear,
> Why thus compelled I seek not to divine,
> At man's command I stir,
> I, his stem messenger![93]

The Victorians, in other words, had become as powerful as the sorcerers of old. The same supernatural metaphor figured in American reactions to the first railroads. One Chicago resident described them as 'talismanic wands'. Their power to transform landscapes sccmed to draw upon 'a mysterious creative energy that was beyond human influence or knowledge'.[94]

    This fantasy of flight was not wholly fanciful. The need for a level permanent way meant that railroads were quite often elevated above the terrain they tra-

43. G. F. Bragg, lithograph, 1836. The London–Greenwich Railway on its continuous viaduct as it crossed the Surrey Canal.

versed. The London–Greenwich line, London's first railway, was on a viaduct for almost its entire length. At Liverpool Road station on the Liverpool–Manchester line, a tourist of 1833 elaborated the passenger's experience when entraining:

> Ascending a flight of stairs which rise from the interior of the lower office, we enter upon the railway at a level with the second storey. . . . There is something singularly striking . . . in this change in one's altitude. . . . a moment ago we were in the midst . . . of a busy multitude . . . anon we find ourselves, as it were insensibly, translated to another equally sublunary scene, from which to discern the self-same beings of a previous companionship still plying the self-same stern activity, but in a world that now lies stretched far beneath us.[95]

Elevated stretches of railway of this sort were commonplace by the 1850s inside Victorian cities like Manchester.

According to Fanny Kemble in August 1830, when she travelled on the then unopened Liverpool and Manchester Railway with George Stephenson, the speed of the train at thirty-five miles per hour was, indeed, swifter than the flight of a bird, 'for they had tried the experiment with a snipe'. It was impossible to conceive, she went on to say, what 'the sensation of cutting the air was': when the eyes were closed, it was exactly as if in flight.[96] A related sensation was recorded by Thomas Roscoe in his account of travel on the Grand Junction Railway:

> The train darts through the Newton Cutting in the space of two minutes, following its flying course over one embankment, – through another cutting, – and crossing the Tame again, again, and again, as though the little stream was playing at hide and seek with the giant racer, – now swimming right away from his track, and now again re-appearing directly across his path.[97]

The image of flight was revealed in a rather less comfortable dimension in the depiction of the railroad train as a projectile. The metaphor was used initially to emphasise the train's speed, as witnessed in the name given to Stephenson's most famous locomotive, 'Rocket'. That legendary railway commentator, Dionysius Lardner, likewise equated railway speed with that of a cannon-ball.[98] But the metaphor could also be used to reflect the way the train apparently shot through the landscape: 'Thus the rails, cuttings and tunnels appeared as the barrel through which the projectile of the train passes'.[99] An account of travelling on the Liverpool and Manchester Railway which appeared in *Buck's Gazette* echoed these features:

> The projections, or transits of the train through the tunnels or arches, are very electrifying. The deafening peal of thunder, the sudden immersion in gloom, and the dash of reverberated sounds in confined space, combined to produce a momentary shudder, or idea of destruction – a thrill of annihilation, which is instantly dispelled on emerging into the cheerful light.[100]

This sensation of novelty, thrill, shock and perceived danger is akin to a child's first experience of a roller-coaster. Thus can we begin to appreciate how the railway invited fear as well as fascination. The fun-fair analogy had a contemporary basis in fact, for in 1842 there was exhibited in London the Grand Centrifugal Railway, later called the Flying Railway, a kind of roller-coaster upon which people could ride. Posters were still advertising it in 1844 and in 1848 it appears to have moved to France.[101]

44. Advertisement for a 'novelty' railway, 1842. In its general principle, this would not be out of place in a theme park such as Alton Towers a century and a half later.

Elizabeth Barrett Browning invested the experience of railway travel with sexual overtones in her poem 'Through the tunnels' from *Aurora Leigh*:

> So we passed
> The liberal open country and the close,
> And shot through tunnels, like a lightning wedge
> By great Thor-Hammers driven through the rock,
> Which, quivering through the intestine blackness, splits,
> And lets it in at once: the train swept in
> Athrob with effort, trembling with resolve,
> The fierce denouncing whistle wailing on
> And dying off smothered in the shuddering dark,
> While we, self-awed, drew troubled breath, oppressed
> As other Titans underneath the pile
> And nightmare of the mountains. Out, at last,
> To catch the dawn afloat upon the land![102]

The spectacle from the lineside was not much different in the drama of its impact:

> First, the shrill whistle, then the distant roar,
> The ascending cloud of steam, the gleaming brass,
> The mighty moving arm; and on amain
> The mass comes thundering like an avalanche o'er
> The quaking earth; a thousand faces pass –
> A moment, and are gone, like whirlwind sprites,
> Scarce seen; so much the roaring speed benights
> All sense and recognition for a while;
> A little space, a minute, a mile.
> Then look again, how swift it journeys on;
> Away, away, along the horizon
> Like drifted cloud, to its determined place;
> Power, speed, and distance, melting into space.[103]

45. A. F. Tait, lithograph, 1848, of Newton station on the Liverpool and Manchester line.

Yet again the images are of flight, cataclysm and inhuman power, while space and time apparently fuse as miles become minutes in 'melting space'. At the Legh Arms at Newton in Lancashire, a spacious inn adjoining the Liverpool–Manchester railroad, Sir George Head described the coming and going of trains:

> Each train, as it approaches, is preceded for many seconds by a sound as if a legion of winged horses were cleaving the air at a distance; and as one continues to listen, they seem, as they advance, as if furiously panting and clapping their pinions against their sides, till whizzing along, like skyrockets, they pass, one after another, – a succession of moving objects glancing onwards, in the variety of a magic lantern.[104]

Even terminal stations had their own distinctive version of high drama, as apparent from Sir Francis Bond Head's account of the arrival of a train at Euston Square:

> About four minutes after the up-train has been authorized by the air-pipe to leave Camden station, the guard who stands listening for it at the Euston tunnel . . . announces by his flag its immediate approach . . . the Company's porters, emerging from various points, quickly advance to their respective stations; and this suspense continues until in a second or two there is seen darting out of the tunnel, like a serpent from its hole, the long dark-coloured train, which by a tortuous movement is apparently advancing at full speed . . .[105]

By night, the experience of observing a train passing through a station was more spectacular still and potentially more terrifying:

46. T. T. Bury, aquatint, 1831, of the entrance to the railway tunnel at Edge Hill.

47. John Martin, *The Last Judgement*, oil on canvas, 1853 (detail of pl. 255). The railway train tumbles into Chaos.

. . . the sights and sounds grow more strange and awful. Every now and then a great flaming eye makes its appearance in the distance: the gradual boom of its approach grows louder and louder; the thunder of its tread reverberates from afar; the sickly hue of the buffer light is surpassed by the red light of the furnace, as it glares below the wheels. . . . As the iron gullet of the monster vomits aloft red hot masses of burning coke, the thundering, gleaming mass rushes past at some fifty or sixty, perhaps seventy, miles an hour; and as it rolls off into darkness again on the other side of the station, with its three red eyes gleaming behind, it seems to burn its way through the sable livery of night with the strength and straightness and fury of a red-hot cannon-ball.[106]

Where railway lines passed through industrial districts, the images of the supernatural could be overwhelming. Between Birmingham and Wolverhampton, travellers on the Grand Junction Railway could observe 'on all sides, as far as the eye can reach, the land . . . blazing with innumerable furnaces'. The heavy sound of steam hammers signalled the 'continual war of forges', while from the centre of the earth came the 'hoarse thunder of the miners' blasts'. It was 'a picture more stupendous and terrific than fabled *Lemnos*, with its burning fires and colony of supernatural blacksmiths'.[107] These were the images that inspired the painter John Martin in his vast biblical canvases, with all their apocalyptic terror, the fame of which soon spread far and wide through the medium of mezzotint.[108] The Black Country presented to the artist a whole set of 'formal symbolic precedents for the transformation of the face of the earth and its natural resources into satanic "fabrics huge".'[109] Within one of these canvases, *The Last Judgement* (1853), a railway train can be seen tumbling into Chaos.[110] For Martin, the steam locomotive was no less a source of satanic imagery than the fiery furnaces of the Black Country. As railway trains rushed headlong deep through the earth, they offered a flight into the underworld, a terrible experience of the infernal regions. Klingender thought the Edge Hill railway tunnel might easily have been the site of John Martin's more spectacular cataclysms, its three portals apparently leading into the bowels of the earth, flanked by great chimney stacks, 'decorated like columns in honour of some long-dead Roman Emperor'.[111]

A produced nature

... from out of the midst of darkness a new era
was ushered to the wondering world. It was the
birth-struggle of a giant power, destined ere long to bear
down, like the rushing of a mighty torrent, all existing
barriers, and give a direction hitherto unknown to
the leading features of our social institutions;
to annihilate – or, at least, immediately extend – the
bounds of time and space; to convert our hills and
valleys into level plains; – to throw up towering
mountains, and scoop out dead depths ... from the
very bounds of the earth.[112]

If Victorians had to resort to the image of flight to capture the railroad's speed, they were unambiguous about the material transformations that it forged. That populist reformer, Lord Brougham, talked of 'the gigantic power of man penetrating through miles of solid mass, and gaining a great, lasting, an almost perennial conquest over the power of nature'.[113] For Carlyle, the railroads became part of a war with 'rude nature'.[114] They were a tribute to man's power to conquer nature and to forge a second or *produced* nature.[115] John Ruskin, however, was appalled by the way railroads brutally amputated every hill in their path and raised mounds of earth across meadows vaster than the walls of Babylon.[116] Railway architecture

48. J. C. Bourne, lithograph, 1839, showing rocks being blasted at Linslade on the London and Birmingham Railway, October 1837.

49. J. C. Bourne, lithograph, 1839. The vast, extending mound of earth intended to carry the London and Birmingham Railway across the Wolverton valley, June 1837.

appeared deliberately to play on this comparison with ancient antiquity, as witnessed in the triumphalism of many of its edifices. Artists, too, used it as a basis upon which to forge a distinctive railway iconography (see chapter eight).

Many of these features were revealed in disarmingly stark fashion on the line of the Liverpool and Manchester Railway. The five miles of boggy fen known as Chat Moss were celebrated by Michael Drayton as having their origin in the Deluge,[117] but the Moss was successfully traversed by constructing a floating embankment: 'the railway, for the most part, floats on the surface of the heathy ocean; and where it was softest, branches, brushwood and hurdles formed by twigs and heath, twisted and plaited in frames, were made a foundation'.[118] Nearer to Liverpool, the line cut a ravine seventy feet deep and two miles long through Olive Mount. Then, between Edge Hill and Wapping, it burrowed through rock for two thousand yards, to reach the terminus close to Queen's Dock. When Fanny Kemble reflected how such 'great masses of stone had been cut asunder to allow . . . passage thus far below the surface of the earth', she felt 'as if no fairy tale was ever half so wonderful' as what she saw.[119] Sir George Head, likewise, was full of wonder when in 1835 he rode on the rope-worked incline of the Edge Hill tunnel:

> As we passed along, a train came rumbling downwards, by its own gravity, in an opposite direction. The effect was awfully grand at the approach of so stupendous a body rushing towards us in the dark, with a sound like that of distant artillery; while the conductor sat in front, holding in his hand a small glimmering lantern. The scene brought the regions of Pluto to the imagination . . .[120]

Dickens offered another picture in his inimitable prose fashion in *Dombey and Son* (1846–8) on the occasion of Dombey's journey with Major Bagstock on the newly constructed London and Birmingham Railway. The railway was 'defiant of all paths and roads, piercing through the heart of every obstacle . . . through the fields, through the woods, through the corn, through the hay, through the mould, through the clay, through the rock'. When it was not passing through obstacles, it

50, 51 (above and opposite). Edwin T. Dolby, c. 1850, two views of the western entrance to Abbotscliffe tunnel on the London and Dover Railway.

was going *over* them.[121] Moreover, it 'breasted' away 'wind and light', 'shower and sunshine', working with such a 'storm of energy and perseverance' that the motion in tunnels could even seem backwards – 'until a ray of light on the wet wall, shows its surface flying past like a fierce stream'.[122] In February 1843, the *Illustrated London News* carried an account of some of the London and Dover Railway Company's works on the Channel coast. Here, when the engineers dynamited part of the cliff, it was as 'a mountain cast into the sea'. The nobility and gentry of the neighbourhood flocked to witness the event, while the lower orders in Dover were terrified at the anticipated destruction of their windows.[123]

In William Pickering's *Railroad Eclogues* of 1846, even the railroad prospectors fitted the destructive mentality, as expressed in the lament of one Rector:

> O, they have favoured me again this morning,
> And Huns & Chouse and Co. have given me warning,
> A grand competing line will tunnel under
> My rectory, and cut my glebe asunder,
> The Church they don't intend to touch at present;
> The experiment as yet might scarce be pleasant.
> But, by and by, should it be deemed expedient
> To *change their line*, to make it more convenient,
> The Church itself must go – thus coolly runs
> The notice I've received from Chouse and Huns.[124]

More than half a century after the first railroads, the power of the invention in the face of nature appeared undiminished. Harold Munro wrote of the 'Wild Engine' in the following manner:

> Every time I sit
> In a train I must remember it
> The way it smashes through the air; its great
> Petulant majesty and terrible rate:
> Driving the ground before it, with those round
> Feet pounding, beating, covering the ground.[125]

The ultimate representation of the railroad's war with nature was in the clocks, which observed railway time – instead of local time, as measured on a sun-dial. As Dickens so acutely remarked, it was 'as if the sun itself had given in'.[126] Initially, the standardisation of time was a clumsy process. Bagwell describes how, on the Grand Junction Railway,

> each morning an Admiralty messenger carried a watch bearing the correct time to a guard on the down Irish Mail leaving Euston for Holyhead. On arrival at Holyhead, the time was passed on to officials on the Kingston boat who carried it over to Dublin. On the return mail to Euston the watch was carried back to the Admiralty messenger at Euston once more.[127]

After the setting up of the Railway Clearing House in 1842, this rather absurd procedure gave way to the observance of Greenwich, not local, time at stations around the country, a practice made easier by the spread of the telegraph. Greenwich, or 'railway' time, became standard in Britain by the 1850s.[128] At the Prime Meridian Conference in Washington in 1884, twenty-five countries settled on Greenwich as the zero meridian. British 'railway' time thus became 'world' time.[129]

52. London and South-Western Railway 2-2-2 locomotive 'Frome', built 1859.

To talk of railroads and the conquest of nature is, of course, to see nature as external. But nature does not exist independently of man: it is a social construction. What the railroad became part of was thus a transformed nature and, more particularly in the eyes of Marxist commentators, a nature tied to the imperatives of capitalism.[130] Putting it slightly differently: the human mind had discovered nature's secrets and was converting her material resources into productive usefulness.[131] In his short story *Mugby Junction* (1866), Charles Dickens senses features of this transformation with uncanny facility. There were so many railroad lines that they appeared to be 'the work of extraordinary ground spiders that spun iron'.[132] There were iron-barred cages full of cattle . . . the drooping beasts with horns entangled, eyes frozen with terror'. There were 'half-miles of coal'.[133] Signalmen had been reduced to puppets which 'popped out of boxes in perspective, and popped in again'.[134]

The triumph of machine and of capital was re-echoed in the erasure of the distinction between night and day. Much as the factory defied the rhythms of sun and stars (vividly captured in a painting of Cromford Mill at night by Joseph Wright of Derby), so did the railroad. In the *Lazy Tour*, Dickens remarked how the junction station was, by day or by night, either totally unconscious or wildly raving. When unconscious, it was lifeless, as if 'the last train for ever, had gone without issuing any Return tickets'. Then, there was a 'shave of the air' (as the signal went up) and all changed.[135] At night, activity broke out as 'a constellation of gas', followed by 'lurid torches' as the trains wailed and shrieked into the station.[136] Railroad operation, in other words, took no cognizance of the dawn or of the setting sun, whereas stage-coaches and canal-boats had typically moved in daylight hours.

In some commentaries, the steam locomotive alone became the cardinal representation of the production of nature – in its description as an automaton, for example. But it was sometimes difficult to find the appropriate means of describing steam locomotion. One contribution in *Buck's Gazette* could say of its 'belchings or explosions' that they more nearly resembled 'the pantings of a lion or tiger' than any familiar vibrations. The same contributor went on to observe how the automaton appeared sometimes to labour 'like an animal out of breath', especially as it sought higher elevations. Once over the summit, though, the automaton was 'flying down the declivity like lightning', with the wind appearing to 'be blowing a hurricane, such was the velocity with which we darted through the air'.[137] Leon Faucher, in his observations of railways in the centre of Manchester, seems to have had the same difficulties. He heard 'nothing but the breathing of the vast machines, sending forth fire and smoke through their tall chimneys, and offering up to the heavens, as it were in token of homage, the sight of that labour which God has imposed upon man'.[138] Fanny Kemble, likewise, seems to have found considerable difficulty in straying from animate imagery when describing her trip on the Liverpool and Manchester Railway. The engine she described as a 'fire-horse'. It went upon two wheels which were 'feet'. These feet were moved by bright steel 'legs' called pistons. The pistons were propelled by steam and as more steam was applied to the extremities of the pistons, the 'hip-joints', the faster the wheels went. The 'wonderful beast' had 'reins, bit and bridle' in the form of a small steel handle so simple that a child could manage it, so the writer claimed. Finally, the fire-horse was provided with coal in place of oats.[139]

Anxieties over the death of nature

We are unaware of the degree to which the Victorian
consciousness – and especially the sub-conscious – was
haunted by fear and worry, by guilt, frustration
and loneliness.[140]

The conquest or production of nature had profound implications for Christian belief. Railroads easily became part of the inhuman and godless 'circlings of force', recorded by Charlotte Brontë upon her reading of the Atkinson–Martineau letters (1851) on man's nature and development, in which the full creed of scientific materialism was laid out.[141] This found acute expression in the vexed question of whether railway trains should be run on the Sabbath. Some clergymen, share-holders, Parliamentarians and literary figures like Trollope brought pressure on companies either to abandon Sunday trains or to refrain from running them in hours of divine service.[142] However, their campaign met with very mixed results. Sabbatarian observance was greatest in Scotland where by 1914 the proportion of lines closed on Sundays reached nearly sixty per cent. In England, the figure grew from five per cent in 1860 to around twenty-two per cent in 1914,[143] but there were significant variations among the different companies. The London, Brighton and South Coast Railway, for instance, recorded only six miles closed on Sundays in 1914, whereas the North Eastern had 610 miles out of service, more than a third

53. J. C. Bourne, lithograph, 1846, of the interior of Box tunnel on the Great Western Railway.

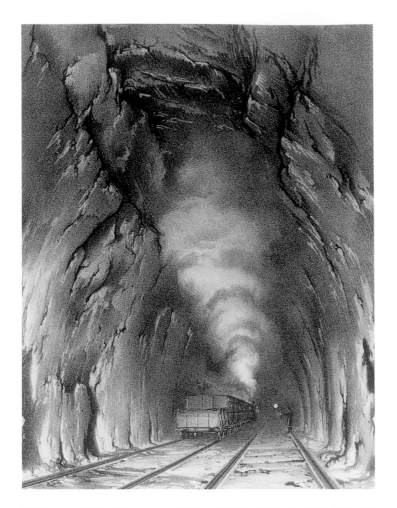

54. T. T. Bury, aquatint, 1831. One of several versions of the interior of the Edge Hill tunnel on the Liverpool and Manchester Railway. This view was soon replaced, because it erroneously showed a locomotive in steam when trains were in fact hauled through the tunnel by steam-worked cable.

of its network.[144] One prime difficulty facing the Sabbatarians was the fact that the public at large showed no particular inclination not to travel on Sundays. It was, as Dr Grantly famously remarked in *Barchester Towers* (1857), easy to withdraw trains if you could withdraw passengers.[145] As the century went on, Sunday closure on some company lines became less about observing the Lord's Day than about issues of profit and operation.

The railroad 'juggernaut' also caused people to fear for their bodily wellbeing. It was not just the fear of being run down by a train, as the death of the MP William Huskisson at the Liverpool and Manchester Railway's opening so forcefully demonstrated, but the fears for human safety in travelling, psychological as well as physical. One objector to the Great Western Railway's Bill claimed in relation to the tunnel at Box that 'no person would desire to be shut out from the daylight with the consciousness that he had a superincumbent weight of earth sufficient to crush him in case of accident'.[146] Another argued that the noise of two trains passing inside the tunnel would have a devastating effect on the nerves of passengers.[147] That these objections had a broader basis of sentiment is illustrated by the precautions that the Liverpool and Manchester company took in its tunnel at Edge Hill. The interior was painted white and it was illuminated by gas jets at regular intervals, to allay insecurities in the minds of passengers as well as in the minds of the spectators who were invited to view it.[148] Arthur Freeling's guide to the London and Birmingham Railway contained a serious and lengthy piece about the supposed evils of tunnels, but assured passengers that these were all imaginary.[149] Even so, there remained a somewhat disturbing resemblance between the first engravings of the interiors of tunnels like Box and Edge Hill and the picture *Bridge over Chaos* that John Martin had made for an illustrated *Paradise Lost* a few years before. Another way in which efforts were made to try to convince the public that the railroad was not as dangerous as it looked was by its architecture, as in the case of Liverpool Corporation when it insisted that the Lime Street station

55. John Martin, *Bridge over Chaos*, 1826, illustration to Milton's *Paradise Lost*.

56. J. C. Bourne, lithograph, 1839, of the making of Tring cutting on the London and Birmingham Railway, June 1837.

of the Grand Junction Railway harmonize with St George's Hall.[150] In Dickens's *Martin Chuzzlewit* (1844), Mrs Gamp's famous account of the many miscarriages allegedly induced by railroad travel was a further indication of its potential terrors. And it was quite widely believed that railroad travel induced 'suicidal delirium' among those of a nervous disposition.[151]

As to the physical dangers, 'John Bull', as late as 1835, found it impossible to imagine how people would find any pleasure in being 'dragged through the air . . . all their lives being at the mercy of a tin pipe, or a copper boiler, or the accidental dropping of a pebble on the line of way'.[152] Others claimed that the noise and stench of the steam would 'disturb the quietude of the peasant, the farmer and the gentleman', not to mention the chronic effects upon farm livestock. In sum, railway lines were 'odious deformities' which increasingly tattooed the face of the country; they were among the 'most dangerous and disfiguring abominations'.[153]

It has been claimed that the Victorians 'were utterly unprepared for the radical crisis in thought and society which burst upon England in the thirties and forties'.[154] When, late in his life, Froude remembered the 1840s, it was to recall how, all around, 'intellectual lightships' were being broken from their moorings. He went on to say how new generations would never know what it was like 'to find the lights all drifting, the compasses all awry, and nothing left to steer by except the stars.'[155] There is hardly an aspect of this intellectual and social crisis which was not in some way connected to the railroad. The thrusting lines of permanent way, with all their attendant engineering works, were integral to Lytton's 'age of visible transition', 'of disquietude and doubt'.[156] Dickens captured something of this interesting juxtaposition in his accounts of Stagg's Gardens in Camden Town on the London–Birmingham line. The building of the railroad brought 'a hundred thousand shapes and substances of incompleteness, wildly mingled out of their places, upside down, burrowing in the earth, aspiring in the air, mouldering in the water, and unintelligible as any dream.'[157] Within a few years, though, the neighbourhood had discovered a 'powerful and prosperous relation' in the railroad.[158] The old Stagg's Gardens had vanished from the earth, amidst the palaces and granite columns of the 'Railway world'.[159]

Meanwhile, for those travellers familiar with Lyell's newly published *Principles of Geology* (1830–33), the great exposed rock sections flanking parts of the lineside between London and Birmingham offered a potentially stark reminder of Lyell's challenge to biblical teaching and the triumph of Uniformitarianism.[160] Victorians bought and read Lyell's book as if it were a novel: 'there was no better popular encyclopaedia of geological information'.[161] The strata crossed by the London and Birmingham line extended from the clay of the Thames Basin to the borders of the coal measures. Northwards from the station at Tring, the route cut through the great chalk ridge of Ivinghoe in an excavation two and a half miles long and up to almost sixty feet deep, forming an 'immense chasm'.[162] Emerging from Beechwood tunnel, further north towards Birmingham, the eye was arrested by the 'jagged and salient' sides of the deep sandstone strata.[163] According to one writer, geologists had flocked to study these great exposures.[164] John Ruskin, whose dislike of railways was legendary, came close to the mark when he opined that 'all that you can know, at best, of the country you pass is its geological structure'.[165] During the first decades of the nineteenth century, geology was at the leading edge of science.[166] What made it distinctive was the exceptionally rapid development of stratigraphic palaeontology – that is, the co-relation of geological formations from their fossil contents. By the 1840s, as railway cuttings were in the making all across the country, it became possible to observe whole sequences of strata, with all their distinctive fossil remains, for the first time. A correspondent of Charles Lyell wrote in February 1838 of the fascinating sections uncovered in making parts of the Forfar–Dundee railroad, urging Lyell to come and examine

57. F. Swanson, water-colour, 1849, of Blisworth cutting on the London and Birmingham Railway.

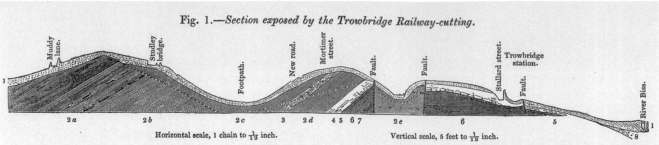

Fig. 1.—Section exposed by the Trowbridge Railway-cutting.

Horizontal scale, 1 chain to $\frac{1}{13}$ inch.   Vertical scale, 5 feet to $\frac{1}{13}$ inch.

1. Drift, 3 feet, with *Serpula vertebralis* and other shells from the Oxford Clay, and with pebbles of Cornbrash.
2. Oxford Clay.
   a. Bituminous slaty clay, with *Belemnites, Belemnoteuthis, Ammonites,* and *Rostellaria.* Septaria and veins of stone, the latter containing *A. Reginaldi.*

2. Oxford Clay (continued).
   b. Blue clay, with a fossil tree in the portion overlying the Kelloway rock.
   c. Mottled clay, altered by atmospheric agency.
   d. Blue clay.
   e. Blue clay, with *A. Kœnigi*; and with shale near the surface containing *Trigonia costata.*
3. Kelloway Rock.   Sand and sandstone.

4. Cornbrash.   Brashy stone and soft bed, 4 feet; solid rock, 3 feet; with three species of Ammonites, and numerous shells.
5. Lignite, 6 inches to 1 foot, containing large and small trees.
6. Blue marl, with very few organic remains.
7. Forest marble.   Limestone in patches, with minute *Ostreæ.*
8. Gravel.

58, 59. Drawing of a geological section exposed near Trowbridge, Wiltshire, and illustrations of fossils found in the railway cutting. They accompanied observations published by R. N. Mantell in the *Quarterly Journal of the Geological Society* (1850). One of the engineers of the Great Western branch railway from Chippenham to Westbury, Mantell stated: 'the spectacle presented to my view, during the many months I was engaged in the construction of this railway, strongly impressed on my mind the conviction that I was exploring a mud-bank of an ancient ocean, to which terrestrial plants and trees, and the shells of littoral and shallow water species of mollusca, had been transported by currents, and promiscuously intermingled with the exuviae of the inhabitants of the profound depths of the sea.'

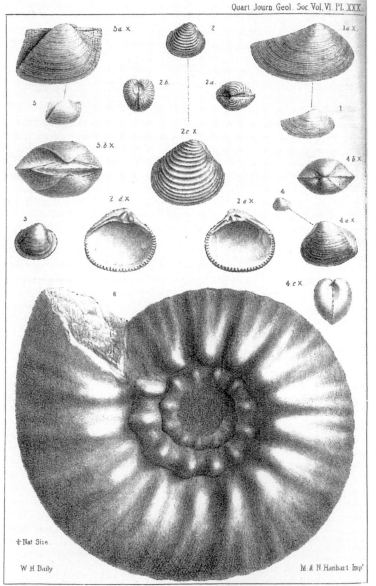

Quart. Journ. Geol. Soc. Vol. VI. Pl. XXX.

W. H. Baily   M. & N. Hanhart Imp'

Fig. 1 *a* Nucula Phillipsii.— Fig. 2 *a–c* Astarte carinata. Fig. 3 Astarte ?
Fig. 4 *a–c* Corbula Macneillii.— 5 *a b* Arca subtetragona.— 6 Ammonites Reginaldi
The figures marked X are magnified

them for himself.[167] When the Blisworth cutting was in progress on the London and Birmingham line, geologists came from all parts of the kingdom to search for fossils thrown up from the layers of oolitic limestone and from the long un-disturbed clays.[168] Early railway guides were quick to pick up on the potential interest of amateur geologists in travelling by train. Wyld's *Great Western Railway Guide* of 1839 talked of the glory of the geological district through which the line ran. Meanwhile, that most distinguished of early railway artists, J. C. Bourne, in *The History and Description of the Great Western Railway* (1846), claimed that 'it would be difficult to select a line or district possessing greater geological interests and better fitted for the convenient study of the science itself'. Even the ordinary populace who observed railway excavations could not have failed to be struck by the vivid colours of the newly exposed strata. Thomas Roscoe described how, as travellers emerged from the abyss of the Linslade Tunnel on the London and Birmingham line, the vivid red slopes of the ironsand excavation, coupled with the sudden transition from darkness to light, produced the most powerful effect on the vision.[169] Further south, the London clay was a bright cobalt blue when first cut through, changing with exposure to orange. Elsewhere, there were yellow gravels, black and white flint courses, not to mention the myriad sandstone hues.[170] Botanists also found railway excavations a rich source of speculation. Joseph Hooker wrote to Darwin in July 1845 about the way cutting open railways caused a change of vegetation: first by turning up buried live seeds and, secondly, by affording space and protection for the growth of transported seeds. 'What a curious principle life must be', he commented, 'and what an uncomfortable abode it must often have'.[171] So the railway, albeit unwittingly, offered a spy-hole into a distant and shadowy past, a past which extended beyond the Flood and grappled with the murky science of evolution. Along with famine, Chartism and political revolution, the 1840s was transformed into a decade when there no longer appeared to be any benevolence in either history or nature.[172]

60. J. C. Bourne, litho-graph, 1846, of the cavernous eastern approach to Long Tunnel, Fox's Wood, on the Great Western Railway. The geology is laid bare for all to see.

2

THE 'MARCH OF INTELLECT'

By 1850, the railways had reached a standard of
performance not seriously improved upon until the
abandonment of steam in the mid-twentieth century,
their organization and methods were on a scale
unparalleled in any other industry, their use of novel
and science-based technology (such as the electric
telegraph) unprecedented. They appeared to be several
generations ahead of the rest of the economy, and indeed
'railway' became a sort of synonym for ultra-modernity
in the 1840s, as 'atomic' was to be after the
Second World War.[1]

THE AGE OF SCIENCE AND STATISTICS

THIS PARALLEL, drawn by the historian Eric Hobsbawm between the railway in
1850 and the harnessing of the atom a century later, is an intriguing one. The
atomic age appeared to those who observed its inception as an era of limitless
power. It was almost as if mankind had uncovered an artificial energy. The railway,
too, was regarded by contemporaries as having prevailed against the forces of
natural energy. Whereas draught animals became exhausted in travelling, steam
power was 'inexhaustible and capable of infinite acceleration'.[2] The railroad broke
the 'age-old restrictive relationship between biological energy and movement'.[3]
The frictional effect of distance on movement, whether regarded in mileage or
in terms of natural obstacles, was denied much of its significance by the railway.
'Natural space' was replaced by a very different sort of spatiality, one part of which
was the straight line. In the process, the traveller seemingly lost contact with the
landscape, a feature that was dramatically enhanced in cuttings and tunnels and
on elevated track sections. This signified the interjection of what has been
described as a 'machine ensemble' between the traveller and the landscape.[4] Henry
Booth perceived the phenomenon in his fascinating account of the line of the
Liverpool and Manchester Railway around the time of its opening in 1830:

> the passenger by this new line of route having to traverse the deepest recesses,
> where the natural surface of the ground is the *highest*, and being mounted on
> the loftiest ridges and highest embankments, riding above the tops of the
> trees, and overlooking the surrounding country, where the natural surface of
> the ground is the *lowest*.[5]

The extreme novelty of features of this kind is well demonstrated in the
curious, almost contrived, language in which some early railway passengers
described their journeys. Fanny Kemble, on first seeing the Liverpool–Manchester
line, remarked how 'the wheels were placed upon two iron bands, which formed

61 (opposite). *Opening of
the Buxton and Matlock
Railway, Illustrated
London News*, 1863: the
line afforded a scenic
spectacular. Shown from
the top are the Manchester
Junction Tunnel, Wyedale;
Cressbrook; Monsal Dale,
and Millersdale Station.

62. Monsal Dale on the
Midland Railway, an early
photograph from a roughly
similar viewpoint as that
shown in the *Illustrated
London News* on the
opening of the original
line (opposite).

the road, and to which they are fitted, on the same principle as a thing sliding on a concave groove'.[6] Another tourist on the Liverpool–Manchester line noted how the railway was 'formed with an entire double way of parallel lines . . . . one of them is used in going, the other in returning'.[7] Such an arrangement was soon familiar, but to early rail travellers it was strange and hence excited comment. The same tourist went on to remark upon the singularity of other aspects of the railway's operation. The Company kept 'a police establishment' which had 'station-houses at intervals of about a mile along the road'. In turn, these stations were 'depots for passengers and goods'.[8] What these particular comments reflected, of course, was the exclusivity of the railway company's control, a sharp deviation from pre-existing transport undertakings. Edward Stanley's fascinating account of travelling on the line on the day of its opening enshrines many similar perceptions. On looking out of the side of the carriage, 'the earth, with its iron stripes on which we shot along, seemed like a vast riband unrolling itself rapidly as we went'.[9] Here again was the sharp linearity and the railroad as machine ensemble.[10] In 1835, Sir George Head travelled on the Stockton and Darlington Railway, by then inaugurated ten years. On a particularly straight section of the route, he observed how the rails converging in perspective seemed to form the track of a terrestrial zodiac: 'lines terminating in points on the horizon, whence at prescribed periods earthly objects rise and perform their transit . . .'[11]

Hobsbawm's reference to the science of the telegraph (quotation, page 57) provides a further reminder of the machine idea. Experiments had been conducted with the electrical telegraph in the later years of the eighteenth century. A charge of frictional electricity was applied to one end of a wire and detected at the other end by a pith ball electroscope, a separate wire being used for each character to be transmitted.[12] In the early nineteenth century, frictional electricity was replaced by simple voltaic piles and the multiple wires were abandoned as cumbersome. Telegraph codes were then developed based on two possible directions of deflec-

63. Isaac Shaw, *Railway office, Liverpool*, pen, brown ink and brown wash, 1830.

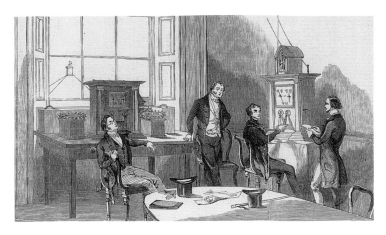

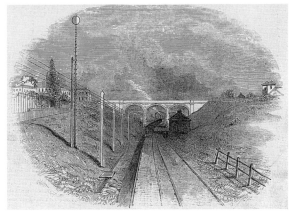

tion of the magnetic needle.[13] The first railway telegraph seems to have been installed on the Great Western Railway betwen Paddington and West Drayton and was operating by the spring of 1839.[14] The line consisted of five wires, insulated with cotton and gutta-percha, the whole encased in an iron pipe and laid on the ground beside the track. In 1842, an 'improved' telegraph, consisting of double-needle instruments needing only two wires, was ordered by the Great Western Board. The wires were no longer to be cased in an iron pipe but suspended over-head on upright standards of cast-iron and at intervals of up to 150 yards.[15] The history of the telegraph on the Great Western was initially somewhat chequered but, by 1848, 1,800 miles of railway were so equipped in the country as a whole.[16] This afforded telegraphic communication to some two hundred principal towns and allowed the telegraph wires to be compared to a nervous system, the rapidity and precision of which were comparable to that of the human frame.[17] As Lord Salisbury remarked in 1889, the telegraph enabled the combining together at one moment of 'the opinions of the whole intelligent world with respect to everything that is passing at that time upon the face of the globe'.[18] It offered a wholly novel simultaneity of experience.[19]

It was not long before the lineside wires became a feature of literary comment. Charles Dickens, in *Hard Times* (1854), had Mrs Sparsit in a railway carriage observing the electric wires of the telegraph ruling 'a colossal strip of music-paper out of the evening sky'.[20] The lines of the wires repeated the linearity of the permanent way. The landscape became enframed, much as the graticule of Renaissance maps enframed the world, thereby adding to the sense of separation from nature and, simultaneously, symbolizing man's command over it.[21]

The satirical magazine *Punch* labelled steam and electricity (that is, the steam engine and the telegraph) 'the two giants of the time' and produced a cartoon together with a set of verses that formed an imaginary conversation piece between the two.[22] The opening verse was full of optimism:

> 'What can we two great Forces do?'
> Said Steam to Electricity.
> 'To better the case of the human race,
> And promote mankind's felicity?'

Later verses were more sanguine, questioning, for example, whether the world got on much better for going faster. But this was written in 1857, by which time some of the novelty of steam had faded.

64. The telegraphy room at Nine Elms station on the South Western Railway, *Illustrated London News*, 1845. The illustration depicts a long-distance chess game played between London and Portsmouth on 10 April 1845.

65. Telegraph wires alongside the South Western Railway, *Illustrated London News*, 1845.

66. Cartoon from *Punch*, 1857.

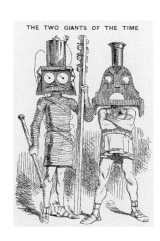

THE TWO GIANTS OF THE TIME

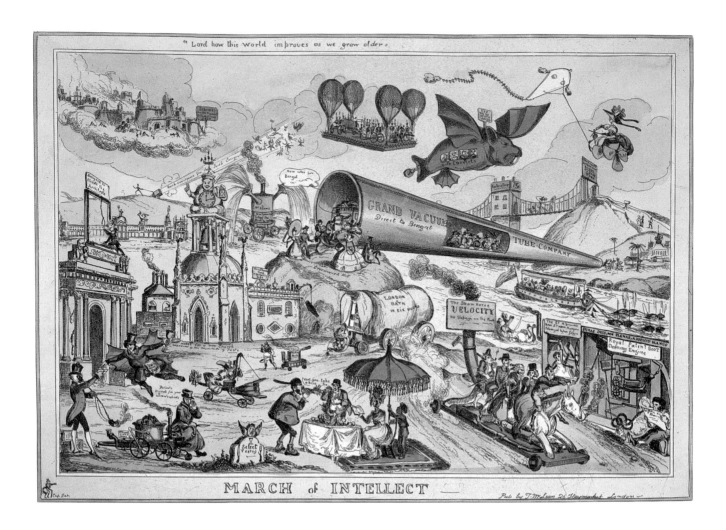

67. Paul Pry, *March of Intellect*, 1829. Within the panorama, steam power and its metaphors appear to have permeated almost every aspect of living – from the steam-razor in the booth in the bottom right-hand corner to the vacuum tube that takes you from Greenwich Hill direct to Bengal.

The fascination with scientific technology that the railway came so powerfully to exemplify had been presaged in a wonderful panorama of 1829 by Paul Pry, *March of Intellect*. It evokes the association of steam power with flight and gives comic epitaphs of the death of the old social order, the composition as a whole bearing witness to the inventiveness of the Victorian mind in relation to scientific application and to Carlyle's later claim that, if there was a single epithet that characterised the age, it was *mechanical*.[23] In case it is thought that the examples in this panorama strained reality to the point of sheer fancy, it is worth remembering the range of steam household contraptions that the Victorians had experimented with by the end of the century, as well as the extraordinary Atmospheric System patented by the Samuda Brothers in 1839.[24] This system was employed first on the Kingstown and Dalkey line near Dublin, later on the London and Croydon Railway and, perhaps most famously, by Brunel on the South Devon Railway.[25] It involved making the pressure of the atmosphere available as a propelling force, achieved by sucking air from a continuous line of pipe laid along the permanent way, so creating a partial vacuum. The Croydon line ran experimental trips in 1845, achieving a speed of 30 miles per hour with a train of sixteen carriages. Later trials produced a reputed speed of 75 miles per hour with a train of twelve carriages.[26] Passenger trains began running on the South Devon line in September 1847 and a maximum speed of 68 miles per hour was recorded with a train of 28 tons.[27] According to Brunel's biographer:

the motion of the train, relieved of the impulsive action of the locomotive, was singularly smooth and agreeable; and passengers were freed from the annoyance of coke dust and the sulphurous smell from the engine chimney.[28]

On the Croydon line, it was shown that the system could operate successfully on gradients of 1 in 50.[29] However, all these experiments proved short-lived because of a critical technical problem with the leathers of the travelling piston.[30] Paul Pry turned out to be a poor prophet, however, in his depiction of the application of steam power to road vehicles: steam road carriage was quickly stifled by reactionary turnpike trustees who applied prohibitive tolls.[31]

The nature of the 'rail-way', though, proved, in the first instance, to be a highly contested realm. Early British railway development was not characterized by a uniformity of gauge (the distance between the running rails). Most of the initial lines were built to a gauge of 4 ft 8½ in. This accorded closely with track dimensions that had existed since the Roman era, being close to the width required between the wheels on a road vehicle when it was drawn by a horse in shafts. Many colliery lines also followed this pattern, and the gauge of the Liverpool and Manchester Railway was said to have been taken from that of the railways around Newcastle.[32] It was the preferred choice of gauge for George and Robert Stephenson. However, their great engineering rival, Isambard Kingdom Brunel, convinced the Board of the Great Western railway in 1835 that a gauge of 7 ft (actually 7 ft ¼ in) was technically superior.[33] As a result, the ten years from the mid 1840s saw a dramatic struggle among railway proprietors for the supremacy of one gauge over the other, the 'broad' over the 'narrow', with the Great Western as the principal protagonist.[34] The picture was made still more complex by the fact that a number of other companies adopted yet different gauges. The Eastern Counties

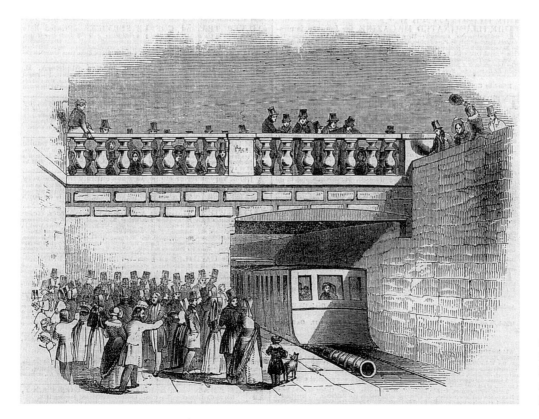

68. *The Kingstown and Dalkey Atmospheric Railway – starting of the train, Illustrated London News, 1844.*

70. The broad gauge at Newport, Monmouthshire, in the summer of 1855. Notice the stone sets between all the rails, and the way the pointsman and other workers have posed for the photographer.

69. Isambard Kingdom Brunel (1806–59), one of the central figures of the railway age.

71. Cartoon from Angus Reach, *Comic Bradshaw, or Bubbles from the Boiler*, 1845. Here are a version of Thomas the Tank Engine and friends a century before their creation by Wilber Awdry.

THE BROAD GAUGE AND THE NARROW GAUGE.

line, for instance, was first built to a 5 ft gauge.[35] Some short Scottish lines adopted 6 ft. In Ireland, the Ulster Company took up the recommendation of the Irish Railway Commissioners and completed part of their line to Dublin on a 6 ft 2 in gauge. Coming north to meet them, though, the Drogheda Company, setting out from Dublin, adopted a gauge of 5 ft 2 in. [36] Eventually the national gauge for Ireland was fixed at 5 ft 3 in, although a plethora of 3 ft gauge light railways by the end of the century made the idea of a uniform gauge something of a dead letter.

Brunel arrived at his 7 ft gauge during the course of his surveys of the projected Great Western line from London to Bristol. As the leading historian of that company has observed,

> being endowed with a vivid imagination and distinctly original turn of mind, he became impressed with the great possibilities of the extraordinary straight and level road he was laying out, and hence the desirability of getting rid of the limitations imposed by rails less than five feet apart.[37]

He regarded Stephenson's narrow-gauge machines as too small in relation to the masses and velocities that he anticipated would be attained.[38] The 'battle of the gauges' thus soon became a leading scientific debate. Although a Royal Commission accepted the technical capabilities of the broad gauge, it viewed the narrow gauge as best suited to the general needs of the country and recommended the compulsory extinction of Brunel's broad gauge. However, Parliament did not adopt the Commission's findings in their entirety. It favoured the general enforcement of the narrow 4 ft 8½ in gauge in the future, but did not see fit to require companies to convert broad-gauge lines that already existed. Further, when those companies sought extension of their broad-gauge lines, it was also not felt possible to insist on the narrow (now standard) gauge.[39] Thus the broad gauge continued to expand its domain after the Gauge Act of 1846. By 1866, broad-gauge rails ran from Paddington to Penzance, to Milford Haven, Hereford, Wolverhampton and Weymouth.[40] However, their eventual extinction had by then been well forecast. The Great Western Railway Company progressively lost its campaign to consolidate the territory of the broad gauge in the south and south-west as well as in the north.[41] As Robbins has remarked, its failure was not one of technical competence but of lack of 'administrative imagination'.[42] Or, as a much earlier commentator observed, 'a line that was handicapped by a different, though it might be better, gauge could never hold its own'. The Railway Clearing House calculated that each change, or break, of gauge and the transshipment necessitated, added the equivalent of roughly twenty miles to the cost of carriage.[43] By 1866, there were no fewer than thirty places where breaks of gauge occurred.[44] Queen Victoria, travelling between Balmoral in Scotland and Osborne in the Isle of Wight, had to change trains twice, at Gloucester and at Basingstoke.[45] There is little doubt, however, that the general public preferred broad-gauge trains. The *Penny Cyclopaedia* commented how the superiority of the 'enlarged gauge' was apparent in the increased speed and power of the engines, and the stability and convenience of the carriages.[46] On the Great Western's line from London to Swindon, expresses were sustaining a travelling rate of over 61 miles per hour in 1848. On the same company's more difficult run from London to Exeter, the figure was still 53 miles per hour. Express trains from London to Liverpool, on the narrow gauge, could manage only 36–38 miles per hour. The closest that any narrow-gauge rival came

72. The turmoil of the break of gauge at Gloucester, *Illustrated London News*, 1846.

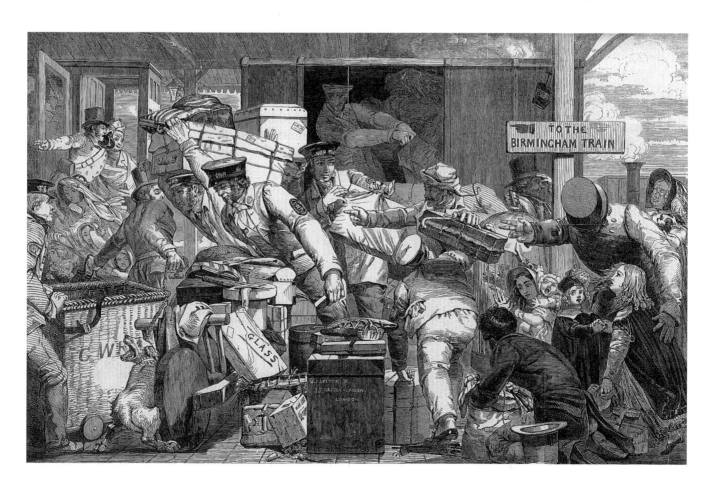

to the Great Western was on the London and South Western's line to Southampton, where trains sustained a rate of 52 miles per hour.[47]

If it was not fascination with the gauge controversy that occupied people's minds, it was the awesome scientific and mechanical power of the locomotives, whether broad-gauge or narrow, rendered the more remarkable because expressed in multiples of horse power. The Great Western's *Lord of the Isles*, for example, exhibited at the Great Exhibition of 1851, was capable of up to 1,000 hp.[48] It towered over its narrow-gauge competitors, in its gleaming green livery and polished metal. Even so, one of its rivals, *Liverpool*, exhibited alongside, boasted 1,140 hp.[49] The naming of engines reinforced the sense of inhuman or unnatural energy. Among the Great Western's locomotive stock in January 1839 were *Vulcan*, *Atlas* and *Apollo*, all recalling power and might in classical myth. Names like *Thunderer* and *Neptune* evoked the forces of the raw elements. *Snake* and *Viper* signified the perils and dangers of steam locomotion.[50] Ten years on, the same company's locomotive department had produced names like *Wizard*, *Dragon* and *Lightning*. But alongside were more earthly appellations: *Great Britain*, *Great Western* and *Iron Duke*.[51] The growing practice of naming engines after people or places registered the measure by which steam locomotion became accommodated in popular minds. In time, it became less alien and more familiar. The London and Southampton opened its line in May 1840 with the engines *Mars* and *Venus*, while in the same month *Mercury* was derailed near Winchester.[52] The London and South Western locomotive department boasted such names as *Minos*, *Pegasus* and *Pluto*, not to mention another *Vulcan*.[53] The Grand Junction Railway had engines named *Falcon*, *Lynx*, *Eagle*, *Sirocco*, *Wildfire* and *Dragon*, all dating from 1837–8.[54]

Locomotives exhibited at the Crystal Palace in 1851 and a battery of names from classical myth were not, of course, a proper substitute for the experience of seeing the steam monster in action. In 1852 F. S. Williams remarked that a striking peculiarity of locomotive agency was its extraordinary power on the one hand, but the facility of its management on the other. Its velocity outstripped the wind; its

73. South Devon Railway 'Hawk' class 4-4-0 locomotive *Hawk*, built 1859.

strength defied all living forces. Its endurance was measured only by the supply of a simple vapour and the capacity of its machinery to resist the expansive power of that vapour. The steam locomotive exhibited 'enormous bulk and terrible power', but the ease and certainty of its control was 'marvellously disproportionate'.[55] Charles Mackay captured these reactions in verse when observing a train arriving at Dartmouth Arms station on the Croydon Railway in April 1844:

> Behold, smoke-panoplied, the wondrous car!
> Strong and impetuous, but obedient still;
> Behold it comes, loud panting from afar,
> As if it lived, and of its own fierce will
> Ran a free race with wild winds blowing shrill!
> Fire-bowell'd, iron-ribb'd, of giant length
> Snake-like, it comes exulting in its strength
> The pride of art – the paragon of skill![56]

Likewise, Sir George Head caught similar reactions among the population who saw his train pass by on the Leeds and Selby Railroad in 1835:

> The sensation created by our transit . . . was particularly striking. Had the double-tailed comet passed that way, the country-people would hardly have been more interested by the spectacle; the men at work in the fields and quarries stood like statues . . . in attitudes of fixed attention, and immoveable

as if turned by the wand of a magician into blocks of stone; and women in troops, in their best gowns and bonnets, fled from the villages, and congregated at the corner of every intersecting lane.[57]

The 'march of intellect', as well as demonstrating the powerful ingenuity of the day, also bears testament to an increasing fixation with achievement, which was perhaps the central hallmark of the Victorian age. In 1830, Henry Booth was already predicting how 'from west to east, and from north to south, the mechanical principle, the philosophy of the nineteenth century' would spread and extend itself.[58] Writing in the early 1840s, John Francis was drawn to speculate how soon there would be railway streets in London, with the carriages overhead and the foot passengers and shopkeepers underneath. In the country, meanwhile, steam engines on the atmospheric principle would not only perform all the work of the lines, but employ their surplus power 'in impregnating the earth with carbonic acid and other gases, so that vegetation may be forced forward'.[59] It has been observed that 'no century in all human history was ever so much praised to its face for its wonderful achievements, its wealth and its power'.[60] Dickens caught the tone in his inimitable fashion in *Household Words* (1853–4) when describing the London and North Western Railway Company.[61] It was 'wealthier than any other corporation in the world'. Its stock-in-trade had a value greater than the whole capital of the East India Company, and came close to the total outlay upon the entire three thousand miles of canal in Great Britain and Ireland. Further, it conveyed every year more passengers than there were people in Scotland, and the value of the goods it conveyed to and from Liverpool was 'fully a match for the whole import and export trade of Belgium and Portugal'. One of the earliest handbooks for travellers on the London and Birmingham Railway (1839) repeated the tone. Euston's Doric portico was said to be 'the largest in Europe, if not the world'.[62] The diameter of the columns was 'eight feet six inches; their height forty-two feet; the intercolumniation twenty-eight feet . . . and the total height, to the apex of the pediment, seventy-two feet'.[63] The engineering works on the line were described in a host of superlatives. The oblique arched bridge near Box Moor station had no previous counterpart in its design.[64] The Tring excavation was 'one of the most stupendous cuttings to be found in the country'.[65] The Wolverton embankment, averaging 48 feet in height and comprising 500,000 cubic yards of material, was cast in similar vein.[66] All was 'wonder and admiration'. Another contemporary commentator marvelled at the scale of the goods depot at Camden:

> the extent of the area of the principal warehouse will be understood when it is stated to be twice that of Westminster Hall, being about 230 feet long, by 140 width. The roof, divided into three sections, and supported by two rows of pillars, has nearly an acre of slating, and 100 skylights. The whole is erected on vaults, and out of the 3,000,000 bricks employed in the building, a large proportion was expended in their construction.[67]

No less remarkable was the range of equipment that Pickfords had in their receiving shed at the Camden depot, including 24 steam-cranes, a steam-lift, a travelling crane on the roof, and a steam capstan for hauling trucks along the rails. Moreover, to prepare food and water for the 222 horses employed, there were four steam hay-cutters which could prepare 50 trusses of hay an hour and a 16 hp steam engine which raised water from an artesian well almost 400 feet deep.[68]

Such zest for bigger and better, for more tons of coal carried and more railroads built, was ridiculed by Matthew Arnold in a passage in *Culture and Anarchy* (1869).[69] Was this an adequate measure of cultural attainment? Carlyle repeated the tone: it was not just the 'external and physical' that was 'managed by machinery', but the 'internal and spiritual also'.[70] Dickens picked up the theme in the character of Gradgrind in *Hard Times* (1854).

> 'You are to be in all things regulated and governed', said the gentleman, 'by fact. We hope to have, before long, a board of fact, composed of commissioners of fact, who will force the people to be a people of fact, and of nothing but fact. You must discard the word Fancy altogether.'[71]

What all the statistics, facts and superlatives signified, however, was a society that held no satisfaction with what it was, or a society that was satisfied only with 'what it was becoming'.[72] Thus the London and Birmingham Railway met 'the wants of a vastly-improved people'; it was 'the triumphant invention of Science, trained and disciplined under severe study, and gathering accelerated strength from the successful experiments of each succeeding year'.[73] Elizabeth King, writing in her old age of a journey made from Liverpool to Birmingham in May 1839, remembered her father continually 'holding his watch in hand marking speed by the mile posts', such was the fascination and preoccupation with the surging march of time.[74] *Punch* echoed the theme in a splendid piece of comic satire in 1845. Not satisfied with going with the 'march of intellect' at a jog-trot, it preferred running before it and produced a railway map of England as it would appear in a year or two. England would 'never be in chains', but would 'soon be in irons', such was the testament of new railway prospectuses then current.[75] The railway became the genius of the age: 'like a mighty river of the new world . . . full, rapid, and irresistible'.[76]

The pioneers who made the railways were likewise accredited with genius. Men like George Stephenson and his son Robert, along with I. K. Brunel, Joseph Locke, Thomas Brassey and others, were soon transfigured into popular heroes,

commemorated in print, pictures and all manner of other ways – much as the railway lines they engineered and the locomotives some of them designed. Samuel Smiles's *Lives of the Engineers* later elevated such men to a status that was often hard to justify and, in some cases, patently misleading. George Stephenson, for instance, was not the inventor of the railway, as Smiles initially tried to claim.[77] Moreover, the depiction of such men as shining illustrations of 'self-help' tended to underrate their mental abilities. What Stephenson and others besides him demonstrated above all was the successful planning and execution of vast enterprises: 'only the Royal Navy afforded a parallel in those days to the complex organization that had to be created for the Liverpool and Manchester Railway'.[78]

A preoccupation with statistics was reflected in rather a different guise in the railway timetable. Hobsbawm claims that all subsequent 'timetables' took their name and inspiration from it.[79] One of the earliest users of the term may have been the Grand Junction Railway: in *Osbourne's Guide* of 1838, the times of arrival and departure are given under the heading 'Time Table'.[80] Not all railway companies, however, followed this practice; some, like the Liverpool and Manchester, offered lists of departures only, the implication being that arrival times were not always certain.[81] George Bradshaw produced his first railway timetable in 1838, and by the later Victorian period the name 'Bradshaw' had become synonymous with 'railway timetable'.[82] Even as early as 1850, people were poking fun at it and mocking it for its complexity and impenetrability, except to the most tested brains. Humorists suggested that the most useless thing in the world was 'last month's Bradshaw'.[83] *The Comic Bradshaw: or, Bubbles from the Boiler* (1848) contained a speculative piece about Bradshaw a century on, in 1948.[84] On the Eastern Countries line (as distinct from the notorious Eastern Counties line), a train left Shoreditch station in London at 6 a.m. and arrived in Pekin in China at noon the

77. The engineer George Stephenson (1781–1848), in what became a widely disseminated portrait. This version appeared in a German text around the turn of the century.

78. Handbill advertising trains of the Liverpool and Manchester Railway.

79. Title page of one of George Bradshaw's first railway timetables, 1841.

same day.[85] In 1856, *Punch* offered its readers a farcical mystery play based on Bradshaw.[86] *Punch* had earlier proposed that learning to read a railway timetable should be an integral part of the school curriculum.[87] There should be 'a regular course of railway trains', in the same way that there were 'guides to knowledge' of every kind. The reading of a railway timetable required training in youth: it had to be taught, or else it was akin to a dead language. *Punch* suggested, too, a course in 'railway arithmetic'. There was only one contemporary publication that *Punch* was prepared to concede as perhaps being more powerful in its non-intelligibility than a Bradshaw – the official catalogue of the Great Exhibition.[88]

Educational novelties proferred in the satirical press aside, the speed with which the railroad permeated the regular realms of education was striking (children's literature, in particular, is examined in chapter seven). It was soon accommodated, too, within the burgeoning range of writing on science and culture, as encapsulated in the imprints of the *Society for the Diffusion of Useful Knowledge*, under the enterprising eye of its publisher Charles Knight.[89] The new steam-powered printing presses were causing prices to plummet and, with newspaper tax down to a penny, the streets were soon awash with all kinds of radical tracts and all sorts of 'self-improvers'.[90] Among the Society's output was the *Penny Magazine*, which first appeared at the end of March 1832. The first volume incorporated material based on Dionysius Lardner's published lectures on the steam engine, including accounts of the Liverpool and Manchester Railway and its rising measure of profitability. By the end of 1831, the Company's original £100 shares were selling for twice that figure.[91]

The *Penny Magazine* was complemented from 1833 by the *Penny Cyclopaedia*, issued in alphabetical sequence over the ensuing ten years.[92] The 'Railway' entry, appearing in 1841, ran to some 23 pages.[93] The nature of the commentary makes no mistake about the continuing novelty of virtually every aspect of the railroad, one example being the case of the so-called 'skew bridges' which made a frequent appearance on railway works.[94] These were introduced where the

80. *An Educational Novelty*, Punch, 1850: learning to read a railway timetable.

81. J. C. Bourne, lithograph, 1839, of the 'oblique bridge' at Box Moor on the London and Birmingham Railway.

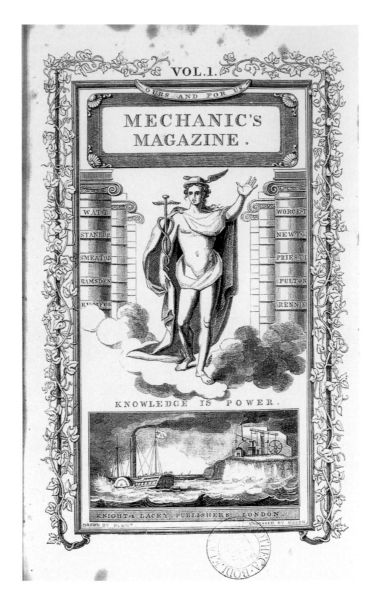

railways intersected another line of communication at an acute or oblique angle.
Thomas Roscoe, in his account of the London and Birmingham Railway, noted
how the science of bridge-building had made rapid strides in association with the
railway, citing the case of an arch near Tring in which 'the square span' across the
road was 20 feet, but the 'obliquity' on the face of the arch lengthened it to more
than 39 feet.[95] Such arches had been constructed before the introduction of
railways, but were not used generally. However, since straightness was of great
importance on a railway, it frequently became necessary when bisecting other
roads or ways to adopt such skew forms. The idiosyncracy of this kind of construction made it a favourite subject of artists and engravers, many of whom also
made use of the straight line of the railway track itself, employing a recessional
perspective and often adding an approaching train.

As might have been anticipated, the *Penny Cyclopaedia* dealt specifically with
the sharp linearity of the railway's permanent way. The railway engine, it recorded,

> runs upon very hard and smooth surfaces, and has only very gradual changes
> of level to surmount. Its precise track is determined by flanges upon its
> wheels, and that track never deviates suddenly from a straight line . . .[96]

RAILWAY EXHIBITION.

The Public are respectfully informed that an Exhibition is

NOW OPEN

Every Day from Ten till Dusk, at the

BAZAAR,
BAKER STREET,

PORTMAN SQUARE,

Representing by Mechanical and Pictorial display that

CELEBRATED WONDER

OF

ART AND SCIENCE,

THE

Manchester & Liverpool
RAILWAY.

This Exhibition is quite of a novel and instructive, as well as pleasing nature, and will enable persons who have never seen the Railway, to form a more accurate idea of this Wonderful National Work, than can be gained by any written description, as the principal Plans and Views on the Route from Manchester to Liverpool are delineated on a Picture of several Thousand square feet of canvas, which is in constant motion, and Locomotive Engines are also at work in a similar manner to those they are copied from on the Railway.

It must be also interesting to those who have been on the Route, as they will no doubt feel pleased at the accurate manner with which this Great Exhibition has been got up, and to persons interested in Railways, it gives a better description than can be got unless they go to the Great National Work itself.

This Exhibition has been many months in preparation, and neither pains expense has been spared to render it worthy the patronage of the Public, and exhibited in a handsome Theatre built expressly for the occasion.

Admission One Shilling.

** Explanatory Catalogues with numerous Descriptive Plates,
PRICE ONE SHILLING.

May 1834

83. The Liverpool and Manchester Railway as exhibition, a handbill of 1834.

To the late twentieth-century observer, such an explanation may appear banal in the extreme, but in the eyes of someone living in the 1830s straight lines were relatively rare occurrences in transport undertakings and were still more unusual in nature. Their association with railroads goes as far back as the early 1820s: in an article in the *Mechanic's Magazine*, Thomas Gray wrote of the establishment of 'a general iron railway in a direct line . . . instead of the ridiculously winding course the stage and mail coaches now daily run'.[97] Another feature discussed in *The Penny Cyclopaedia* was the method of laying permanent way. The most common practice was 'to fix rails into iron chairs which are spiked down to blocks of stone', following the pattern of early plateways or tramways. However, the stone blocks, being isolated from each other, could be deranged by vibration or subsidence, thus 'some railways have substituted cross wooden sleepers . . . the rails cannot thus lose their parallelism'.[98] Another mode of laying permanent way was to install a continuous support to the rail, as practised on the Great Western lines.

The spread of scientific knowledge was also assisted through its progressive institutionalization. Philosophical and Learned Societies mushroomed in the first decades of the nineteenth century. The spirit of scientific enquiry permeated all classes and, within this, the railway and its engineers formed a consummate focus. Leon Faucher remarked in his account of Manchester in 1844 how science appeared to have 'fixed itself in Lancashire' – Manchester had a Statistical Society and chemistry was 'held in honour' – but that literature and the arts had become a 'dead letter'.[99] In many towns and cities Mechanics' Institutes were formed. In 1823 the *Mechanic's Magazine* was launched, the frontispiece of its first issue on 30 August bearing the motto 'Knowledge is Power'.[100] Priced at threepence, the magazine was directed to those manually employed and was intended to acquaint them better with 'the history and principles of the arts they practise'.[101] Successive issues recorded the moves to found Mechanics' Institutes up and down the land. The Glasgow institute, formed in 1823, had its own weekly paper.[102] As the railway age was slowly born, so the *Mechanic's Magazine* came to be among its most ardent champions. In an issue of 1836, it recorded how the ten best engines of the Liverpool–Manchester railroad were each averaging 538 miles per week by 1834,[103] a prodigious demonstration of the effectiveness of steam traction, of 'self-acting locomotion'. The vicissitudes of the early Railway Bills in Parliament were detailed in many issues,[104] as were the enormous engineering difficulties experienced in laying out some lines, the London and Birmingham Railway among them.[105] This company's seventh half-yearly report caused a 'great sensation in what may be called the railway world' on account of the vast escalation in the line's estimated costs.[106] By 1840, another very different measure of this 'railway world' became manifest when a correspondent urged uniformity among railway clocks: 'Railways are said to "annihilate both time and space"; this they can only do safely and satisfactorily by keeping time'. Further, he remarked, 'want of punctuality annoys the man of pleasure and injures the man of business in no ordinary degree.' Another correspondent of 1840 bemoaned the 'unfitness' of the Greenwich terminus of the London and Greenwich Railway at Easter

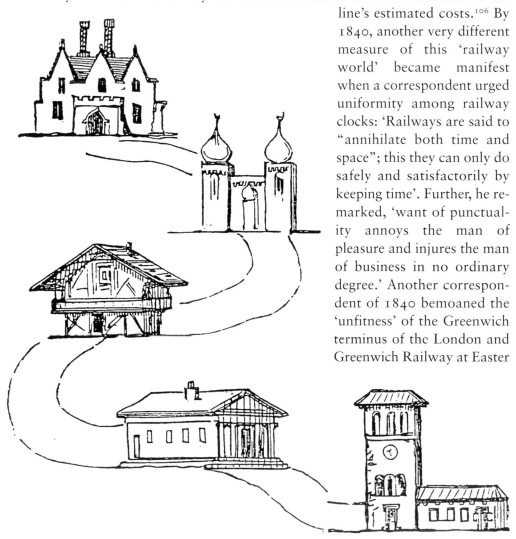

84. *Railway Architecture, Punch,* 1848.

holiday time when the rush of travellers was 'shocking to witness'.[107] The Bank Holiday crush had already materialized, even though the railway was only a decade or so old.

The railway was also popularized very rapidly through exhibitions. Pride of place must go to the Bazaar in Baker Street, Portman Square, London, where the 'Liverpool railroad' was represented in a 'mechanico-graphicorama' or 'disyntrechon'.[108] This comprised 10,000 square feet of canvas 'painted by artists of acknowledged talent, from sketches made upon the spot', presenting 'a faithful delineation of all the prominent and interesting features of the road'. Alongside this canvas picture operated a real railway with locomotive engines and trains of carriages of corresponding proportion with the view – perhaps it was among the very first toy railways. The early and rapid growth in the publication of railway prints (first aquatints, then lithographs and chromolithographs) was another facet of the exhibition idea (explored fully in chapter eight). One social historian has seen their increasing numbers as a direct reflection of the need among railway proprietors to reassure the public in the face of the hostility that the early railways faced.[109] The railway also found representation in commemorative medals, mugs and jugs, printed handkerchiefs and jig-saw puzzles,[110] a trend parodied by Dickens in *Dombey and Son*.[111] There were 'railway patterns in drapers' shops'. There were railway 'wrappers, bottles, sandwich-boxes'. In effect, the railway had become a new kind of religion or church: nobody hesitated to acknowledge it; those who had formerly hesitated were now 'wise and penitent'.[112]

The notion of the railway developing a quasi-religious aura was reinforced in a number of other ways. The choice of saints' names for stations, as in the case of St Pancras in London and St Enoch in Glasgow, was one example; neo-Gothic for station architecture was another. Station train-sheds, with their vast arched canopies and vaulted columns, could not fail to inspire comparison with cathedral naves. Indeed, a commentary in *Building News* in 1875 claimed that railway termini and their hotels were to the nineteenth century what monasteries and cathedrals were to the thirteenth.[113] This remark was in part prompted by the building of the fantastic neo-Gothic façade of the Midland Grand Hotel at St Pancras, the Midland Railway's new London terminus. But St Pancras was the apotheosis of a general pattern.

The architecture of the early railways lays claim to study in its own right.[114] *Punch* viewed the eclecticism of style on early railways with some disdain:

> The various lines of Railway accordingly present specimens of nearly every order; and the traveller cannot keep his ideas or his imagination within any consecutive train, for almost every place he arrives at presents some deviation from the style of architecture he has just left behind him.

As if to presage the railroad's conquest of space, however, the article claimed:

> on the great lines of Railway one may fancy one's self traversing all the countries in the world within half-an-hour, for he is very likely to encounter an old English ticket-office, a Turkish water-tank, a Swiss engine-house, a Grecian goods depôt, and an Italian terminus, all within the limits of fifteen miles of railway.[115]

Punch instead looked towards a uniformity of practice in architectural style and adornment.

85. Earthenware jugs commemorating the Liverpool and Manchester Railway.

86. J. C. Bourne, *Tunnel No. 2, near Bristol*, lithograph, 1846. Brunel's design for the tunnel mouth was perhaps inspired by John Martin's paintings of the ancient world.

What the Moorish Arch at Liverpool and the Doric Arch at London Euston embodied, though, was a strong sense of the exotic and, in parallel, a desire to form a spectacle. It was not just that termini in the Italianate style or neo-Gothic façades appealed to contemporary emotions, to a burgeoning current of romanticism. Equally, their scale appealed to the Victorians' need for a vision that was physically real.[116] As one contemporary remarked: 'All must be made palpable to sight, no less than to feeling'.[117] It was Gradgrind as much as it was heroic myth.

Brunel's spectacular architectural designs for the Great Western Railway appear to have owed something to the painter John Martin, who became famous for his vast canvases of the ancient world, composed in the manner of the industrial or machine age, forming part of an artistic genre known as the apoca-

87. J. C. Bourne, *Wharn-cliffe Viaduct, Hanwell*, lithograph, 1846, another of Brunel's designs to echo the fashion of the ancient world.

88. John Dobson's original design for Newcastle central railway station.

lyptic sublime.[118] Thus some Great Western tunnel portals and the great viaduct at Hanwell came to echo Martin's renderings of Egypt and Babylon. Nor was Brunel alone in this. His great engineering rival, Robert Stephenson, carried the Chester and Holyhead Railway across the Menai Strait in a bridge of classic Egyptian style. Meanwhile, many a great railway station of the 1840s seemed to mimic John Martin's extravagant rendering of Belshazzar's Feast (1821).[119]

89. John Martin, *Belshazzar's Feast*, oil on canvas, c. 1821.

90. T. Picken, lithograph (n.d.), showing part of 'unbuilt Oxford', a bird's eye vision of the proposed station for the Oxford, Worcester and Wolver-hampton Railway. The collegiate style is unmistakeable.

91 (opposite, top). J. C. Bourne, lithograph, 1846, of Brunel's hammer-beam roof for Bristol station and trainshed.

92 (opposite). *The Great Western Railway new terminus, at Paddington, Illustrated London News,* 1854. Note the fine tracery at the openings of Brunel's iron trainshed and the distinctive variable curvatures of the roof girders, the whole made more powerful by the uncluttered platforms below.

Railway architecture can be viewed as prescribing three generally distinctive realms or projections: the Functional, the Social and the Hieratic.[120] The Functional addressed the novel engineering demands that the railways made – for example, the provision of train-sheds or shelters at stations. Many of these began as little more than glorified cattle-sheds. It was left to Brunel to rise to the architectural challenge – seen in his remarkable Tudor-style passenger train-shed at Bristol, with its elaborately carpentered timber roof, complete with mock hammer-beams. Soon, though, railway architects replaced timber with iron, the first iron train-shed being built at Newcastle Central in the mid 1840s. The massive passenger train-sheds at Paddington, Cannon Street and York stations all repeated the pattern.

The Social projection reflected the needs of many early railway companies to humanize their enterprises. It was the architect's task to counter the anxieties and terrors that characterized many of the first public reactions to the steam railway. At Liverpool, the station at Lime Street was designed deliberately to harmonize with the adjacent classical buildings. Elsewhere, there was a reliance upon the vernacular. Some architects built in the Italianate manner with remarkable success, a style to become more familiar through the Prince Consort's design for Osborne, Queen Victoria's summer residence on the Isle of Wight. At Dover, Lewis Cubitt's striking tower or campanile indicated not a place of worship but the town railway station. The use of the Tudor or Elizabethan style clearly reflected sociability. Carlisle Citadel station became the 'finest piece of railway architecture in the sixteenth-century collegiate manner'.[121] Another remarkable composition was the station at Shrewsbury, which might easily have been mistaken for the façade of an Oxford college.

The Hieratic projection symbolized not the old but the new. Here railway magnates sought to represent themselves as part of a new leadership breed, the Victorian capitalist class. The most powerful evocation of this role came in the use of groups of classical columns, as colonnades or as porches. Most stunning of these was the free-standing portico, as at Euston. Here the eye was drawn not to the station complex itself but to the screen front of seven stone blocks linked by iron railings, the main block (or propyleum) forming the central 'incident'.[122]

It is quite evident that the old Geographies and Road-Books must be getting useless, except as guides to the antiquities of our country . . . . The geographical questions which will shortly be in use have reference to nothing but railways. Instead of saying, 'What is the capital of England?' – the instructor of youth will inquire, 'What is the capital of the London and Birmingham Railway?' 'Name the chief towns in the West', is to be expunged, and 'Name the chief stations on the Great Western' is to be the substitute.

Distance, of course, will no longer figure in the maps, but time will be the substitute. 'How many miles?' will be altered into 'How many minutes?'[123]

93. A spirit flask got up to look like a railway chronometer: the choice of disguise testifies to the railway's annihilation of space by time.

95 (opposite). Owen Jones, design for St Pancras station, lithograph (n.d.), showing Barlow's overall roof lettered to mark the destinations served by the new London extension of the Midland Railway. The roof structure, as built, was not embellished in this way; nor were the terminal buildings constructed to the design shown here.

The annihilation of space by time must be among the most familiar concepts associated with railways in nineteenth-century Britain. This concept did not become a commonplace in the academic discipline of geography until the last decades of the twentieth century,[124] but it was already in general usage in the 1840s and Marx used the expression in *Grundrisse* (1857–8).[125] Christian Anderson wrote in 1847 of how the 'magic horse' (the railroad engine) caused space to disappear.[126] The Liverpool *Railway Companion* of 1833 refers to the annihilation of the 'bounds of time and space'.[127] Henry Booth, writing about the line in 1830, considered that the most striking result of its completion was 'the sudden and marvellous change which has been effected in our ideas of time and space . . . what was quick is now slow; what was distant is now near'.[128] For Samuel Smiles, the railroad had effectively reduced England to one sixth of its size.[129] With the annihilation of space, moreover, came homogenization. Regions, towns and villages came to be more and more like each other. Anthony Trollope's *Barchester Towers* (1857) encapsulated the process wonderfully: when the old Bishop dies, the Archdeacon sends the news to London by telegraph; the new Bishop and his wife make their appearance in the novel in a first-class railway carriage hurtling to Barchester at fifty miles per hour; Mrs Proudie descends upon the quiet cathedral close of Barchester like a modernizing tornado, demanding gas lighting and piped hot water on all floors.[130]

The first of the quotations above, though, has a rather more subtle message than this. It introduces the notion of relational space, what might also be called 'railroad space'. As one recent commentator has written, 'compared to the eo-technical space-time relationship, the one created by the railroad appears abstract'.[131] A new space-time consciousness was born, one that, in turn, was embedded in the imperatives of Victorian capitalism. The railway timetable was the ultimate embodiment of the idea of relational space. As Hobsbawm observes, it symbolized 'the gigantic, nationwide, complex and inter-locking routine' that the railways forged.[132] And this was underpinned further in the electric telegraph, with its annihilation of time *and* space. However, some parts of the country did not obtain railway communication until very late. Such places clearly could not figure in 'railroad space'. They became isolated backwaters. Much the same was true of the country through which railway lines passed but where no stations were provided to gain access to them. The railway then became nothing but a useless spectacle.[133]

The division of railway operation among different private companies, often serving discrete geographical realms, meant that the major termini, especially those in London, effectively became a kind of spatial synonym for those realms. In Paris, this was reinforced in terminus names like Gare du Nord and Gare de Lyon.[134] But Paddington, Euston and Waterloo were quickly vested with spatial meaning – as gateways, respectively, to the West, the industrial provinces, and the European continent. At Euston, Philip Hardwick designed eight bas-reliefs of symbolic representations of the cities and towns through which the line passed: London, Liverpool, Manchester, Birmingham, Carlisle, Chester, Lancaster and North-ampton.[135] That famous railway commentator, W. M. Ackworth, in an unracter-istic piece of parody, saw the London and North Western Railway as a quasi territory or state. Its seat of government was London, but its capital Crewe. Its Civil Service numbered not far short of 60,000. Its President was Sir Richard Moon (Chairman) and its Prime Minister George Findlay (General Manager). The revenue flowed into the Exchequer at the rate of £26 a minute. Echoing the satire of *Punch*, Ackworth went on to suggest that it would be

> in some such words as these that, once the conservative mind of the British schoolmaster has awakened to the fact that counties and Lord Lieutenants are anachronisms, and that the United Kingdom has been divided and given to great railway companies, the Board School pupil of the future will be taught his geography.[136]

John Ruskin suggested that the idea of the terminus station as spatial synonym meant that people were no longer real travellers but human parcels: they proceeded to their destination untouched by the space they traversed.[137] While this

94. The Great Western Railway as gateway to Europe, 1892.

may be eminently true of the disappearance of all the familiar rigours of travel (it is no accident that so many commentaries of the 1840s talk of railroad travel in itself as 'gliding'[138]), it is not appropriate in relation to the spaces they saw through the carriage window. Not only did travellers see nature 'in a wider extent' and 'in longer draughts',[139] but they could not fail to become aware of spatial contrasts. Dickens, in 'The Lazy Tour of Two Idle Apprentices', captures this dimension vividly:

> The pastoral country darkened, became coaly, became smoky, became infernal, got better, got worse, improved again, grew rugged, turned romantic; was a wood, a stream, a chain of hills, a gorge, a moor, a cathedral town, a fortified place, a waste. Now, miserable black dwellings, a black canal, and sick block towers of chimneys; now, a trim garden, where the flowers were bright and fair; now a wilderness of hideous altars all a-blaze; now, the water meadows with their fairy rings; now, the mangy patch of unlet building ground outside the stagnant town, with the larger ring where the circus was last week. The temperature changed, the dialect changed, the people changed, faces got sharper, manners got shorter, eyes got shrewder and harder.[140]

This remarkable succession of pictures was a product of the speed of railway travel and of the semi-detached vantage that it afforded. Such panoramas were a critical adjunct to the emergence of the 'condition of England' question in the 1840s.[141] Whereas in *The Pickwick Papers* (1836–7) a bad smell was a bad smell, by the time of *Our Mutual Friend* (1864–5) a bad smell had become a social problem.[142] Victorian society was made suddenly aware of 'otherness' (to use the postmodern idiom),[143] of difference, within its geographical realm. It was recorded in 1852 that 'men became better acquainted with the condition and habits of their fellow men'.[144] The railroad topographies were naturally part of this appreciation, whether read in pocket versions inside the railway carriage or in the solitude of the home. Thomas Roscoe's guides to the London and Birmingham and Grand Junction Railways were bound together, for example, and re-issued as *Home and Country Scenes on each side of the line of the London and Birmingham and Grand Junction Railways*.[145] The scenic plates within it satisfied most senses of the picturesque (even those depicting industrial centres like Warrington). 'Distance lends enchantment to the view', so the commentary ran.[146] However, the experience of railway travel greatly enlarged these particular kinds of perceptions to include much that did not satisfy any conventional sense of the aesthetic or the picturesque. It was not merely, as Disraeli recorded in *Sybil* (1845), the attitude that viewed railway stations as the 'least picturesque of all creations',[147] but the black, sick misery of the industrial districts that travelling on the railway exposed to view, much as Dickens cast them. At night, such areas may well have presented visions of Dante's inferno, and prompted all kinds of artistic and poetic inspiration. But, by day, they were grim indicators of the filth and the social squalor that accompanied large-scale industrialism. A. F. Tait's 1848 lithograph, initially unpublished but later widely reproduced, of Stockport viaduct on the London and North Western Railway was conceived very much in the tradition of the picturesque. Subsequent commentators, though, have viewed it more as a representation of the pollution of nineteenth-century industry. And this, of course, is what railway travellers of that date would, above all, have registered as they passed along the viaduct.

The shrinking of space that the speed of railroad travel afforded also had a reverse dimension: 'space was both diminished *and* expanded'.[148] In *Household Words*, an article in the late 1850s expressed a plea for 'omnibus trains'. These, it

97. A. F. Tait, *Stockport Viaduct (London and North Western Railway)*, lithograph, 1848.

suggested, would offer a sixty-mile trip for a shilling and allow the scattering of the homes of the whole population across the face of England. The undue growth of towns would be halted as they became what 'market places used to be – places to which men resort to do their business with each other; and to which crowds go for the amusement that it offered'.[149] The effect on spatial consciousness was that places sixty miles distant from the metropolis would become mere suburbs of it – London would soon be all of England, or so it seemed. As one contemporary remarked in 1852:

> the extremities of the island are now, to all intents and purposes, as near the metropolis as Sussex or Buckinghamshire were two centuries ago. The Midland counties are a mere suburb. With the space and resources of an empire, we enjoy the compactness of a city . . . . For questions of distance, we are as mere a spot as Malta, St Helena or one of the Channel Isles.[150]

RAILWAYS AND THE WORLD OF EVERYDAY LIVING

> . . . even idleness is eager now, – eager for amusement;
> prone to excursion trains . . .[151]

The revolutionary speed of railway trains naturally had implications for the speed of living. As early as 1843, the average speed on all lines was 21½ miles per hour. On the London and Birmingham Railway, the average was 27 miles per hour; on the Great Western, it was 33.[152] Top speeds were recorded as high as 60 miles per hour,[153] six times the rate of travel in a fast stage-coach. Lamenting the loss of 'Old England', William Pickering penned the following lines in 1846:

> No longer now we prize 'retired leisure',
> That 'in trim gardens' used to 'take his pleasure',
>
> Time's precious – up! – would you your future make,
> Your maniac journey by express train take.[154]

Victorians increasingly felt they were living without leisure and without pause, a life of haste, a life so filled that no time was left to reflect upon where they had been and what they were becoming – and certainly no time to know the value or the purpose of what they had done or seen.[155] The anxiety to be 'in time', 'the hurrying pace – often the running to catch trains', may have contributed to the increase in deaths from heart failure between 1851 and 1870.[156] Max Nordau has claimed that inventions wore down the nervous system:

> every line we read or write, every human face we see, every conversation we carry on, every scene we perceive through the window of the flying express, sets in activity our sensory nerves and our brain centres.'[157]

Punch picked up the same theme in a comic piece about 'The Wonders of Modern Travel' in 1864,[158] in which it was implied that travelling by rail had become one long succession of anxieties. When Charles Darwin took his first railroad journey in August 1838, he found the many changes of train required were a dreadful plague, not to mention the 'glorious' scramble for luggage when the train reached London.[159] About another journey, in January 1839, he wrote to his sister Emma:

THE WONDERS OF MODERN TRAVEL.

TO THE STATION.

WONDER if my watch is right, or slow, or fast.
Wonder if that church clock is right.
Wonder if the cabman will take eighteenpence from my house to the Station.

THE STATION.

Wonder if the porter understood what I said to him about the luggage.
Wonder if I shall see him again.
Wonder if I shall know him when I *do* see him again.
Wonder if I gave my writing-case to the porter, or left it in the cab.
Wonder where I take my ticket.
Wonder in which pocket I put my gold.
Wonder where I got that bad half-crown which the clerk won't take.
Wonder if that's another that I've just put down.
Wonder where the porter is who took my luggage.
Wonder where my luggage is.
Wonder again whether I gave my writing-case to the porter, or left it in the cab.
Wonder which is my train.
Wonder if the guard knows anything about that porter with the writing-case.
Wonder if it *will* be "all right" as the guard says it will be.
Wonder if my luggage, being now labelled, will be put into the proper van.
Wonder if I've got time to get a sandwich and a glass of Sherry.
Wonder if they've got the *Times* of the day before yesterday, which I haven't seen.
Wonder if *Punch* of this week is out yet.
Wonder why they don't keep nice sandwiches and Sherry.
Wonder if there's time for a cup of coffee instead.
Wonder if that's our bell for starting.
Wonder which is the carriage where I left my rug and umbrella, so as to know it again.
Wonder where the guard is to whom I gave a shilling to keep a carriage for me.
Wonder why he didn't keep it; by "it," I mean the carriage.
Wonder where they've put my luggage.

THE JOURNEY.

Wonder if my change is all right.
Wonder for the second time in which pocket I put my gold.
Wonder if I gave the cabman a sovereign for a shilling.
Wonder if that was the reason why he grumbled less than usual and drove off rapidly.
Wonder if any one objects to smoking.
Wonder that nobody does.
Wonder where I put my lights.
Wonder whether I put them in my writing-case.
Wonder for the third time whether I gave my writing-case to the porter or left it in the cab.
Wonder if anybody in the carriage has got any lights.
Wonder that nobody has.
Wonder when we can get some.
Wonder if there's anything in the paper.
Wonder why they don't cut it.
Wonder if I put my knife in my writing-case.
Wonder for the fourth time whether I gave, &c.
Wonder if I can cut the paper with my ticket.
Wonder where I put my ticket.
Wonder where I *could* have put my ticket.
Wonder where the deuce I put my ticket.

I suspect I have to thank you, that I am a living man, for if you had not given me the sandwiches I should have died from starvation in one of the rail road carriages. We only got to Birmingham, five minutes before the London train started, so that by the time I had got my luggage all safe and a ticket, the bell rung to be off.[160]

This was a man who had recently returned from all the privations of a circumnavigation of the globe! By the close of the Victorian era, the increased importance of punctuality had become manifest in the widespread diffusion of the pocket

99. *Fatal railway accident at Kentish-Town, on the Hampstead Junction Line, Illustrated London News, 1861.*

watch, especially among urban dwellers.[161] Moreover, there was as great a pre-occupation with the calculability of time as with punctuality. People increasingly paid new attention to short intervals of time.[162]

When passengers were not anxious to be 'in time', or scrambling for their luggage, they were worrying about the prospect of instant death. For with the railways came what has been described as the 'technological accident'.[163] Before the railway era, accidents were 'natural', the result of floods, thunderbolts and similar catastrophes of nature. The 'technological accident' was where the technological apparatus destroyed itself by means of its own power. The more efficient the technology, the more catastrophic was the potential scale of its destruction.[164] When things went wrong, the power of the express train in the early railway era must have seemed lethal against a 'peaceful, bucolic England of coach, plodding wagon or silently gliding canal boat'.[165] As railway travel became habitualized, of course, the fear of accidents receded. The transformation of the railway carriage into a kind of parlour on wheels, along with the added comforts of railway luncheon baskets, railway rugs and foot warmers, soon helped passengers form a new 'psychic layer' in which old fears lapsed.[166] But still, from time to time, memories were revived by the sudden death and destruction caused by major accidents, which the newspapers and weeklies pulled no punches in reporting. The *Illustrated London News*, describing the dreadful disaster to the Irish Mail in North Wales in the summer of 1868, claimed that 'a rush down the crater of Vesuvius into the fiery gulf beneath' could hardly have been more appalling. The Mail ran into some detached goods waggons, one laden with barrels of petroleum:

a momentary crash – a dense cloud, blacker then night, of suffocating vapour – an all-enwrapping, all-consuming flame of fire – and between thirty and forty human beings . . . all rejoicing but a minute before in life and its pleasures . . . were transformed into a heap of charred and indistinguishable remains.[167]

The first thirty or forty years of the railway age were indeed a black era for accidents. Some passengers lost their lives through mere foolishness – they leapt from moving trains or rode on the roofs of carriages (especially on excursion trains). At other times they were mown down by trains because they failed to hear them approaching or else misjudged their speed. Some companies initially locked passengers into their compartments or carriages to prevent them from alighting while the train was in motion. But once it was seen how fatal this could prove in the event of fire the practice was soon abandoned. Accidents to trains themselves arose from inadequate operational organization and from the unreliability or stupidity of some personnel. In September 1845 the *Illustrated London News*, shocked by the increasing frequency of railway accidents, called for Parliament to adopt measures requiring companies to improve their operational management.[168] The difficulty was that the early railway era used the time interval rather than the space interval system for train operation.[169] The latter, more familiarly known as 'block working', was by far the more foolproof method, but the communication systems of the time were not adequate to achieve its widespread application. Thus it was very easy for a train to run into the back of the one before it if, for any reason, the first had come to a standstill. On single-line working, the time interval system could have horrendous consequences, as some head-on collisions testified.

100. *Goods-train on fire run into by an express mail-train* on the Caledonian Railway, *Illustrated London News*, 1867. Fire was one of the most terrifying hazards associated with railway accidents. Oil-lamps easily fed the flames, as did the largely wooden rolling stock.

Punch, predictably, was quick to pick up these weaknesses, adapting a nursery rhyme accordingly:

> Air – 'Dickory, Dickory, Dock'
> Smashery, mashery, crash!
> Into the 'Goods' we dash:
> The 'Express', we find,
> Is just behind –
> Smashery, mashery, crash![170]

Another issue carried a cartoon showing a railway director as the ultimate patent safety railway buffer, a clear gibe at what was perceived to be the failure of many railway boards to address the issue of accidents seriously. For Victorian fathers away on business, *Punch* could not resist dwelling upon the anxieties that railway travel brought:

THE PATENT SAFETY RAILWAY BUFFER.

101. Cartoon from *Punch*, 1857, showing a railway director strapped to the front of the engine to act as a buffer.

> I'm going by the Rail, my dears, where the engines puff and hiss;
> And ten to one the chances are that something goes amiss;
> And in an instant, quick as thought – before you cry 'Ah!'
> An accident occurs, and – say good-bye to poor Papa![171]

At the time of this verse, in 1851, the actual chance of being killed on the railways was 1 in 420,437,[172] so *Punch* was making liberal use of artistic licence. People's perceptions, though, clearly leaned more towards the magazine's view than towards statistics. As William Pickering observed in 1846:

> . . . the papers day by day
> Tell us how railroad screws have given way
> Now bursts a boiler. O'er the embankment's ridge
> Rushes the hapless train; now falls a bridge;
> Now sinks a viaduct; or wrapt in fire,
> Or plunged in torrents, passengers expire.[173]

Anxieties about death aside, one of the strange paradoxes of the railroad's annihilation of space by time was that people actually spent much more of their lives travelling – in one observer's words, travelling was increasing in geometric progression.[174] The populace generally became much more mobile, and they also journeyed over far greater distances: railways both contracted *and* expanded space. The increase in travelling meant a great extension of leisure time, even if it was an enforced leisure. For some, the journey became an obligatory tedium – a time for sleeping, for recovering from the hectic pace of life that the railways seemed to engender. For Anthony Trollope, the railway carriage became a place where, after a little practice, he could write as quickly as he could at his desk. Much of *Barchester Towers* (1857) seems to have been written while he was travelling on trains.[175] For others, the railway carriage afforded reading time. Sir Francis Head described how, immediately after a train's departure from Euston, its passengers began reading – men of business intently studied the City news, while men of pleasure read the newspaper leaders.[176]

As Raymond Williams states, the railway helped to 'revolutionize the distribution of not only magazines and newspapers but books'.[177] Among those who were able to read and who could afford to do so, taking books, magazines or newspapers on trains became habitual. In 1848, W. H. Smith was granted exclusive

102. *The Christmas excursion-train, Illustrated Times*, 1859. These two views, of first and second class, demonstrate clearly the habit of reading on railway journeys (they appear to be a pastiche of Abraham Solomon's paintings of 1854, shown on page 229).

THE CHRISTMAS EXCURSION-TRAIN.—FIRST CLASS.

THE CHRISTMAS EXCURSION-TRAIN.—SECOND CLASS.

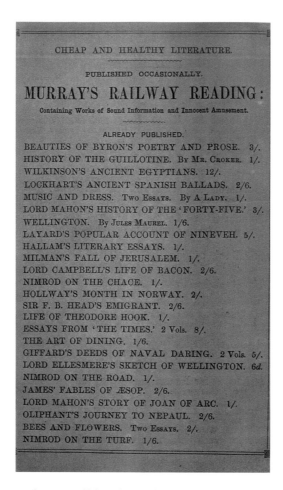

CHEAP AND HEALTHY LITERATURE.

PUBLISHED OCCASIONALLY.

MURRAY'S RAILWAY READING:

Containing Works of Sound Information and Innocent Amusement.

ALREADY PUBLISHED.

BEAUTIES OF BYRON'S POETRY AND PROSE. 3/.
HISTORY OF THE GUILLOTINE. By Mr. Croker. 1/.
WILKINSON'S ANCIENT EGYPTIANS. 12/.
LOCKHART'S ANCIENT SPANISH BALLADS. 2/6.
MUSIC AND DRESS. Two Essays. By A Lady. 1/.
LORD MAHON'S HISTORY OF THE 'FORTY-FIVE.' 3/.
WELLINGTON. By Jules Maurel. 1/6.
LAYARD'S POPULAR ACCOUNT OF NINEVEH. 5/.
HALLAM'S LITERARY ESSAYS. 1/.
MILMAN'S FALL OF JERUSALEM. 1/.
LORD CAMPBELL'S LIFE OF BACON. 2/6.
NIMROD ON THE CHACE. 1/.
HOLLWAY'S MONTH IN NORWAY. 2/.
SIR F. B. HEAD'S EMIGRANT. 2/6.
LIFE OF THEODORE HOOK. 1/.
ESSAYS FROM 'THE TIMES.' 2 Vols. 8/.
THE ART OF DINING. 1/6.
GIFFARD'S DEEDS OF NAVAL DARING. 2 Vols. 5/.
LORD ELLESMERE'S SKETCH OF WELLINGTON. 6d.
NIMROD ON THE ROAD. 1/.
JAMES' FABLES OF ÆSOP. 2/6.
LORD MAHON'S STORY OF JOAN OF ARC. 1/.
OLIPHANT'S JOURNEY TO NEPAUL. 2/6.
BEES AND FLOWERS. Two Essays. 2/.
NIMROD ON THE TURF. 1/6.

rights to sell books and newspapers on the London and Birmingham section of the London and North Western Railway. Within three years, Smith had acquired an exclusive concession over all that company's lines. Little more than ten years later, he had gained a monopoly of bookselling on the stations of most of the leading company lines.[178] By 1902, there were 777 W. H. Smith bookstalls on stations.[179] Nor did Smith miss the publishing opportunities that his retail outlets offered. The *Railway Anecdote Book* of 1852, for example, provided the railway traveller with 'a collection of the best and newest anecdotes and tales to the present day.'[180] Within its 192 pages, there were reminders of the startling range of items that passengers accidentally left behind on trains or in railway halls.[181] More seriously, there were accounts of the commercial benefits of the electric telegraph.[182] It was fiction, however, that became the stock-in-trade of the station stall. Simms and Macintyre started their *Parlour Library* in 1847, a monthly series of one-shilling titles. This was followed in 1849 by Routledge's *Railway Library*.[183] Both were hugely successful, but in the face of rising social criticism. 'Railway literature' became a term of abuse and disapprobation.[184]

Samuel Phillips, writing for *The Times* in 1851, commented that the larger proportion of railway readers lost their accustomed taste the moment they entered the station. In London, he asserted that 'unmitigated rubbish encumbered the bookshelves of almost every bookstall we visited'.[185] The railway travelling public were a captive audience and thus it was claimed in 1857 that 'no small amount of literary rubbish travels by rail'.[186] While cheap editions of much of what we now regard as literary classics of the century were available, there were also many volumes that have since vanished from public and critical notice. Easily the most popular author of the day, for example, was G. W. M. Reynolds, whose writing appeared in periodicals like the *London Journal* and his own *Miscellany*. He was more popular than Dickens, and yet his work is largely unread a century later.[187] Among the more popular non-fiction works sold at Euston were Macaulay's *England* and Murray's sketch of the London and North Western Railway, *Stokers and Pokers*. Weale's series of practical scientific works found a significant sale among the mechanics and engine-drivers.[188] At Waterloo in 1859, commuters snapped up Darwin's newly published *Origin of Species*, much to its author's consternation.[189] Although the literary tastes of railway passengers appeared (if we are to believe Samuel Phillips) to depend more upon the salesman than upon the locality, there were cases where taste varied from one particular part of the country to another; even stations had their idiosyncracies. Yorkshire was not partial to poetry. At Bangor, all books in the Welsh language had to have a strong dissenting or radical savour, while English books at the same station had to be High Church and Conservative. It was difficult to sell any valuable book on the stations between Derby, Leeds and Manchester. Religious books could find no sale in Liverpool, whereas they were in high demand in Manchester. Phillips went on to conclude that it was not possible to promise 'to instruct by steam', but it was at least possible to provide cheap and good books 'and make the most of that anxious and welcome desire for knowledge which locomotion has mainly introduced'.[190]

104. Young man selling newspapers and magazines at Euston station, London, 1908.

3

CAPITAL

> The railway magnates have shown greater genius in inventing fantastic species than have botanists or zoologists. The classification of goods on British railways, for example, fills volumes, and rests for its general principle on the tendency to transform the variegated natural properties of goods into an unequal number of transportation ailments and pretexts for obligatory impositions.[1]

STEAM RAILWAY CAPITALISM

BRITAIN'S RAILWAYS in the Victorian era were embedded in the contemporary workings of capital. We need look no further than Karl Marx's monumental work on capital, where it is made plain in his comments on 'the general classification of goods' of the Railway Clearing House. The classification for 1869 covered 28 pages and was marked 'private and not for publication'. Under the letter 'B', it encompassed items from boilers, bolts and bomb-shells to bonnets, boots and books.[2] This was part of what Marx termed the 'fetishism' of the commodity, and 'no one entity came so close to being the key to all the mythologies of Victorian life'. For Marx, representing commodities was almost a theological problem. The commodity was 'present everywhere, but fully concentrated nowhere'.[3] The railway classification of goods became the target of a rising barrage of criticism from traders in the later decades of the nineteenth century, prompting various Parliamentary investigations.[4] Many people were incensed by the secrecy or mystery that appeared to surround railway commodity rates which, in a sense, almost formed a mythology of their own.

Detailed use of railways was a feature of Marx's ideas about the life-span of fixed capital. He quoted the life of wooden sleepers as between twelve and fifteen years. In 1867, the life of a locomotive was between ten and twelve years.[5] Marx used the railways to exemplify his concept of 'fictitious' capital – in 1846, the demand for capital for the establishment of railways did not increase the value of money: there was merely a 'condensation of small sums into large masses'.[6] Railway labour, likewise, was an object of Marx's critique. He recited the evidence of railway workers who declared how the progressive lengthening of the working day was bringing their labour power to breaking point.[7]

The generalized function of improved transportation, according to Marx, is to accelerate the circulation time of capital and to do so with greater efficiency and greater reliability. As more and more of the production regime comes to be based on exchange, so the physical nature of exchange becomes more critical. The ultimate impulse was the total annihilation of space so that, to use Marx's own

105. The Midland Railway's goods depot at Nottingham, 1922.

106. Page from the Railway Clearing House's general classification of goods for the year 1869. Commodities were charged according to the class in which they fell. As a general rule, class rates reflected what it was perceived the traffic would bear.

GENERAL CLASSIFICATION OF GOODS.						17
ARTICLE.	Class.	ARTICLE.	Class.	ARTICLE.	Class.	
Blocks, *Rough Cast Steel Horn*	S	*in waggons, to be carried only by special agreement.*		Borate of Lime	S	
do., *Ships'*	3	Boilers, *Copper*	3	Borax...............	2	
Blood, *in casks*	2	do., *Furnace*	2	Borings, *iron*	S	
Blowing Engines ...	3	do., *do., at Owner's risk*	1	Bottles, *blk. & green, or common glass* ...	1	
Blubber	1	do., *Kitchen*	3	Bottles, *Glass, white*	4	
Boards, *Paraquet Flooring*	2	†do., *do., at Owner's risk*	2	Bowls, *wooden*	3	
Boats, Canoes, and Cobles, *minimum charge, 1 ton per waggon. S. to S.* ...	3	do., *Locomotive* ...	2	Boxwood	1	
		Bolts, *fang*............	S	Bran	S	
		do., *iron*	S	Brass	2	
Boats, *Life, actual weight. S. to S.*	1	do., *Railway*	S	*Brass Dust............	2	
		Bomb Shells (*not loaded*)	1	do. Nails	2	
Bobbins	3	Bone Ash	S	do. Pipes	4	
Bobbin Blocks	1	Bone Flats	2	do. Scrap	2	
Boiler Lorries, *sent by boiler-makers with boilers, to be charged on the outward journey the same rates as the boilers which they accompany, and returned free.*		Bone and Horn Waste, *if in less quantities than 2 tons per truck, S. to S.*	1	do. Tubing, *except Locomotive Tubes*	4	
		do., *in truck loads of not less than 2 tons...*	S	do. Wire	3	
Boiler Plates, *Iron*... (*See Undamageable Iron List, p. 50*).	S	Bones, *loose, other than for size or manure* ...	2	Bread	2	
Boilers, *weighing less than a ton, occupying only one waggon*	2	do., *packed*	1	Bricks, *common and fire*	M	
		do., *calcined*	S	do., *Bath, Flanders, or Scouring*	1	
do., *45 feet and above, S. to S.*	3	do., *common, for size or manure*	S	do., *do.,at Owner's risk*	S	
do., *30 feet and under 45 feet, S. to S.*	2	Bonnet Fronts	5	Bridge Work *of iron plates made up in parts, above 15 feet and not exceeding 30 feet* ...	1	
do., *under 30 feet, S. to S.*	1	do., *at Owner's risk*...	4	do., *do., do., at Owner's risk* ...... (*See Damageable Iron List, p. 50*).		
do., *requiring more than one waggon, to be charged not less than as for 2 tons per waggon; to be loaded by sender, and unloaded by consignee, and carried at Owner's risk.*		Bonnet Shapes	5			
		Bonnets	5			
		Books............... (*See note, p. 51*).	3	do., *do., above 30 feet (As Girders*).		
do., *requiring a special train to be charged the ordinary rate, plus a minimum of 5s. a mile for the train.*		Book Muslin	4	Brimstone, *Roll*......	1	
		Boothing or Stalling	5	do., *crude or unmanufactured*	S	
		do., *at Owner's risk*...	4	Bristles	3	
do., *of peculiar shape, or extraordinary dimensions, requiring alterations to be made*		Boots and Shoes (including Goloshes) *in hampers (except white rod hampers at Owner's risk)*	5	Bristle Waste	1	
				Britannia Metal Goods	4	
		do., *in white rod hampers, at Owner's risk*..	4	Bronze Powder	4	
		do., *in casks, cases, and boxes*	3	Broom and Brush Blocks	1	
				Brooms, Broom Heads, and Brushes	3	
		Boracic Acid ..:........	2	Broom and Mop Handles	2	
				Buckles, *iron or brass*	2	

† When carried at Owner's risk, and damaged in transit, to be returned free, and the articles sent to replace the same to be carried free also, provided the whole transaction is completed within one month, reference being made in each case to the original invoice.

metaphor, circulation time can be reduced to 'the twinkling of an eye'.[8] It is plain that the battle over the Liverpool and Manchester Railway Bill in the 1820s arose in part from the desire among certain of its supporters to increase the rate of circulation of capital in its commodity form. It was no use that goods spent as long in transit from Liverpool to Manchester as they did on the 21-day Atlantic crossing.[9] The railway objectors might cite the practice among manufacturers of stockpiling supplies,[10] but such stockpiles of goods impeded the circulatory motion and diminished capital's reproducibility. Leon Faucher was remarkably alive to these various pressures when he wrote his account of Manchester in 1844. Cotton manufacture could not remain stationary: it was 'a system without limits' requiring 'a field of action boundless in extent . . . in no department of society [was] the law of progress more inexorable'.[11] Fourteen years earlier, Henry Booth, in one of the first detailed accounts of the Liverpool and Manchester Railway, remarked how the 'race of competition' was 'universal and unceasing – every manufacture striving against each other, and against themselves . . . . Every class, and every individual, in every department of industry, hurrying along, struggling with fortune and the times, and jostling his fellow sufferers . . . . and especially the never-ceasing race of population against subsistence'.[12] Booth ultimately saw this 'new theatre of activity and employment' as healthy for society,[13] but his observations of the workings of capital might easily have been penned by Friedrich Engels.

The particular nature of railway technology, with its dedicated permanent way and exclusive rolling stock, involved extensive outlays of fixed capital. Indeed, it is hard to over-estimate the scale of the railway's 'built environment'. On many early lines, the volume of fixed capital required was inflated by over-exacting engineering standards. The London and Birmingham Railway, for example, cost £53,100 per mile.[14] Laid out by Robert Stephenson, its gradients rarely exceeded 1 in 300 and curves were of a generous radius.[15] Up to 1844, the average cost of British passenger railways was over £34,000 per mile, three to four times the average for Germany, double that for Belgium and 50 per cent higher than the average for the most expensive French lines.[16]

Costs were high not just because of very exacting engineering requirements. Parliamentary and legal expenses also inflated the figures, as did the cost of land. Railways were highly unusual among nineteenth-century industrial enterprises in that they were legislated into existence. This forced railway promoters into the hands of the complex hierarchy of lawyers who held the key to private bill procedures in Parliament. As a result, many railway schemes became lawyered in a manner akin to complicated law-suits in the Court of Exchequer.[17]

> . . . in the absence of centralised state planning, the country's railway capitalists had no choice but to engage in a prolonged Parliamentary free-for-all for complete incorporation, commercial territory, and the power to expropriate land.[18]

Worst of all, perhaps, railway Bills were subject to double sets of investigative hearings – in the Lords as well as in the Commons.[19] The railway boom thus created a windfall of business for the Parliamentary Bar. By 1862, the railway industry had expended some £30 million on Parliamentary business.[20] The problem with land costs was that the provisions to expropriate land, enshrined in every railway Act, represented a dramatic infringement of private property rights. So pervasive had railway projects become by the Mania of the 1840s that railway promoters soon became embroiled in a far wider social and political conflict with landed proprietors, the largest of whom enjoyed powerful representation in Parliament. The outcome was inflated compensation for the land that railway companies needed to make their permanent ways. The first Eastern Counties line, for instance, involved an outlay of above £12,000 per mile for purely agricultural land.[21] The London and Dover gave for 27 acres of farmland a sum that amounted to four times its agricultural worth.[22] As the railway industry became more competitive, even small parcels of land could involve large payments in compensation. This was especially true of urban land. The Earls of Derby, for instance, got nearly £500,000 between 1864 and 1892 for a series of small plots in Liverpool.[23] In some cases, excesssive payments became a thin disguise for buying off Parliamentary opposition among individual landed proprietors. After 1845, moreover, the landed

107. J. C. Bourne, lithograph, 1839, showing part of the heavily engineered London and Birmingham line at Berkhamsted, Hertfordshire, in the summer of 1837.

interest strengthened its position with the passing of the Land Clauses Consolidation Act which, according to an infuriated railway lobby, was a licence for still higher levels of compensation.[24] By 1850 escalating land costs were being blamed for the decline in profitability even of leading companies like the Great Western and the Midland.[25]

For Marx, the building of railways involved outlays of fixed capital that would attain their term of reproduction only after a period of some years. This could not be 'just any sum of money'; it had to be 'an amount of a certain size'.[26] Such capital yielded an interest (a dividend) rather than an entrepreneurial profit. In the case of the Railway Mania, these large capital sums flowed from what Marx described as 'Lancashire's streaming surplus value'.[27] The sums were used to underwrite such a vast array of railway enterprise that the capital needed beyond the initial calls could be acquired only by means of credit. Subsequently, the market in railway shares crashed, as the shaky nature of many initial schemes became apparent.

Marx constructed his analysis of the political economy of capitalism with the benefit of almost two decades of hindsight. However, he was not the first to pick out the interlocking dimensions of railway and capital. 'Capitalism' had been used as a term describing a particular economic system from the early nineteenth century. The noun 'capitalist' had a slightly older usage, Arthur Young having employed it in the 1790s to refer to 'money men'.[28] In the 1830s and the 1840s, it was this latter usage that was most often associated with railways. However, at least as early as 1844, there were critical commentators who appeared to see railways as part of a distinctive set of socio-economic relations, in the manner of Marx's ideas about society. A pamphlet on railway reform of that year described how the capitalist railway proprietors had been granted a monopoly of channels of communication of the most secure kind and how this placed the community in the power of such capitalists in one of its more important matters.[29] The author foresaw 'ruinous effects . . . . on the poorer classes and their deprivation to a great extent of the manifold advantage which the establishment of railways is calculated to confer on them'.[30] Another pamphleteer, in an open letter to Gladstone the same year, described railways as 'legalised' and 'grasping monopolies', 'invading private property and wringing enormous profits from an injured community'.[31] It is clear that these commentaries were part of the movement to secure better train accommodation for the working classes and that they were, more widely, linked to the controversial issue of public ownership of the railways which Gladstone sought to address in his 1844 Railway Bill.[32] The case of Belgium's publicly owned railway system was cited in one of the pamphlets.[33] Such commentaries generally bore sentiments that did not sit ill alongside Friedrich Engels' exactly contemporary *Condition of the Working Class*, with its depiction of the social evils of industrial capitalism.[34] The well-known cartoon in *Punch* of 1843, illustrating the misery that accrued from the particular relations of capital and labour, repeated the picture of exploitation.[35]

108. *Capital and labour, Punch*, 1843. The occasion of this composition appears to have been publication of the Report of the Children's Employment Commission, the intention to show the 'pleasing picture of aristocratic ease' to which labour in the mines gave rise.

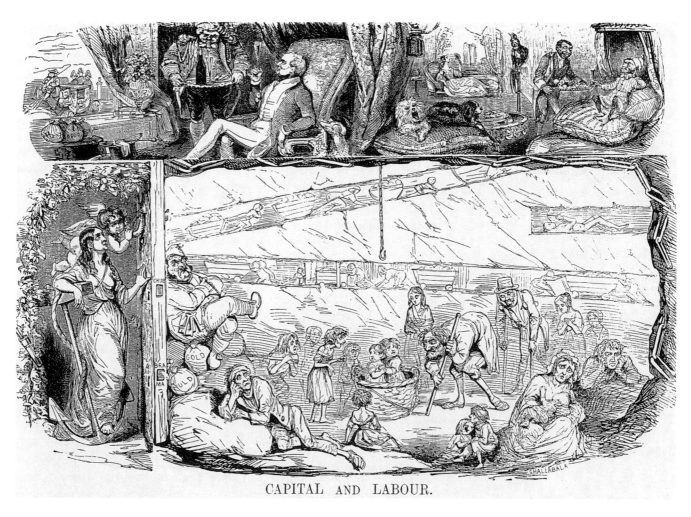

CAPITAL AND LABOUR.

Railways became a focus of interest for capitalists or 'money men' when it became apparent that they had the potential to yield a higher rate of return than the average 4 per cent for government stock. Without state direction or subsidy, English steam railway capitalism inaugurated 'an almost archetypal form of industrial capitalism'.[36] Railway enterprises were joint stock companies of private shareholders. More particularly, the 9½ per cent dividend paid out regularly to investors in the Liverpool and Manchester Railway proved to be the critical watershed.[37] Francis Whishaw's comprehensive account of the railways of Great Britain and Ireland, published in 1840, had on its dedication page the words: 'To the Railway Capitalists of the United Kingdom'.[38] William Pickering caught the tone in verse some six years later:

> Take my advice: so fresh and fair a field,
> Well tilled, may more than barren laurels yield;
> May fill your pockets when the corn-rents fail:
> Take my advice and cultivate the rail.[39]

Pickering's comparison with farming was not just a poetic device. In the poor harvest years of the late 1830s, several key trunk lines were completed and opened. By 1845, the London and Birmingham Railway was yielding a 10 per cent dividend, the Great Western and the London and South Western each 8 per cent.[40] As Marx observed, it was in the industrial north, especially Lancashire, that accumulated capital had attained greatest proportions by this date.[41] In 1835, the *Circular to Bankers* claimed there was no other part of Britain where could be found 'so many opulent competitors in railway projects'.[42] Lancashire money interests were underwriting not only the railway projects of their own localities (roughly half of the Liverpool and Manchester Railway shares were accounted for by citizens of Liverpool and Manchester),[43] but also supporting railway schemes much farther afield. The London and Birmingham Railway, for instance, drew more capital from Lancashire and Cheshire than from London and Birmingham together; half of the total of £2,500,000 was provided by Liverpool alone.[44] Lancashire capital was prominent in financing the Canterbury and Whitstable, the London and Southampton, the Great Western and the Eastern Counties lines.[45] In 1836, the *Circular to Bankers* recorded Lancashire capital as being involved in the promotion of projects as far distant as Edinburgh and Glasgow, Dublin and Drogheda.[46]

The scale of Lancashire's interest in the railway capital market soon led to the development of formal share markets in both Manchester and Liverpool. The *London Mercantile Journal* of 1836 even suggested that railway shares were becoming 'almost as current a commodity as cotton'.[47] Subsequently, broking in railway stocks became widespread throughout provincial towns, especially as the railway capital market increasingly became a speculative one.[48] Whereas the market for government stock was a near-monopoly of London brokers, railway stock suffered no such restriction. Thus railway investment became a central means in the development of a national market in company securities.[49] Indeed, the *Circular to Bankers* of 11 July 1845, citing the existence of new markets for railway shares in Leeds, Wakefield, Bradford, Halifax, Huddersfield, Leicester, Birmingham and many other inland towns, claimed that the market in government securities had become 'an object of inferior interest'.[50] In a sense, then, railway securities had become synonymous with the capital market. Even as early as 1844, they boasted a level of paid-up capital almost twice that of the joint-stock banks.

Investment in railway securities had a range of attractions. Those 'moneyed men' who backed the Liverpool and Manchester scheme were soon rewarded with a regular return on capital that competed more than favourably with the return on government securities. Many of the investors in some of the early trunk lines were likewise persuaded by the prospect of high operating dividends. However, the railway securities market was dominated by investors who were most of all interested in speculating in partly-paid shares. Often these shares constituted no more than the initial 'capital call', with no dividend in sight, let alone even any construction work. Such investors relied on making quick capital gains as the shares moved in response to market conditions. An extreme form of such speculative activity was the gambling in letters of allotment and scrip certificates.[51] Here, almost anyone could become a speculator or 'stag'. It has been claimed, moreover, that the single most important asset of most railways floated at the height of the Mania of the 1840s was the public standing of its principal promoters: in effect, it was a case of social status being transformed into capital.[52] Here was the 'bubble' company *par excellence*. Contemporary business commentators typically argued that trading in such 'light' railway stocks, which accounted for the lion's share of Stock Exchange dealings in the 1840s, was critical in opening the way for the more substantial investors who naturally weighed the risk of new ventures much more heavily.[53] Even so, it is a fair contention that by the last months of 1845 the promotion of new railways by joint-stock companies had become almost completely detached from *bona fide* capitalism.[54] In December 1845, the *Illustrated London News* contained a memorable engraving of the mad rush to deposit railway plans at the Board of Trade, Parliament having fixed 30 November as the last date for submissions during that session. Alongside were published the names of over 600 plans or projects. The paper went on to remark how it was:

109, 110. The desperate rush to correct final plans for new railway ventures, and deposit them at the Board of Trade in time for the 30 November 1845 deadline, *Illustrated London News*, 6 December 1845.

111. Fifty-pound share
certificate in the
Middlesbro' & Redcar
Railway Company, issued
at the height of the mania
in April 1846.

impossible to conceive the amount of business connected with Railway Illustration that has been carried on, particularly in London, within the last fortnight . . . . Surveyors and levellers have made quite a harvest of it, many of them getting from six to fifteen guineas per day . . . . lithographic and zinco-graphic engravers have also been collected from every large town, not only in England, but from France and Germany.[55]

William Wordsworth attacked the cupidity of the railway speculators in a famous letter to the *Morning Post* in 1844. He was not against railways themselves but against the abuse of them and the way the mask of 'Utilitarianism' was being offered as justification for what was none other than sheer gambling. It was a shameful 'Thirst of Gold that rule[d] o'er Britain like a baneful star'.[56]

Dealing in railway securities began in earnest in the early 1830s, in the wake of the huge financial success of the Liverpool and Manchester scheme. The number of railway company shares quoted on the London exchange was four in 1830, eight in 1833, and 62 by 1836. Over the ensuing period to 1844, the figure stabilised at around 40.[57] However, in the mid 1840s dealing in railway securities really accelerated. By the spring of 1844, according to one contemporary, there was a more plentiful supply of money available for railway investment than even the oldest capitalists could recall.[58] By September 1845, according to a report in the *Illustrated London News*, the volume of railway business already prepared for the House of Commons in its ensuing session was more than it could possibly get through properly. The report went on to suggest that perhaps the House might choose to sit permanently – like the French Convention during the political convulsions of the Revolution. The Railway Mania lasted from 1844 to 1847 and saw Parliament authorize some £250 million on railway schemes, involving some 9,500 miles of line.[59] Bank of England rates of 2½ per cent, coupled with other favourable economic indicators, encouraged an unbounded optimism in the potential of railways.[60] By 1847, railway investment was 6.7 per cent of national income, or 'two-thirds of the value of all domestic exports'.[61]

On the London Stock Exchange, dealing was revolutionized by the Railway Mania. Whereas railway share-dealing had formerly been the preserve of a small number of minor brokers, as the business grew so leading brokers entered the fray and government stocks, previously the life-blood of the market, faded rapidly in their appeal.[62] Meanwhile, on the newly emergent provincial share markets, the impetus of the Mania soon brought formally constituted stock markets into being.[63] It was the growth of these regional securities markets that help to explain how the Mania attained such remarkable proportions.

THE WIDER CULTURE OF CAPITAL

> ... this century is hardly awake of a morning before
> thousands of newspapers, speeches, lectures and essays
> appear at its bedside, or its breakfast table ...[64]

Whether the focus is upon capitalism at large, or steam railway capitalism in particular, it is impossible to disengage such materialist analyses from sections of the wider cultural profile. This is not to invoke a primitive form of economic determinism, but to point to the complex relationships between forms of economic organization and aspects of culture, the latter embracing art, literature and the press, as well as the world of attitudes and ideas. 'Cultural materialism' has been defined as a 'particular application of the Marxist method of historical materialism to cultural studies'.[65] Its primary exponent, Raymond Williams, has seen 'determination' not as something that occurs in relation to a static mode of production, but as part of a more active, conscious historical experience, grounded in human agency, and yet enframed within a clear set of historical conditions.[66] The Railway Mania, for instance, was in significant measure transacted through what became known as the 'railway press'. This was not some organ of the railway companies, but a spontaneous growth of the ordinary press. In itself and in its contents, the railway press reflected all the familiar 'norms' of *laissez-faire* capitalism, but connected them to the wider *zeitgeist*. Indeed, it might be claimed that relations between the two were indissoluble.

By October 1845 there were at least sixteen railway journals, one of which (the *Iron Times*) appeared daily, while the rest were weekly.[67] John Francis parodied the phenomenon by remarking how there were *Railway Expresses*, *Railway Worlds*, *Railway Examiners*, *Railway Globes*, *Railway Standards*, *Railway Mails*, *Railway Engines*, *Railway Telegraphs* and so on.[68] The most prominent

112. *The Railway Times*, 3 February 1844, easily the most widely sold of the railway weeklies.

WAITING FOR "THE RAILWAY TIMES."

(AFTER HAYDON.)

journals were the *Railway Magazine* and the *Railway Times*, the former first produced in 1835, the latter in 1837.[69] By 1842, the *Railway Times* had attained (by its own account) a circulation of some 27,000 copies.[70] In 1836, the *Railway Magazine* was taken over by John Herepath and re-titled the *Railway Magazine and Annals of Science*.[71] As well as presenting detailed acounts of railway 'intelligence', including lists of Railway Bills reported, committed and passed, and railway share prices, the journal also contained, as its amended title indicated, analyses and speculations reflecting the scientific preoccupations of the age. Issue number three, for instance, incorporated an editorial on the effects of the atmosphere in resisting a train. Also included were suggestions on the practicability of employing wind as an auxiliary on railways. Another article even addressed the physical constitution of the universe. Here, then, was the steam railway not just as capital enterprise but as cultural emblem.

As well as railway weeklies, there were railway yearbooks. The *Railway Almanac* of 1846, published by Richard Groombridge and Sons, gave details of railway dividends payable on continental as well as English lines, offered share tables for calculating amounts of premium, included a digest of railway law, and provided would-be investors with a directory of Parliament together with lists of London and provincial stockbrokers.[72] At the end was an advertisement for yet another railway newspaper, the *Railway Herald*. This was published thrice weekly, priced sixpence. F. S. Williams, writing in 1852, went so far as to regard the railway press as a species of literature of its own: 'Patriotism and poetry, paragraphs and pamphletts, essays and articles, aided in the work of exalting the value of railways'.[73]

Railway Mania can also be traced in the comic and satirical press of the day, especially in *Punch*, which treated it as 'rollicking farce, larded with occasional moral strictures'.[74] Later, it has been claimed, *Punch* adopted the stance of advocate of the middle classes against the unscrupulousness of railway directors and officers, particularly over the carelessness of organization that led to accidents.[75] However, this is to miss some of the significance of the subject material that provided the focus of *Punch*'s comedy and criticism. The public house scene of 1845, 'Waiting for "The Railway Times"', offers a vivid portrait of the widespread preoccupation with railway speculation.[76] The picture is a pastiche of Robert Haydon's celebrated portrait, *Waiting for The Times*, which depicts two men in the White Horse Cellar in Piccadilly digesting news about the Parliamentary debate on the famous Reform Bill in October 1831. In *Punch*'s version, the caricature on the right appears to be that of a workman (his hand rests on a spade), whereas the figure immersed in the newspaper is clearly of a higher social station. On both tables there are ink-pots. On one is an application form for shares. The juxtaposition of classes is important:

> Old men and young, the famish'd and the full,
> The rich and poor, widow, and wife, and maid,
> Master and servant – all, with one intent,
> Rushed on the paper scrip . . .[77]

Another *Punch* cartoon of 1845 styled the railway as a new Lord of the World, or Juggernaut, with speculators throwing themselves under the wheels of the advancing steam locomotive. According to one parody, among the populace at large almost everyone appeared to have some piece of paper called scrip, which entitled them to 'a certain proportionate part of a blue, red, or yellow line drawn across a map and designated a railway'.[78] If the coloured scratch ran from south to north it was a trunk line; if it turned and wheeled about in all directions and led

THE RAILWAY JUGGERNAUT OF 1845.

114. Cartoon from *Punch*, 1845.

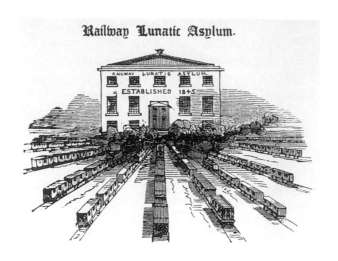

115. Cartoon from *Punch*, 1845. Even at this date, not long into the mania, *Punch* viewed some new schemes as so 'impracticable, and useless' that they cast doubt on the sanity of their proposers.

nowhere, but interfered with every other railway in its path, it was a Grand Junction line; and if it lay at full length along the shore, it was a coast line. It was perhaps no wonder, then, that *Punch* later followed its Railway Juggernaut with a scheme for a Railway Lunatic Asylum, to reflect contemporary enlightenment and public spirit regarding the impracticable, useless and insane railway schemes that were being touted.[79] The same tone of benevolent indulgence featured in the *Illustrated London News* in a more sober account of the railway magnate George Hudson, who had come to personify Railway Mania and was known as the 'railway king'. He was 'the creature of an immoral system', it was argued. He had been elevated into the dictatorship of railway speculation in 'an unwholesome ferment of popular cupidity, pervading all ranks and conditions of men'. Thus it was too much 'to expect of him that he should be purer than his time or his associates'.[80] William Pickering reflected the same attitude in 1846:

> Say what you please of railroad speculation,
> Prospectus, shares, scrip, humbug, malversation:
> Fertile's the subject, novel is the theme;
> What Muse before e'er sang of smoke and steam?[81]

Against an index value of 100 in 1840, railway shares had risen to 149 by 1845, a 50 per cent gain. By 1848, however, they were down to 95.5 and by 1850 to 70.4.[82] By 1853, it appears that roughly 2,000 miles of line sanctioned by Parliament had been abandoned by their promoters.[83] This is in addition to the vast array of schemes that failed to get beyond a first reading in Parliament. In other words, the railway bubble of the mid 1840s soon burst, bringing financial ruin to many a speculator. One caricature in *Punch* in late 1845 had the young Queen Victoria devotedly asking Prince Albert if *he* had any railway shares.[84] A satire dedicated to the 'pillaged and plundered shareholders of Great Britain', written by 'a Lancashire victim' in the 1850s, perhaps said it all:

> If there's a hell on earth for imps to range,
> Earth has that hell here in the Stock Exchange,
> Which lies at many a root of many a crime,
> Polluting widely with its with'ring slime –
> 'Tis Satan's kingdom, where his subjects meet,
> To kneel in abject worship at his feet – [85]

116. Cartoon from *Punch*, 1845. Queen Victoria anxiously asks: 'Tell me, oh tell me, dearest Albert, have *you* any Railway Shares?' Railway share mania was seen to affect all ranks of society.

THE MOMENTOUS QUESTION.

The invective was no less harsh for the railway directors, especially the chairman:

> Does any dare his Godship to arraign?
> Audacious wretch! against a God declaim!
> At him, ye pimps and panders, drown his voice –
> Clamour and insult, stop him with your noise – [86]

But the cupidity of the shareholders and speculators did not escape censorship either:

> What sin unwhipped, what crime, say, to atone,
> Plunged thee in deep – in Railways like this one?
> With thy discernment, thy foresight so clear,
> In name of wonderment, what does thou here?
> To plain, straightforward dealings from thy cradle
> So used, what brings thee to the gambling-table,
> Where loaded dice's dull, rattling sound is heard – [87]

The disheartened investor went on to cast railway speculation as a 'reeking', 'festering . . . cesspool'.[88] His verses concluded with the call to 'put the Railway Charlatan to flight'.[89]

In the *Illustrated London News* of spring 1846 appeared a set of verses under the title 'Lays of the Line; the Song of the Engine'. Its ultimate tone verged on catastrophe: the transformation of nature, using imagery taken from the supernatural, left a torrent of destruction in its wake:

> Roaring o'er the trembling land,
>   Mountains piercing, vallies crossing,
> Right and left, on either hand,
>   Glowing embers madly tossing:
> Like some fettered fiend of Hell
>   Sped I on my reckless way,
> Shouting aye, to wood and fell,
>   My infernal roundelay
> Over moor and pasture screaming
> Whilst the tired world is dreaming,
>   Ho! Ho!
>   Away I go
> With my train of weal and woe![90]

For one modern commentator, however, it was the law and the legal profession that 'made and unmade the Railway Manias'. The ranks of lawyers, far more than any other social group, 'contained men with the blend of technical skills, busines savvy, commercial contacts, and raw avarice needed to promote bubble railway companies at a profit'. Lawyers 'understood the thinking, mores, and vulnerabilities of the monied classes'; they also were familiar with stock markets and pioneered the marketing of railway shares.[91] In the wake of the collapse of the railway share market, therefore, it was the lawyers, above all, who felt the invective of litigants and other ruined investors. Initially, lawyers had not figured as either the sole or main proprietors of railway companies. Typically, railway projects had been floated by members of the business community and by private persons. After spring 1845, however, lawyers began to appear as the sole pro-moters of new railway schemes or else to feature prominently among the lists of promoters. The *Railway Gazette* branded them as 'bubble' lawyers, accusing them of 'concocting' railway schemes in a manner that was delinquent and self-interested.[92] Other organs of the railway press were equally condemnatory. The lawyers, it was claimed, had lined their pockets with fees ten to twenty times what was normal.[93] In turn, when panic gave way to collapse, many of these same lawyers were exceptionally well placed to take on the 'hurricane of litigation' visited on the railway investment sector.[94] There appeared to be no clear way for abortive railway companies to be dissolved. The result was a 'vicious cross-fire of law-suits' which brought the legal profession 'a huge windfall of profitable employment'.[95] Evidence implicating lawyers found its way into the columns of *The Times*. It was said that there was not a projected railway with a respectable solicitor connected with it.[96] Lawyers, it could thus be argued, were instrumental in *dis*-organizing steam railway capitalism.[97]

Dickens offered a fascinating satire on the waste and propaganda of the 1840s railway boom in an article in *Household Words* in 1858. Entitled 'Railway Nightmares', it presented a prophetic picture of an abandoned undertaking:

> The long, silent panorama of the Direct Burygold Railway passes before me: the whole line in Chancery; choked and stiffened by the icy, relentless hand of legal death. The Burygold station, once so full of life, is now an echoing, deserted cavern; its crystal roof is an arch of broken glass; its rails torn away; its rooms and offices are empty and boarded up; and its walls are defaced with old ghastly time-bills, the mocking records of its former wealth and activity.[98]

The Direct Burygold line had been stifled out of existence by a competitor, the Great Deadlock Railway, a general fate that was to become all too familiar a century on from the time Dickens was writing.

The nightmare of the Direct Burygold Railway underscored, of course, the risks that even 'money men' took in backing railway schemes. Dividends on share capital, for instance, declined significantly in the wake of the Mania. By 1850, at 3.31 per cent on average, they had fallen below the 4 per cent return on govern-ment stocks.[99] Marx cast the Mania of 1844–7 as 'the first great railway swindle'.[100] Drawing on evidence given before the Parliamentary Committees on Commercial Distress of 1847–8, he recounted how railways steadily diverted money away from other business activities.[101] Loans were increasingly made on railway shares at a high rate of interest. Initially, the expenditure was not nearly so rapid as the calls, but in the second half of 1847 the opposite was the case. Enormous pressure on the money markets followed, compounded by poor harvests in 1846 and 1847 and a hike in the bank rate from 3–3.5 per cent in January 1847 to 7 per cent in April and 10 per cent in November.[102] According to the House of Lords, the crisis year of 1847 saw the value of railway stock decline by £19.5 million; the parallel fall in government stocks was £93.8 million.[103] Those holding railway shares soon no longer cared for their profit or loss – they sold them just to make themselves safe. The scripholders, those who held only the preliminary share certificates, lost everything.

The railways, then, far more than any other business sector, demonstrated the expansionary power of capital and the pecuniary rewards that it could bring to investors. It was not that the cotton industry, for instance, had failed to yield equivalent returns to its proprietors, but the railways obtained a wider, more ubiquitous, public profile. By the same token, they also demonstrated the innate tendency of capital to crisis. If one needed an emblem of the vicissitudes or perpetual state of flux of the workings of capital within Victorian society, the railways surely provided it, especially over the middle decades of the century. By 1848, the Parliamentary report on commercial distress among the general population was citing the railway as a proximate cause: it had diverted capital from its ordinary employment in commercial transactions.[104] Two years before, a pamphlet had suggested that there should be Railway Exchequer Bills, Bills with a fixed value which would effectively become a national currency. This, it was claimed, had the potential to offer a remedy for the 'railway embarrassments', the adverse currency fluctuations that the Mania brought in its wake.[105]

CENTRALIZATION AND COMBINATION OF CAPITAL

> For one who grows rich ten are ruined, and a hundred
> placed at a greater disadvantage then ever.[106]

As well as demonstrating the boom and bust of capitalist accumulation, the railways also afforded powerful illustration of the centralization of capital. Not only did the railway command a monopoly of its right of way, which brought much adverse criticism, but there was a progressive trend during the later 1840s for companies to amalgamate or for larger ones to swallow up smaller ones. In some measure, this arose through the increasing fragility of the railway share market from 1846, but it also reflected the growing struggle for territory and, notably, the need to consolidate trunk lines. Having lambasted the profligacy and waste of the Mania, *Punch* quickly targeted what it saw as the undesirable consequences of railway amalgamations. In a parody of a scene from *Macbeth*, appearing in 1848, it

A DANGEROUS CHARACTER.

MAC—BULL AND THE RAILWAY WITCHES.

117. Cartoon from *Punch*, 1847, showing the railway as a fallen idol, which has 'done quite mischief enough'.

118. Cartoon from *Punch*, 1848, a satirical rendering of railway company amalgamation inspired by Shakespeare's *Macbeth*.

119. Cartoon from *Funny Folks*, 1879, expressing unease about the growing monopolistic tendencies of private utilities. The Gas Monopoly warns Water and Railway, 'Ah, it's all very well to laugh at your customers as I did; but take warning by me – *your turn will come!*'

THE MONOPOLIES.

regarded the wave of amalgamations as a certain route to higher fares, fewer trains and poorer facilities.[107] For the shareholders, of course, it meant a potential rise in profits and more guaranteed dividends. Centralization through combination extended the work of capital accumulation, according to Marxist theory. The railway company that, according to Dickens, was by 1853 'wealthier than any other corporation in the world',[108] was created in 1846 from an amalgamation of the London and Birmingham, Grand Junction, Manchester and Birmingham, and Liverpool and Manchester companies. By 1848, the London and North Western Railway covered almost 1,000 miles of route. The Great Western was a close second in mileage, having swallowed up or absorbed no fewer than seven major enterprises, including the Bristol and Exeter railway and the South Wales Railway. Of the total 4,982 miles of railway open in 1848, five companies alone (the London and North Western, the Great Western, the Midland, the London and South Western and the Great Northern) accounted for 3,430 miles.[109]

Centralization of capital was also apparent at a very early stage in the matter of railway construction. The sheer scale of the building enterprise and its relative indivisibility made this almost inevitable. Thus emerged the remarkable band of contractors which for most of the middle years of the century dominated railway building. Samuel Morton Peto, one of the largest, had a labour force in 1850 of 14,000 men, 'a larger number than the New Model Army which fought at Naseby'.[110] Such 'legions' of navvies took time to assemble, with all their attendant equipment and draught power, not to mention their expertise and experience. The contractors effectively became partners in railway promotion for, in the crisis of investor confidence that followed the Mania, the primary means of continuing construction was for the promoters to pay the contractors by giving them bonds on the new lines. In turn, these became the security on which banks provided the cash to pay for wages and construction materials. The outcome was an array of additions to the network that became known as contractors' lines. In an effort to minimize capital costs, some of these lines were engineered with quite severe gradients. Among them was the Portsmouth Direct, built by Thomas Brassey in the mid 1850s which, until electrification in the 1930s, remained the curse of enginemen.[111]

The process whereby a few railway companies obtained a monopoly of ownership and control continued after the initial phase of combination and absorption of the late 1840s. In 1874, the four largest companies owned 39 per cent of the track mileage and earned 47 per cent of gross receipts.[112] This was against the background of a mileage total almost three times the figure of 1848. The scale of these leading companies as capital units was awesome by the standards of the day. The London and North Western railway attained a capital value of £117 million by 1898.[113] The Midland Railway, by 1911, was worth £120 million, almost seven times as large as the biggest firm outside the railway industry, Imperial Tobacco.[114] Some commentators have argued that still greater concentration of ownership and control would have occurred had it not been for the 'determination of Parliament, egged on by a vociferous and suspicious trading public, to enforce competition'.[115] Others of a Marxist persuasion have proposed that the centralization process will continue only until some equilibrium of production organization has been attained, whereupon opposing tendencies of decentralization become apparent, with portions of capital becoming disengaged and beginning to function independently.[116] In any event, as late as 1913, the share of gross receipts of the four leading companies remained as it was in 1874.[117] Amalgamation continued in the intervening years, as did various forms of working unions, but so also did the formation of new companies. The entry of a new main line railway into London in 1899, the Great Central, certainly bucked the trend towards centralization of capital organization, as did the launch of companies like the Hull and Barnsley Railway.

For the travelling public and especially the traders, the leading railway companies were increasingly viewed as monopolistic, whether or not their competitive positions were unchallenged. The antagonism towards railways as capital ventures which had become manifest in the wake of the investment collapse of the later 1840s took on a more particular guise in the struggle over the small parcels trade.[118] In the early 1840s, a number of companies had commenced vigorous campaigns to capture from the hundreds of independent carriers the lucrative business of handling small parcels. As the round of company amalgamations gathered momentum in the later years of that decade, even greater efforts were made to secure regional monopolies over the small freight business. For some Victorian business commentators, such commercial trends were quite contrary to the free market assumptions of Adam Smith whereby competition was seen as the pivot of a productive economy. The problem was compounded, moreover, by the very limited influence that Parliament exercised over railway freight rates. The response of the independent carriers was to bring a long series of law-suits against the railway companies. In general terms, judges and juries in these cases favoured the market conditions of the pre-railway era – that is, they were against the corporate monopolies that the new railway companies were forging. The outcome, so the railway interest claimed, was a further dent in the profitability of the railway

120. Private owner
wagons mingled with
railway company wagons
at New England yard,
Peterborough, on the
Great Northern Railway,
11 May 1908.

industry. The same issue developed into an epic struggle, lasting more than twenty years from the 1870s, over the contentious question of railway rates. This centred on the issue of differential rates, whereby a place, a district, or even an individual, could be quoted a preferential rate over another.[119] There were detailed and lengthy investigations of the issue in Parliament. Chambers of Commerce and local trade associations were vigorous in their opposition to what were regarded as unfair and bureaucratic practices in the setting of rates. However, the matter was never satisfactorily resolved and rate discrimination remained a constant irritant in the relationship between the companies and their customers right up until 1914.[120]

One area where it might be claimed that the small business community did win out over the railway companies was in the matter of 'private owner wagons'. The facility existed for anyone in the business community to own a freight wagon, a legacy from the early railway age when traders were expected to provide their own rolling stock.[121] For someone with a few hundred pounds to spare, such an investment could be highly attractive: once the initial outlay had been made, a private owner wagon required little or no attention or maintenance.[122] Coal merchants accounted for the bulk of private owner wagons, and up to 1914 roughly half of all railway wagon stock was in the hands of private individuals.[123] For the railway companies, this arrangement was a nightmare. Not only was there the problem that such wagons could not be moved around at will. More seriously, given the increasing economic pressures on companies to introduce larger and more efficient vehicles, they represented a form of built-in obsolescence. Private owner wagons thus became a thorn in the side of railway management. Indeed, it would be hard to conceive of a more inappropriate context for the enactment of the principle of private property.

As well as being far in advance of their time as giant capital ventures, the leading railway companies also evolved forms of internal organization that became commonplace among other firms only in the twentieth century; in fact, they provided the model for the modern business corporation. They were forerunners of managerial capitalism, the system whereby ownership became separated from control.[124] Management became departmentalized, a hierarchy of management functions was formed, elementary systems of staff training were introduced. Shareholders were effectively derogated to the role of observers; real power rested in the hands of the General Manager and the Board of Directors. And while the pressure for dividend performance remained strong, so too was the pressure to consolidate and extend the company's domain. In other words, the maximization of profit was not necessarily paramount, and this could elicit cries of conspiracy from shareholders. The Boards of Directors quite often comprised business leaders from the areas served by the railway company.[125] Some were local 'money men' or capitalists. In helping to forge decisions to enlarge railway company activities, they were simultaneously benefiting the enterprises that they themselves owned and operated. In effect, therefore, the railway company could become a kind of regional holding company.[126] New extensions or branches could benefit local capital interests, but yield not a penny to shareholders. Thus did the manager of the North Staffordshire Railway Company effectively declare that he was running a sort of regional development agency.[127] Not dissimilar motives lay behind the entry of many leading railway companies into the dock and harbour business, short-sea shipping services and the hotel trade.

CLASS AND CLASS CONSCIOUSNESS

Even historians who reject the Marxist answers . . . are
still attracted by the questions set by Marx.[128]

Before the first railways, the term 'class' appears to have had no currency in passenger travel. Stage-coach and boat travellers had only the choices, respectively, of 'inside' and 'cabin' accommodation, or 'outside' and 'deck'.[129] But, relative to the average working wage of the time, all categories of travel were expensive. Poorer members of society were rarely among those who travelled by stage-coach; they went either on foot or in stage-wagons carrying goods.[130] The process whereby railway proprietors extended the spectrum of travel accommodation to encompass them was a protracted and, at times, ambivalent one. Ordinary folk were quite regularly conveyed on the colliery lines of the north-east;[131] and this practice seems to have extended to the evolving railway systems of northern manufacturing districts.[132] On other lines, however, little or no provision was made for the poor. 'Third-class' accommodation, as it became known, did not exist at all

121. Isaac Shaw, first- and second-class trains on the Liverpool and Manchester Railway, aquatint, 1831.

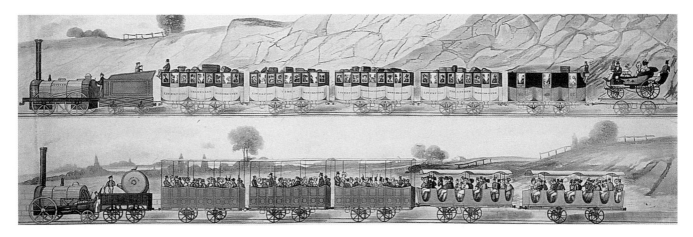

122. Unknown station, c. 1840 (artist unknown). This picture appears to show passenger segregation, the poorer travellers confined behind iron railings while the richer ones, identifiable by their highly coloured clothing, wait directly by the trainshed.

on early lines like the Liverpool and Manchester and the Newcastle and Carlisle.[133] On trunk routes like the London and Birmingham, there was no provision at the time of opening, but subsequently the company altered its policy for the 'convenience of the poor.'[134] The Eastern Counties Railway, perhaps characteristically given its highly chequered financial and operational history, ran 'truck platforms with eight open seats fixed thereon transversely'. Railway proprietors ran third-class trains only as a concession 'for the advantage of the poorer classes', not as a source of profit.[135] On the Great Western, 'persons in lower stations of life' were initially carried in goods trains, following the custom of their travelling by stage-wagon.[136] Other companies with no initial provision for third-class passengers were the London and South Western, the Birmingham and Derby Junction, and the Ulster Railway.[137]

Use of the category 'class' in railway travel seems to date from about the time of the opening of the Liverpool and Manchester Railway in 1830 and was applied largely to trains. First-class trains on the Liverpool and Manchester were coloured yellow, were faster and offered the greatest comfort; second-class trains were blue, were slower and less commodious. Within a few years, however, the modern usage of class, referring to carriage accommodation or tickets, was being applied on many railways.[138] In due course, this was the pattern that prevailed on British railways as a whole, although not in continental practice where differentiation by train persisted. The London and Birmingham had a kind of hybrid system in place around 1840. There were first-class trains, mixed trains (that is, first and second) and third-class trains.[139] A few lines in remote areas adhered for a while to the labels of the coaching era: the Edinburgh and Dalkeith Railway had 'open' and 'closed' carriages, as did the Whitby and Pickering.[140] However, these practices did not last long.

The system of different class trains was temporarily reinforced with the passage of Gladstone's Railway Regulation Act of 1844, which compelled the running of cheap trains with fares of no more than one penny a mile (henceforth these were commonly known as 'Parliamentary trains').[141] The Act was prompted in part by Board of Trade investigations into the means that companies afforded for conveying poor passengers.[142] Its provisions, even though they related to trains, effectively institutionalized the class categorization of rail travel, since they set a datum against which second- and first-class accommodation had to be defined. On the Great Western, for example, the old open second-class carriages were immediately outmoded, since the Act required the carriages of Parliamentary trains to offer protection from the weather.[143]

Class division was not just confined to travel; in some cases, it also figured in ancillary railway facilities. The London and Birmingham Railway Company, for instance, segregated first- and second-class passengers at its Euston Road terminus with separate entrances, booking-halls and waiting-rooms.[144] The Great Western Railway's Bristol station, where the platforms were a storey above entrance level, had separate staircases for first- and second-class passengers.[145] As the century progressed, the larger railway stations typically had different classes of refreshment room, lavatories and other standard offices. So, although the railway station might be seen as a spatial arena in which the different orders of society came face to face, very deliberate efforts were actually made to keep them apart.

123. J. C. Bourne, the trainsheds at Euston station, May 1839.

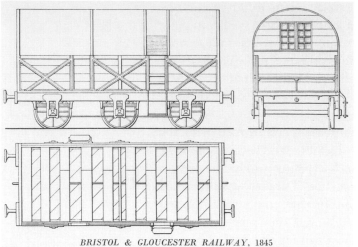

BRISTOL & GLOUCESTER RAILWAY, 1845

No night lamp ; one door only on each side. A sight of the country is confined to the passengers who are fortunate enough to get near the door. No provision is made for the admission of air in bad weather, when the doors and windows are closed. This badly-lighted and badly-ventilated carriage carries 54 passengers

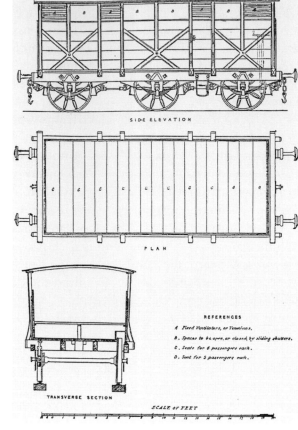

SIDE ELEVATION

PLAN

REFERENCES

A . *Fixed Ventilators, or Venetians.*

B . *Spaces to be open, or closed by sliding shutters.*

C . *Seats for 6 passengers each.*

D . *Seat for 5 passengers each.*

TRANSVERSE SECTION

SCALE OF FEET

124 (above). Third-class carriage on the Bristol and Gloucester Railway, 1845. Holding 54 passengers, it had no side windows or top-lights, nor any night lamp. To the uninitiated passenger, travelling in such a crowded vehicle at night must have been a frightening experience.

125 (above, right). 'Box-cars' for third-class passengers on the Great Western Railway, 1844.

126. The three classes of railway excursion traffic to Epsom Races, *Illustrated London News*, May 1847.

The place that the separation of railway accommodation into classes had in evolving class consciousness, notably among the poor, was clearly underscored by the menial conditions that third-class passengers, even after the 1844 Act, were still forced to endure. Ackworth, commenting on the plight of hapless travellers of the 1840s, claimed that they were conveyed in wagons with pens that even horses and cattle would have disdained to occupy.[146] Whishaw was incredulous at the way no attempt was made on the Manchester and Leeds Railway to distinguish the accommodation for people from that used for 'brute beasts which perish'. The vehicles, common to both categories, were 17 feet long and just under 9 feet wide, divided into compartments by wooden bars and without seats.[147] Even when the 1844 Act stipulated minimum standards for the design of third-class vehicles, some companies merely produced 'box-cars'. The Great Western's officials evidently believed that third-class passengers were uninterested in the scenery, since they were 'encased in a box without windows, only permitting such light to penetrate into the interior as could find its way through the top venetians'.[148] These carriages, just 20 feet long by 8 feet wide, had seats for 59 people. There were eight of them, and they were used on Parliamentary trains between Paddington and Bristol up until 1856. Compared with the low-sided, open wagons in previous use, these carriages were an obvious improvement in that passengers could not fall out. On the other hand, the existence of just one narrow door on the platform side made them potential death-traps, and the absence of spring buffers on some early vehicles was also a serious hazard.[149] The third-class vehicles on the London and North Western Railway's route from Euston to Birmingham had 'the peculiar and interesting

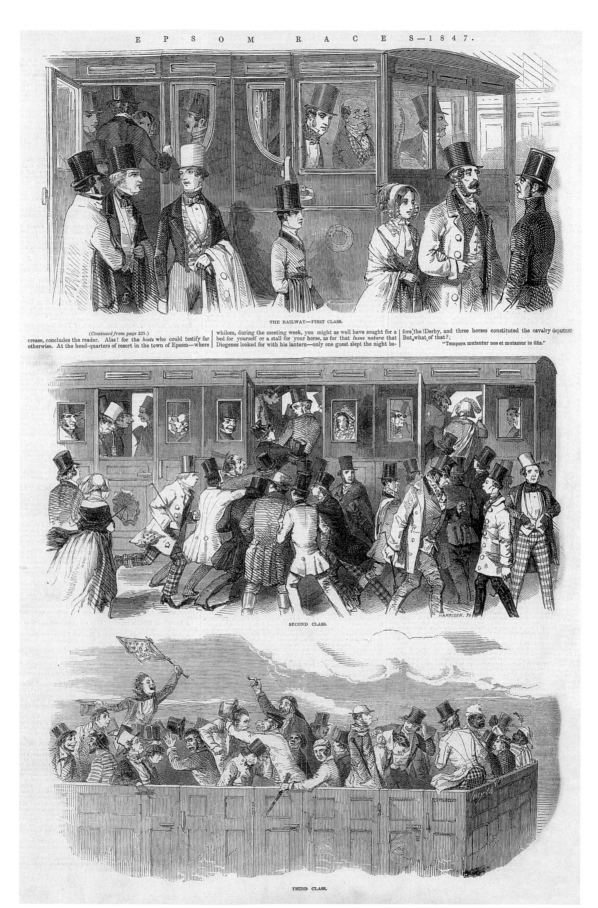

THE RAILWAY—FIRST CLASS.

(Continued from page 325.)

crease, concludes the reader. Alas! for the *hosts* who could testify far otherwise. At the head-quarters of resort in the town of Epsom—where whilom, during the meeting week, you might as well have sought for a bed for yourself or a stall for your horse, as for that *lusus naturæ* that Diogenes looked for with his lantern—only one guest slept the night before the Derby, and three horses constituted the cavalry department. But, what of that?

"Tempora mutantur nos et mutamur in illis."

SECOND CLASS.

HARRISON. Sc

THIRD CLASS.

property, – of always meeting the rain from whatever quarter it may come'; they became 'a species of horizontal shower-bath'.[150]

Primitive standards of accommodation were not especially significant, of course, on short journeys. The dilatory schedules and long stops of the early third-class trains also provided some relief. Initially, only one third-class train ran daily out of Euston for Liverpool and Manchester, with a change at Birmingham, where passengers had to wait from 3 p.m. until 6 a.m. the next day;[151] the time taken to reach Birmingham alone was almost nine hours.[152] On the Great Western, the journey from London to Bristol in 1841 took over nine hours.[153] The 1844 Act set a very low minumum speed of 12 m.p.h. for third-class trains; where company schedules adopted this, journeys were inevitably protracted. On the Great Western, conditions had improved by the late 1850s, with the so-called 'Plymouth Cheap' leaving Paddington at 6 a.m. and taking five hours to Bristol. The one other third-class train to the west, however, took seven hours to Bristol. London to Birmingham also took seven hours.[154] It is tempting to speculate that the restricted service and poor accommodation for most third-class travellers must have severely limited their number; on some lines, however, the picture was quite otherwise. The Manchester and Leeds had five third-class passengers to every one in second class in its first six months, while the ratio of third to first was twenty-eight to one.[155] There appears to have been something of a north–south divide in the proportions of third-class passengers. The Great Western, by 1850, derived only 27 per cent of its passenger receipts from the third class, the London and South Western just 28 per cent.[156] By contrast, the Lancashire and Yorkshire Railway boasted 59 per cent of its passenger receipts in 1850 from third-class travellers, and the Manchester, Sheffield and Lincolnshire a staggering 75 per cent.[157]

If, in their first decades, regular railway services were largely within the province of the middle and upper classes, the same could not be said of excursions or special traffic. An excursion was run by the Liverpool and Manchester Railway only a week after its opening.[158] Excursionists were taken to Newton Bridge where a large hotel was used for their entertainment. It is not clear how far this was aimed specifically at working-class groups, but the arrangement of Sunday School excursions on the line in 1831 suggests that these were soon an important target. On the nearby Preston and Wyre Railway, excursions began at its opening in 1840, and by 1844 cheap third-class trains ran every Sunday in summer between Preston and Fleetwood, with the low return fare of 1s 6d. With the opening of a line to Blackpool in 1846, a wave of working-class excursionists arrived from Manchester and other Lancashire textile towns. Busy summer weekends reportedly brought upwards of 10,000 artisans to the resort's beaches by 1850.[159] William Wordsworth must have had exactly this kind of invasion in mind when he wrote to the *Morning Post* in 1844 of his desire that the Lakes be 'safe from the molestation of cheap trains pouring out their hundreds at a time along the margin of Windermere'.[160]

Further south, the pattern of excursion growth was similar. In Southampton in 1844, the local management of the London and South Western Railway announced an Easter excursion from the town to London, with third-class return tickets costing seven shillings.[161] So successful was the trip that further ones were announced.[162] By 1850, the same third-class return fare by excursion train had fallen to three shillings, with passengers travelling in open carriages.[163] The company won applause in the press for providing 'locomotion for the million'.[164]

It was not just railway companies that organized excursion trips. Many were arranged by employers and institutions. At Birmingham in 1846, roughly half of the 26 excursions from the town in that year were promoted by friendly societies and ostensibly directed at artisanal groups among the working classes.[165] In northern Britain, Sunday Schools, temperance organizations and philanthropic bodies were prominent. For many working-class children, the annual outing arranged by the Sunday School, often by train, afforded one day that could be recorded with pleasure in otherwise grim lives. The textile towns, in particular, excelled in promoting excursions. At Blackburn in 1885, among 39 Whit Monday excursions to the seaside were two organized by temperance societies, three by street committees, three by football clubs, two by friendly societies, one by a cycling club, three described as 'the working men's annual', two arranged by firms and thirteen arranged by Sunday Schools.[166]

The Great Exhibition in London in 1851 demonstrated the full social significance of the excursion train. Leading railway engineers such as Brunel and Stephenson made early efforts to persuade railway companies to run cheap return trips, while all over the country advance subscriptions were organized locally to raise funds to visit London.[167] In September 1850 the *Illustrated London News* recorded how

> already the working classes in Manchester, Liverpool, Sheffield, Birmingham, the Potteries and the great iron districts between Glasgow and Airdrie, as well as other places, have commenced laying by their weekly pence to form a fund for visiting the . . . Great Exhibition of 1851.[168]

Roughly six million visitors filed through the Crystal Palace, most of them having travelled by train, and many of those by excursion.[169] One French commentator observed that whole parishes sometimes came, headed by their clergymen; colonels brought their soldiers, admirals their sailors, schools their pupils, masters their servants, and manufacturers their workpeople.[170] The Exhibition, in effect,

127. Handbill for a temperance gathering at Alton Towers, 1870, using trains of the Midland Railway.

128. Country folk visiting the Great Exhibition, *Illustrated London News*, 1851.

enshrined the railway age. The Crystal Palace appeared (even to its organizers) to be a kind of gigantic railway station, its building techniques largely made possible by the construction industry engendered by the railways. Moreover, steam locomotives were central among its exhibits.[171]

Inevitably, cheap trains to seaside places brought antagonism from those who considered 'trippers' not to be of the right sort. Residential Brighton, 'Dignified Brighton', shut itself up when the day trippers arrived and re-opened when they had gone.[172] In 1850, *Punch* picked on a piece in a London journal about the 'riff-raff' that the Brighton Railway had encouraged by its policy of 'travelling for the million'.[173] Respectable inhabitants were apparently 'fast leaving their houses'. *Punch's* retort was to enquire whether the sea was made exclusively for 'Brightonians'. When Richard Larch, in Arnold Bennett's *A Man from the North* (1898), visited the 'watering place' of Littlehampton in Sussex, he was disappointed to find it as unpicturesque as a manufacturing town, and its summer visitors 'an infestive, lower middle-class folk, garishly clothed'.[174] They were largely Londoners, who had arrived on railway 'specials'. However, one of the functions that the railway also performed was to allow the segregation of the classes in their holiday habits and resorts, mimicking the pattern in their urban and suburban homes. Thus resorts near London became subtly graded in the inimitable hierarchy of middle-class values: Margate was for tradespeople, Ramsgate for a rather higher class, Broadstairs for the socially select, Gravesend and Southend for clerks and artisans.[175] Much the same pattern was repeated on the Blackpool coast. One recent commentator has suggested that the excursion train became part of the process of the conciliation of the working classes and that it assisted the peaceful development of the English 'social system'. The working classes felt that the travel experiences offered by cheap excursions gave them 'a sense of membership of a national community'.[176] There may be some force in this assertion in the particular context of the turbulent 1840s. However, one must also recall that the segregation of classes practised by the railways from their earliest days could not have failed to enhance class consciousness. Railway travel for all may certainly have engendered a sense of being part of the wider nation, but this did not necessarily reduce or erase affiliations of class. The growth of the organized labour movement during the later decades of the Victorian era bears eloquent testimony to this.

129. Ramsgate Sands, *Illustrated London News*, 1864, with the terminus of the London, Chatham and Dover Railway in the background.

THE EMANCIPATION OF THE THIRD CLASS

It is within the mark to say that the third-class 'diners'
running from London to Leeds, Manchester and
Scotland give more luxurious accommodation than the
average first-class carriage of a dozen years ago.[177]

130. Charles Rossiter,
*To Brighton and back for
3s 6d*, oil on canvas (date
unknown).

In the early days of railway travel, the poor accommodation offered on regular
train services to the lower class of passengers was not wholly a matter of class
distinction or class consciousness. It was also a function of taxation. Parliament
had granted third-class trains remission of passenger duty, to encourage a greater
level of provision by companies. However, remission applied only if trains stopped
at all stations, and this limited the measure's impact. During the 1860s, the Inland
Revenue relaxed this rule and a rapid extension of cheap concessions followed.[178]
This was assisted by the contemporary climate of intense competition among
companies and by operational considerations. Companies had to make alterations
in the constitution of trains. The normal carriage stock of composite first- and
second-class vehicles had to be altered to composites serving all three classes.[179]
This was also essential for services between points where traffic did not warrant
attaching independent third-class carriages.

When the Midland Railway opened its London extension in 1868, the accommodation provided for third-class passengers was afforded yet further improvement: the company extended the Parliamentary penny-a-mile fare to some of its

131. Midland Railway express passenger train, c. 1895. The train is hauled by one of the elegant Johnson 'singles'; the pair of driving wheels had a diameter of 7 ft 9 in.

second-best expresses.[180] This put immediate pressure on its parallel competitor, the Great Northern, and that company soon followed the Midland's lead; so, later, did companies like the Great Eastern and the North Eastern which had districts to themselves and faced no competitive pressures. There was a growing realization among railway managers that future traffic growth lay in a much greater democratization of travel. In 1872, the Midland Railway again set the pace of change, by announcing that it proposed to attach third-class carriages to all its trains.[181] Then, in October 1874, it stole an even greater march on its rivals by declaring its intention to abolish second class altogether and to reduce first-class fares to second-class levels.[182] The outcome was a round of rapid fare revisions by other companies to try to maintain their competitive positions. The percentage that the third class represented out of all passenger carryings had been rising steadily over the 1860s, but the changes set in motion by the Midland helped take the figure to 77.5 per cent by 1875, against 17.15 in 1845. There were clear variations from one company system to another, but these had ceased to signify by 1911 when the third class accounted for almost 96 per cent of total passenger carryings.[183]

The eventual rise of third-class travel was complemented by the institution of special fares for workmen, which was required by some metropolitan railway Acts. The Cheap Trains Act of 1883 made these special fares compulsory,[184] consolidating a practice that some companies had been extending on their own initiative (the year before the Act reached the statute book, an average of 25,671 workmen's tickets were issued daily in the London area).[185] By 1913, there were 1,000 'cheap trains' connecting 500 stations with London, with fares at not more than twopence for the return journey.[186] By this time, perhaps a quarter of all suburban rail journeys were on workmen's tickets.[187]

132. Interior view of a third-class 'open' carriage used on Anglo-Scottish services, c. 1905. This was part of the East Coast Joint Stock, a collection of vehicles jointly owned by the Great Northern, North Eastern and North British railway companies.

133. Gustav Doré, workmen's train on the Metropolitan Railway in London, c. 1870.

METRO-LAND

PRICE ONE PENNY

4

URBANIZATION

... it was the influence of the railways, more than any
other single agency, which gave the Victorian city its
compact shape, which influenced the topography and
character of its central and inner districts, the disposition
of its dilapidated and waste areas, and of its suburbs, the
direction and character of its growth; and which
probably acted as the most potent new factor upon the
urban land market in the nineteenth century.[1]

The agglomeration of production within a few large
urban centres, the workshops of capitalist production,
is a tendency inherent in the capitalist mode of
production.[2]

THE AGENCY OF THE RAILWAY in capitalist urbanization is inescapable. While improvements in the means of transportation help to drive down all spatial barriers and open up new avenues for the circulation of capital in all its forms, it does not necessarily follow, notwithstanding Marx's famous phrase 'the annihilation of space by time', that space becomes meaningless. The issue becomes that of 'how and by what means space can be used, organized, created, and dominated to fit the rather strict temporal requirements of the circulation of capital'.[3] A central theme in this process was the concentration of labour and production forces within a restricted space. The statistics on nineteenth-century urbanization and urban growth tell the story unambiguously. In 1831, some 44 per cent of the population of England and Wales was urban. By 1911, the figure was at least 80 per cent. By that date, one half of the urban population dwelt in 36 large towns of over 100,000; London headed the list with 7.25 million within its conurbation.[4] Rural–urban migration was dramatic and continuous throughout this period, facilitated by the spread of railway communication to almost every town of any consequence and many lesser settlements besides. Urbanization and urban growth were critical adjuncts to the emergent factory mode of production in the northern industrial districts, so powerfully symbolized in towns such as Bolton and Preston, with their monotonous regiments of mills, mill chimneys and mill terraces. In London, it was clerical rather than manual work that underpinned the urban condition, and that was reflected socially in the clerkly conformism of its growing middle classes.

134. Suburban paradise:
cover picture from
a Metropolitan Railway
advertising brochure,
c. 1914.

135. Completing the 'monster iron girder-bridge' at London Bridge station, *Illustrated London News*, 1863.

CREATIVE DESTRUCTION

A sudden break with past technological mixes and
spatial configurations often entails massive devaluations
of the pre-existing capital.[5]

Railways were not just agents of spatial concentration, they were vital means in the transformation or re-ordering of urban space itself so as to service the requirements of the urbanization of capital in any one phase of its evolution. Suburbanization was one forcible manifestation of this process, with all its attendant social fragmentation. Another was the destruction and renewal of the pre-existing urban fabric: what some commentators have referred to as the process of 'creative destruction'.[6] 'The capitalist urban landscape lurches between the stabilizing stagnation of monopoly controls and the disruptive dynamism of competitive growth.'[7] There can be no more eloquent testimony to this process than the effects of Victorian railway companies on the central areas of cities. By 1890, the major railway companies had spent over £100 million on the provision of terminals (more than one-eighth of total railway capital), had bought thousands of acres of land in city centres, and had undertaken large-scale works of demolition and reconstruction. In the major cities, they had become the owners of up to 10 per cent of the land in central areas and indirectly influenced the functional land use of up to 20 per cent.[8]

The plans of British towns, no matter how individual and diverse before 1830, were uniformly superinscribed within a generation by the gigantic geometrical brush-strokes of the engineers' curving approach lines and cut-offs, and franked with the same bulky and intrusive termini, sidings and marshalling yards.[9]

This process was most concentrated, most visible and seen earliest in Manchester. There, the railways were almost exclusively on viaducts or, as Leon Faucher put it, upon immense arcades,[10] which at an early stage formed a ring of iron, brick and stone around the central area. By 1836, the Liverpool and Manchester and the Bolton and Manchester Railways had reached to within half a mile of the Royal Exchange; thirteen years later, Victoria and London Road stations had become established. As the century unfolded, Manchester became the focus of intense competition among no fewer than nine railway companies, all seeking central access and facilities. The cotton industry, and the particular spatial separation of its production organization, with a great aureole of spinning and weaving towns to the north and east, ensured that Manchester was a magnet for railway promoters. Faucher wrote in 1844 how Manchester's relation with its textile satellites could be likened to a diligent spider in the centre of its web.[11] Short railway routes soon connected it to this constellation of manufacturing outposts. The outcome was

> a considerable saving of capital tied up in stocks, and a reduction to reasonable physical compass of the urban space demanded by the warehousing associated with an annual output of a million yards of material and a hundred and forty million lb of twist and yarn.[12]

Alongside the cutting of inventory times, the sheer speed of railway transport accelerated the circulation time of capital in commodity form: raw cotton could be

136. A. F. Tait, *A View of Brighouse, Yorkshire*, oil on canvas, 1848. The valley floor is increasingly filled with steam-powered factories and their attendant housing, with the railway threading its way amidst them.

despatched from Manchester for Preston at 3 a.m. and be back as shirting material by 7 p.m. the same day.[13] Entrepreneurs, small masters and salesmen all benefited from the ability to conduct their business more rapidly. Not only could a salesmen collect many more orders than previously, but information on prices and bills of payment came more quickly, oiling the wheels of supply and demand. This was 'railway velocity' – so much so that Manchester Corporation agreed on 1 December 1847 to adjust all its clocks forward by nine minutes to conform to railway time.[14]

The immediate effect of the enormous competition for railway access to central Manchester was the repeated and often wholesale destruction of parts of its physical fabric. When Manchester Central was built for the Cheshire Lines Committee, it involved the clearance, officially, of 312 homes occupied by 1,663 people of the labouring classes (the true figure was probably considerably higher).[15] By 1900, 137 acres of Manchester's central area were occupied for railway usage.[16] Given that 300–400 persons per acre was a common density in working-class districts,[17] it is conceivable that somewhere between 41,000 and 55,000 of Manchester's inhabitants were displaced by the railways over the course of the nineteenth century. Those evicted either crowded into the tenements and cottages that lay immediately either side of the railway routes, or else moved out to adjacent districts. The outcome was deleterious in almost every regard.

Manchester's experience was repeated, if in lesser measure, in many other large cities around the country. At Birmingham, the old London and Birmingham Railway's terminus at Curzon Street was extended to New Street in the early 1850s, to form a through link with the Midland Railway which was in turn being extended from the former terminus at Lawley Street. The mile of line from Curzon Street to New Street alone cost £35,000 and involved extensive demolition. A

137. 'Creative destruction': the London and Greenwich Railway on its continuous viaduct.

BRIDGE OVER THE IRWELL, VICTORIA STATION, MANCHESTER.

138. A. F. Tait, *Bridge over the Irwell, Victoria station, Manchester*, lithograph, 1845. Tait's overwhelming focus in this view of the Manchester and Leeds Railway crossing the River Irwell is not the destruction and squalor with which the railway was associated, but the elegance of its engineering structures.

139. Ivy Street, near Liverpool Road. The railway towers over a working-class terrace in central Manchester.

similar situation occurred when the Great Western began its plans for the station at Snow Hill in Birmingham a few years later: one mile-long section of its approach involved negotiating with the owners of 1,800 properties.[18]

Those residential properties left standing within central districts were, effectively, consigned to dereliction. Landlords considered that money spent on their repair or improvement would be wasted – better to wait for some new round of railway extension, or some competing land use, and capitalize on higher land values. In Manchester, these were the districts that Engels observed in 1844 above Ducie Bridge. The newly built Manchester and Leeds Railway, in sweeping away many courts and lanes, had opened others immediately to view. Here, Engels saw filth and horrors that surpassed all others: 'a chaos of small one-storied, one-roomed huts . . . . kitchen, living and sleeping-room all in one'.[19] By the 1880s, the Medical Officer of Health's reports on the city revealed that, with one exception, in the whole of Manchester and Salford there was no substantial area through which the railways ran that contained housing built or rebuilt after 1830; some property dated back to 1780.[20] This was what middle-class travellers saw at roof-top level as their trains snaked slowly into Manchester's central termini. It was the view that social reformers of the last decades of the century sought to exploit in extending public awareness of the living conditions of the poor.

The potential for a displaced population to migrate to adjacent districts was frequently circumscribed, in geographical terms, by the area of low rents. Pulling down the houses of the labouring classes did not alter the level of rent that they were able to pay. Their need was for cheap accommodation, which was typically found in run-down, sub-divided property. As the railway bulldozed its path of 'creative destruction', there was plainly nothing very creative about the impact it had upon the lives of those lowest on the social scale.

The apparent predisposition of railway companies to 'smash their way through' densely populated working-class areas had a number of causes.[21] First,

140. Hulme locks on the Bridgewater Canal, c. 1900. At the left is one of the 'immense arcades', or viaducts, that carried the railway into central Manchester.

the working classes, being tenants, had no legal basis of objection. The absence of opponents with legal standing made for a much easier passage of urban railway bills in Parliament; this could influence promoters to the extent that they did not necessarily select the shortest or best routes. Secondly, much working-class housing was built on lands belonging to great estates, whose proprietors appear to have had a preference for residential land use.[22] Not only was it simpler for railway companies to conduct dealings with single, large owners, it was also financially preferable to compensate them for residential, rather than industrial or commercial, land. Thirdly, the contemporary concern with sanitary conditions favoured companies in destroying run-down or poor-quality residential housing. In 1855, the Metropolis Management Act made compulsory the appointment of local medical officers of health in London.[23] They were responsible for inspecting and reporting on the sanitary conditions in their parishes, including those arising from overcrowding. The clearance of the worst slum areas by railway promoters could thus be viewed as a public health benefit, even if the basic act of demolition was in itself only the bluntest of reform instruments.

Naturally, some social commentators saw the destruction of working-class housing and the displacement of those who lived in it as a direct and unambiguous product of the workings of capital. Even *The Times* was led to remark that such districts appeared to have a special lure for railway capitalists.[24] Railway promoters would seek out such districts in selecting their choice of route.[25] Parliament appeared to be alive to the problem and set up commissions to investigate metropolitan railway termini and metropolitan communications.[26]

141. *The railway at Leeds from Holbeck Junction, Illustrated London News*, 1868, demonstrates very clearly the railway's occupancy of extensive areas of central urban land. The new Leeds Town Hall stands in the left background.

Whereas in Manchester the railways penetrated the central area at a very early stage, in London the first termini were built on the outskirts. The London and South Western Railway extended its line from Nine Elms to Waterloo on the south bank of the Thames in the mid 1840s, affecting over 2,000 properties, of which 700 were demolished.[27] But generally, through the late 1840s and early 1850s, Parliament successfully resisted efforts by the major companies to extend lines into the centre of the city.[28] But it soon became apparent from the scale of street congestion in central zones that further resistance was impractical. Thus began the great wave of metropolitan railway building which attained its peak in the mid 1860s.[29] From the record of the Demolition Statements, there were in all 69 separate schemes for railways in the metropolis between 1853 and 1901, roughly 70 per cent of them concentrated in the two decades from 1859.[30] *Punch*, predictably, was quick to attack the metropolitan railway mania of the 1860s: 'Are there no means of averting the imminent destruction of the little beauty which our capital possesses?', it commented in early 1864. It cast railway companies as gangs seeking private bills to turn themselves into legalized housebreakers. Its battle cry was

> Petition . . . petition, petition . . . . And be quick about it, unless you want your business broken up, your abodes demolished, your hearths profaned, and all your household goods shivered round you by the confederate money-grubbers who are now exerting all their energies to obtain permission to inflict these injuries by Act of Parliament.[31]

The destruction of the view of St Paul's Cathedral at Ludgate Hill with a 'railway in the air' brought the fiercest invective.[32] For *Punch*'s writer, St Paul's might as well be converted to a railway terminus: 'what else will it be fit for when every Railway runs right into London, and we worship the Terminus?'[33] The tone of *Punch* was countered by that in the *Illustrated London News* which bordered on the adulatory. The latter saw metropolitan railway building as creative destruction, a singular testament to the forces of capital. It added, in 1863, that

> the changes recently effected in London by means of private enterprise alone exceed by far in their extent the large works carried out by Napoleon III in Paris, about which we have lately heard so much.[34]

The *Illustrated London News* had no qualms about presenting the face of destruction, such as the demolition of Hungerford market to make way for Charing Cross railway station in December 1862.[35] Its main preoccupation, though, was with feats of construction, as seen in its remarkable works on the site of Cannon Street station.[36] When the station was complete, a range of superlatives was used to describe the form of its achievement. At 685 feet in length, 202 feet in width and 120 feet high, its train shed was twice the size of the Great Northern's at King's Cross. Two thousand tons of metal were employed in its construction, along with 31 million bricks.[37]

It is very difficult to derive accurate statistics on the scale of population displacement hidden behind these heroic pictures. As early as 1861, a letter to the *Illustrated Times* made clear the potential impact of central railway extension upon London's poor. It claimed that

> by one estimate thirty thousand poor will be dislodged from their present tenements, all in the course of a few months, should these railroad schemes be carried out, and no provision for the expelled is mentioned.

142. Hungerford market makes way for the new Charing Cross railway station, *Illustrated London News*, 1862.

143. Charing Cross railway station under construction, *Illustrated London News*, February 1864. The structure, complete with station hotel, dwarfs all that stands around it.

144. St Pancras station under construction, *Illustrated London News*, 1868, showing the great curved iron roof rising above its surroundings like some temple of the ancient world.

145. The cavernous train-shed of Cannon Street station, South Eastern Railway, shortly after completion, *Illustrated London News*, 1866.

146. The Midland Railway's London extension passes through Old St Pancras churchyard, *Illustrated London News*, 1866. Even the dead did not escape displacement in the process of metropolitan railway construction.

At St Bartholomew's, Moorfields, the Metropolitan Extension involved the destruction of virtually half its buildings, containing 'a population of five thousand persons in five hundred houses'. London's poor, it was claimed, would be ousted from their foul dwellings to still fouler ones for which they would have to pay an increased rent in consequence of the sudden demand.[38] When the Midland Railway's London extension bulldozed its way through Somers, Camden and Agar Towns in the mid 1860s, one source gave a figure of 4,000 houses demolished and 32,000 people displaced.[39] Even the dead were not safe when part of Old St Pancras churchyard was destroyed. The construction of St Pancras station, it is alleged, involved another 20,000 people losing their homes.[40] The Demolition Statements arose out of the concerns of Lord Shaftesbury about the impact of metropolitan railway building on the labouring classes.[41] From 1853, a new Standing Order in all Private Bills involving the destruction of thirty or more dwellings stipulated that a return should be made of the actual number under threat, including the number of occupants. The proponents of Bills were also required to set out what measures thay envisaged to assist the persons displaced. Over the years from 1853 to 1901, these statements record the forced removal of a total of 76,000 people.[42] It is almost beyond doubt that the figure is an under-estimate: few promoters would have been so politically naïve as to present the true scale of the destruction. The East London Railway demolitions between 1865 and 1876 supposedly displaced 4,645 people, but an alternative source put the figure at 6,713.[43] In the railway companies' defence, the population of many of these areas was so fluid that accurate estimates were likely to be extremely elusive.[44] It is beyond dispute, however, that companies put only very limited efforts into re-housing. Eventually, Parliament recognized this failure and made statutory provisions for rehousing in 1885,[45] but these new legal obligations still had to be enforced, and the physical chaos and upheaval of demolition often made strict observance of the law difficult. The inevitable time-lag between demolition and the provision of alternative accommodation also meant that the ultimate occupants were rarely those who had actually been displaced.[46]

The distinctive feature of railway building in London in the 1860s was the construction of the first underground railway. This was not a 'tube' railway in the conventional sense, being very shallow in depth and built on what became known as the 'cut-and-cover' principle. The first line was the Metropolitan Railway between Paddington and Victoria Street, which opened in January 1863.[47] The

147. Construction works on the underground Metropolitan Railway, King's Cross, *Illustrated London News*, 1861.

148. The novelty of underground travel, *Punch*, 1864: 'I'm sure no Woman with the least Sense of Decency would think of going down *that* way to it.'

Illustrated London News described it as somewhat resembling the track of a mole: for much of its course it ran beneath streets, and it had to negotiate a vast network of gas pipes, water pipes and sewers.[48] Later, the Metropolitan was joined by the Metropolitan District Railway Company, and together they constituted the so-called Inner Circle. The Metropolitan's line reputedly carried over 30,000 people on its first day.[49] Even though these early underground lines were mostly beneath the streets, the scale of demolition and reconstruction was still considerable. The 7½ miles of line sanctioned as 'The Inner Circle' in 1864 involved the removal of 234 buildings and interfered with almost 900.[50] Not until the 1890s was this kind of problem resolved with completion of the first real 'submerged' railway, the City and South London. This ran at a depth of forty feet through a tunnel lined with cast-iron rings. It was operated by electrical traction and became the marker for a whole sequence of tunnelling beneath central London to produce the tube railway system which became known the world over as the Underground.[51] London's example was followed, if in more limited measure, in Glasgow over the years

149. The interior of Kensington station on the Metropolitan Railway's western extension, *Illustrated London News*, 1868.

1886–96. *Punch* naturally found in the idea of a subterranean railway a ready source of fun. Twenty years before the first line was opened, it had painted what was described as a prophetic view of a subterranean railway.[52] It suggested that, with a little modification, the sewers under London might answer the purpose. Early surveys had apparently found inhabitants who were agreeable to putting their coal-cellars at the prospectors' disposal. Once the first line was open, there was, of course, the sense of danger and adventure that travelling beneath ground presented. But *Punch* appeared most concerned with the social proprieties.[53]

150. *A prophetic view of the subterranean railways,* Punch, *1846.*

SUBURBIA

'I know practically nothing of London, real London,' she said; 'but I think these suburbs are horrid, – far duller than the dullest village. And the people! They seem so uninteresting, to have no character!'[54]

She had waited over half an hour between eight and nine and in that time she had had full opportunity to understand why those suburban stations had been built so large. A dark torrent of human beings, chiefly men, gathered out of all the streets of the vicinity, had dashed unceasingly into the enclosure and covered the long platform with trampling feet. Every few minutes a train rolled in, as if from some inexhaustible magazine of trains beyond the horizon, and, sucking into itself a multitude and departing again, left one platform for one moment emptying – and the next moment the platform once more filled by the quenchless stream . . . . it was like the flight of some enormous and excited population from a country menaced with disaster.[55]

The novelist Arnold Bennett was among the most acute observers of the effects of capital on Victorian society. In *Anna of the Five Towns* (1902), the constant begetting of money by money perplexes and embarrasses Anna, whereas her father sees the investing of capital as indistinguishable from the planting of rhubarb at the bottom of the garden – tolerably certain of a particular result. To him, the productivity of capital was natural; he never thought to enquire into it.[56] Anna had more imagination than her father and the arrival of remittances out of space, unasked, disturbed her. Moreover, in a disarmingly appropriate metaphor, Bennett notes that 'moneys seemed to pass through her hands with the rapidity of trains'.[57]

One of the cardinal features of capitalist society is its atomization – into pairs of hands and land parcels, for instance. The dullness of London's suburbs – as described by Adeline in *A Man from the North* (1898) in the first quotation on page 133 – reflected the bringing of space under 'the single measuring rod of money value'.[58] Land and building speculation around London saw the population of its suburban ring grow by roughly 50 per cent every ten years between 1861 and 1891.[59] This was to become the territory of the burgeoning ranks of the middle classes, with their stereotyped tastes and manners and their acute self-consciousness, as parodied by a host of contemporary writers including George and Weedon Grossmith in *The Diary of a Nobody* (1892).[60] Railway companies were rarely implicated directly in the suburban building process, but their commuter stations were critical to its viability. Suburbia was no less than 'a railway state', 'a state of existence within a few minutes walk of the railway station'.[61] As early as 1848, a correspondent of the magazine *The Builder* remarked how around London 'houses were springing up in all quarters for the reception of the ever-increasing population of densely-populated London'. Moreover, the same observation could be applied to the vicinities of other large cities 'if they boast the advantage of a railway'. Money was scarce, the whole nation in difficulties, but houses were springing up everywhere – 'as though capital was abundant.[62]

151. Beresford Road, Hornsea, in the late nineteenth century, showing the 'monotony' of London's inner suburbs.

Bennett's Hilda Lessways, on alighting at the suburban station of Hornsey, found 'on her left ten thousand small new houses, all alike. On her right were broken patches of similar houses, interspersed with fragments of green field and views of the arches of the railway'.[63] In *A Man from the North*, Adeline's uncle, Richard Aked, also sees the dullness of the suburbs, their roofs forming 'horrible, converging straight lines', but claims there was character beneath if one was sensitive enough to look for it. He chides his niece that there was more character within a hundred yards of their home than a hundred Balzacs could analyse in a hundred years.[64] Every suburb had an inner spirit, a soul. Moreover, the suburbs *were* London: it was the 'concussion of meeting suburbs in the centre of London' that made the city. The special characteristics of different suburbs exerted 'a subtle influence on the great central spots'.[65] Adeline's uncle even had in mind a book on the 'psychology of the suburbs'.[66] However, the force of his analysis was subsequently undermined by his claim that the play of one suburb on another and on the central haunts was 'as regular, as orderly, as calculable, as the law of gravity itself'.[67] The scientific metaphor, in all its molecular structure, fits more with Adeline's image than with her uncle's.

Leading urban historians in the later twentieth century have likewise contemplated the tensions that Bennett was exploring. London was 'too vast, and the consciousness of the crowd too immanent' to permit any overall identity in community.[68] Its streets succeeded one another 'with a stumbling logic and the names of neighbourhoods they enclosed unrolled with a continuous rhythm across the map'.[69] Its inhabitants appeared governed by a machine rationality. By day they streamed into the centre to work; by night they submitted to a reverse spatial logic as they redistributed themselves for rest. There was social tension, but it was less between classes, or between individual and mass, than between inner life or consciousness and outward behaviour. As Adeline's uncle remarked in *A Man from the North*, if a suburban street contained eighty houses, it contained eighty separate human dramas constantly unfolding.[70]

If the torrent of human beings who daily converged on the suburban station had a sense of collective belonging, it was to the organizing principle of money. Their daily journeys across space were 'tied to the irrigations of commercial capital'.[71] The rigid scheduling of the commuter trains was part of the tightening of the chronological net around daily life that formed a critical part of the rise of industrial capitalism, so as to achieve 'the necessary co-ordinations of profitable production and exchange over space'.[72] People were learning the 'technique of metropolitan life'.[73] The hordes of men who, according to Bennett, daily undertook the journey to work were no less a part of this. The gender division of labour of nineteenth-century capitalism found acute expression on the suburban railway system. The station and train became almost a social centre for the suburban male.[74] Women, typically, avoided the business trains; to do otherwise was 'a sort of indelicacy'.[75] Within the household, the precise scheduling of trains dictated mealtimes and other family activities.[76] Metropolitan living meant precisely that.

The suburbs with which the railways were so closely associated were largely middle-class. Surbiton, Ealing and Sidcup, with their spacious, tree-lined roads and generous gardens, were first in the social order. They were followed by 'lower middle-class' suburbs like Bowes Park, Palmers Green, Wood Green and New Southgate, the home of superior clerks, supervisors and middle managers.[77] The suburbs were predominantly middle-class because it was this group that dominated the exercise of social power within the vast commercial undertaking that London and other provincial centres became over the nineteenth century. In effect, the suburbs became a middle-class bonanza: 'they gave access to the cheapest land to those having most security of employment and leisure to afford the time and money spent travelling up and down'; they presented an 'arena for the manipulation of social distinctions'; and they 'kept the threat of social change beyond the horizon'.[78] Ultimately, it can be argued that the building and populating of the suburbs became the key to the evolution of the entire metropolitan urban realm. For as the inner suburbs were vacated by the middle classes, so those same suburbs steadily became slums, the domain of the working classes, especially of the poorest. Moreover, the volume of surplus capital that went into extending the suburban frontier limited what could be set aside for housing the working classes. As early as 1848, *The Builder* contained a letter from a correspondent that grimly observed how the mania to build villas for the middle classes, to create 'a leaven of aristocracy in the parlour', was consigning the ordinary working man to 'wretched stalls', constructions which men of substance would not even have considered for their beasts of burden.[79] This became the stage upon which an increasingly polarized class consciousness emerged. Urban space displayed steadily greater fragmentation as every stratum of society sought to use whatever powers of domination it could to seal itself off from others. The spectre of the slum thus grew to be a potent factor in suburban consciousness. Moreover, as railway tracks within inner urban areas proliferated in the later decades of the century, there was no more powerful perspective on the nether regions of the city than the one that suburban commuters could observe from the embankments and viaducts that carried their trains to and from the heart of the metropolis. On her way from King's Cross to Hornsey,

No. 1.   *December, 1913.*

"THE MET."

Where can the METROPOLITAN RAILWAY take you?

The answer to this question is:—

ANY WHERE, in and around London.

First let it be remembered that the Metropolitan Railway carries you quickly, quietly and cleanly, wherever you may want to go; and that the frequency of service reduces waiting to a minimum.

For the help of the Londoner who is daily moving about, and also for the "Stranger within our gates," the management of the Company are issuing this series of leaflets, which describe the places and districts covered by their service.

The Metropolitan Service is not liable to interruption by fogs, etc., and the trains are always punctual to time. The carriages are brilliantly lighted, comfortable and warm.

The Metropolitan Railway is, especially in winter time, the best way of getting to the City.

152. Page from a Metropolitan Railway advertising brochure of 1913: part of the 'irrigations of commercial capital'.

Hilda Lessways offered the following account of just such a suburban journey:

> The train, almost empty, waited forlornly in a forlorn and empty part of the huge, resounding ochreish station. Then, without warning or signal, it slipped off, as though casually towards an undetermined goal. Often it ran level with the roofs of vague, far-stretching acres of houses – houses vile and frowsy, and smoking like pyres in the dank air. And always it travelled on a platform of brick arches. Now and then the walled road received a tributary that rounded subtly into it, and this tributary could be seen curving away, on innumerable brick arches, through the chimneypots, and losing itself in a dim horizon of gloom. At intervals a large, lifeless station brought the train to a halt for a moment, and the march was resumed. A clock at one of these stations said a quarter to two.[80]

The dullness and anonymity of the suburbs pervades Bennett's account: the 'undetermined goal' of the second sentence. The way in which the railway apparently swept all before it, leaving an unseemly detritus for the traveller to observe from the train window, is vividly portrayed in his use of the fluvial metaphor. The overall picture is thrown into starker relief by the fact that it is outside the rush hour, yet Bennett cleverly reminds the reader of the tyranny of the clock over suburban commuters' lives and of the way they seemed like armies on a daily march. Naturally, this passage is as much a literary device as it is representational, but this does not diminish the force of the perceptions. The middle classes looked with increasing fear and distrust upon such scenes from the railway arches, upon such a 'visibly fermenting' and 'uncouth laboratory', and this became the springboard for rising political as well as social separation.[81] One commentator has claimed that the class-based politics of the twentieth century was to a large extent grounded in the Victorian commuter age.[82] Railway demolitions in working-class districts in central areas detonated a form of social chain reaction: the poor, displaced by railways and other improvements, in turn displaced the artisans, who then dislodged the lower middle and middle classes from the exclusive suburbs to which they had retreated.[83]

The direct influence of railway companies upon suburban extension was restricted by statute, in that most were debarred from purchasing land in excess of that needed for their lines and their immediate ancillary services. The early main-line companies also showed considerable unwillingness to provide suburban services. Some of the major companies, including the Great Western, the Midland and the London and North Western, refused to make any concessions, either in fare levels or in services, throughout the nineteenth century.[84] Where railways had been constructed as long-distance enterprises, such attitudes were not incomprehensible, at least not in the early decades of operation. Short-distance services with frequent stops were a potential impediment to long-distance traffic which was, in any case, generally the more lucrative. This difficulty was not really resolved until most trunk routes had been converted from double to quadruple track. Some early companies, however, did nothing other than service suburban districts, the London and Blackwall and the London and Greenwich lines among them. The Manchester–Altrincham line afforded a similar example in the provinces, and others served Liverpool and Newcastle. Around London, the earliest major railway company to enter suburban service provision was the London and South Western with its line to Richmond; later in the century, suburban commuters were to become the company's life-blood. Indeed, this became the case for most of the companies running lines into London from the south or south-east. The opening of the Hampstead Junction Railway in 1860 was, according to the *Illustrated London News*, intended principally to enable local passenger traffic on the North London railway to extend west to Kew and Richmond without the need to pass through Camden station and Primrose Hill tunnel, where enormous passenger traffic on the London and North Western's main line presented a serious obstacle to the running of local passenger trains at frequent intervals.[85] *Punch* derided such short branches as a product of the notorious premium on railway property; it proposed in 1858 that 'Cockney capitalists' should lay down money on a 'garden railway' between Kensington and Bayswater, routed right through Kensington Gardens, to reduce a journey of ten minutes to one of two or three.[86] In fact, the 1860s did see something of a railway mania in and around London; this was when Camberwell became one of the new ring of railway suburbs.[87]

154. *Finchley-Road station, Hampstead Junction Railway, Illustrated London News, 1860. The scene could hardly have been more bucolic.*

The Great Northern Railway probably afforded the best example of a main-line company that sought to develop an active policy towards suburban traffic. In the later decades of the century, it sold an unusually large number of season tickets, not to mention half-rate fares typically associated with lower middle-class clerks.[88] These appear to have been connected with the growth of Hornsey, Wood Green and Southgate, suburbs all located directly on the main line out of King's Cross.[89] The company was the first actively to advertise its outer suburban business with a penny booklet, *Where to Live*, published in 1906, offering an illustrated guide to what it saw as some of the choicest suburbs.[90] Even so, the company management was far from being the commuter's champion. When facing complaints from the newly formed London County Council about suburban fares and the timing of trains, the Chairman, Henry Oakley, argued that peak-hour traffic was highly problematic in operational terms, and was not particularly profitable.[91]

A few railway companies were required by their enabling Acts to offer concessionary fares to suburban commuters. The Great Eastern was obliged under its 1864 Act to issue workmen's tickets.[92] Following its extension to Liverpool Street, it was required to issue penny fares to districts like Edmonton and Walthamstow, which consequently experienced a wave of speculative building.[93] By the 1890s, this line had become a sort of workmen's railway, accounting for virtually all of the twopenny return traffic into London.[94] By the turn of the century, it was being paraded by social reform groups as an example that other companies might follow.[95] In 1865, the London, Chatham and Dover Railway Company likewise had introduced penny fares for workmen on its metropolitan extension. Two trains ran daily from each terminus for the exclusive accommodation of 'artisans, mechanics, and daily labourers, both male and female'. Users had to buy a weekly ticket for one shilling, and no luggage was permitted other than a basket of tools or implements of labour.[96] Despite such an interesting experiment in what the *Illustrated London News* called 'social economics', the same company's

155. *Departure of the 12.55 p.m. train to Enfield, Saturday, October 25th, 1884*: the scene at London's Liverpool Street station.

suburban services did not sustain the trend; by the Edwardian period, they had become a public scandal.[97] There was, however, a danger in the successful courting of cheap suburban traffic – the suburbs served could become overcrowded, and thereby indistinguishable from the dilapidated inner districts that they had grown to supplant.

The one early railway company that entered the business of urban property development *per se* was the Metropolitan. It was empowered under the Metropolitan Inner Circle Completion Act of 1874 to grant building leases and sell ground rents.[98] The company began its activity at Willesden Green in the 1880s, and by the first decade of the twentieth century was erecting houses at Pinner.[99] As early as 1885, the policy was bringing in a rent roll of £80,000 a year and around 1,000 tenants.[100] After the 1914–18 war, its property activities were reorganized to form a subsidiary company, Metropolitan Railway Country Estates.[101] This was the umbrella under which the famous Metroland was born between the wars, to be celebrated in posters, magazines, songs and the poetry of John Betjeman.[102] Some ten estates were developed, the first at Rickmansworth and Wembley Park.[103]

The pattern demonstrated by suburban London was replicated in lesser measure in some provincial cities, but not in others. Around Leicester, there were only ever two suburban stations, strictly speaking, and the railway played little part in the city's expansion.[104] This contrasted with Nottingham, where the council had a Railway Committee and sought, among other things, to promote suburban lines as a means of relieving overcrowding in the central area.[105] Eventually, Nottingham

156. *Arrival of the workmen's penny train at the Victoria station, Illustrated London News, 1865.*

157. Metropolitan Railway
advertising brochure's
fold-out map showing the
company's extension lines,
c. 1914.

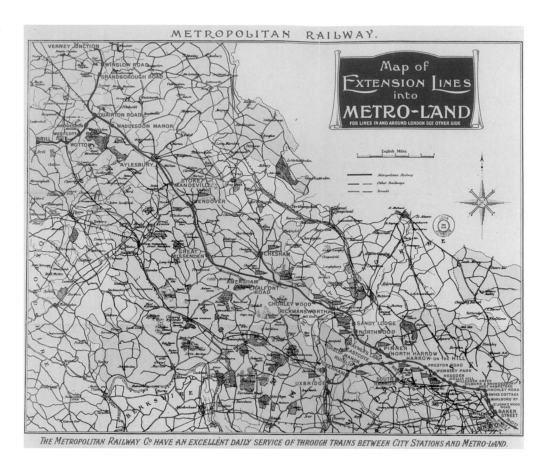

boasted 32 stations within a six-mile radius of the centre.[106] In Manchester, the
main line to Crewe saw the growth of southern suburbs like Cheadle Hulme,
Bramhall and Wilmslow. Together with parallel development on the lines to
Chester and Warrington, and on the Midland's route into Central station, the city
soon displayed – even more sharply than Engels could describe – the segregation of
land uses and residential classes that forms an archetypal manifestation of the
working of the capitalist land market.[107]

CIRCULATION

*The ability to move goods around defines the mobility of
capital in commodity form.*[108]

158. *Comparative length
of Goods Trains from
1845 to 1900,* Railway
Magazine, *1900, showing
the advance of railway
commodity traffic.*

The great city termini of Britain's nineteenth-century railway companies were
uncontestably monuments to the contemporary circulation of capital. This circulation embraced not just commodities themselves, but all the adjuncts of buying and
selling them, including the transmission of orders and bills of payment, the to-ing
and fro-ing of agents and wholesalers, and the vast accompanying world of clerks.
As different railway companies sought constant improvement in their terminal
facilities, so they were playing out the coercive laws of capitalist competition – the
persistent drive to lower costs, to raise volume, and to guarantee speed and
regularity of delivery.

 The term 'panorama' has been used to denote the specific stage of the circulation of commodities that characterized the later half of the nineteenth century.[109]

The large department stores of the period were illustrative of 'panoramic' perception: they enshrined a sales system that gathered 'a mass of heterogenous goods under one roof', arranged 'according to a concept'.[110] The attraction these emporia had for the public gave them an enormously accelerated turnover, and thereby allowed them quickly to render traditional forms of retail outlet outmoded. The initial model for them was undeniably that great palace of commodities, the Great Exhibition of 1851 – perhaps the first shopping mall.[111] In A. J. Cronin's novel *Hatter's Castle*, set in the 1870s, James Brodie eyes up the new chain store setting up in competition next door to his own highly traditional premises, and what offends him most is not the range of goods in the garish window display, but the fact that each article displays its own price-ticket.[112] The visible price-tag was a hallmark of the retail revolution that swept across much of Europe in the later nineteenth century. It symbolized the way that the exchange value of goods had become their intrinsic quality, replacing the tangible qualities of the goods themselves (their 'use' value). In other words, the goods' 'commodity-esthetic' became by far the more dominant value.[113] The commodity character of objects in the department store can be traced directly to the greatly augmented basis of the economic circulation of commodities, a growth underpinned by the railway. The Railway Clearing House's classification of goods represented a 'panorama' in

159. Great Eastern Railway advertisement, showing sea-water as a railway commodity traffic.

160. Crosshall Street goods depot, Midland Railway, Liverpool, 1922.

161. David Hill, litho-
graph, 1831, showing the
goods depot at St Rollox,
Glasgow.

exactly the same way: almost every kind of commodity had its own price-rate. As
Marx observed, the range of these railway rates was fantastic, outdoing even the
species range invented by botanists and zoologists.[114] They were indeed part of a
commodity culture of a fecundity found only in Darwin's theory of evolution.[115] It
is no surprise therefore that the railway became central to the so-called 'scientific
social notions of the epoch'.[116] W. M. Ackworth, one of the leading historians of
the nineteenth-century railway in England, used the analogy of blood circulation to
describe the Midland Railway's system of lines;[117] more widely, this biological
concept, as applied to the social sphere, became an indication of efficiency, of
progress. The railway termini of London and other cities up and down the country
were pulsating hearts within a 'biophysical' system. Here was concentrated 'all
vitality', so John Ruskin wrote; the country was 'passed over like a green sea'.[118]
The 'commodity-esthetic' attained perhaps its most absurd expression on the Great
Eastern Railway, which engaged in the sale of sea-water, for baths, delivered daily
from Lowestoft to any station on the company's lines.[119] The circulation of people
was most vividly (and logically) captured in an advertisment for London's
Metropolitan Railway of 1913–14 which described the Inner Circle line as

> an endless railway, which envelops the heart of London . . . . on this steel
> Circle, electric trains are ceaselessly rotating; speeding round and round its
> circumference, like the rim of a revolving wheel.[120]

The apex or 'citadel' of railway commodity circulation was the goods station,
or depot. David Hill's extraordinarily busy picture of the depot at St Rollox,

Glasgow, published in 1832, offers one of the earliest examples. Coal was overwhelmingly the predominant traffic here but, as similar depots sprang up at railway stations around the country, the commodity range they handled grew. At Camden station, on the London and North Western Railway, the merchandise received in about 1850 from up and down trains each day averaged between eight and nine hundred tons.[121] One contemporary remarked that the area of the principal warehouse was twice that of Westminster Hall, a choice of comparison itself illustrative of the status that the commodity ferment had acquired. In the receiving shed, there were steam-driven cranes, a steam lift and a steam capstan for hauling the railway trucks.[122] Camden Depot was later superseded by the goods station at Broad Street in the heart of London; with an eventual total floor space of nearly 30,000 square yards,[123] it was perhaps 'the largest goods station in the largest city in the world'.[124] The Great Eastern railway's Bishopsgate goods depot was equally remarkable.[125] By the early 1900s, it was employing some 2,000 people on a site covering 21 acres, with nine exits and entrances, divided into three levels. In 1910, in an average day, 725 trucks came inward and 632 went outward, generating around eighty different goods trains in and out daily.[126] The cartage work required a stud of around 1,100 horses and 850 road vehicles, which gave employment to some 800 carmen and van-guards. In addition, there was a contingent of railway police, a brigade of firefighters and a complete ambulance organization.[127] Bishopsgate's traffic was heavily agricultural, as one would expect for a railway serving East Anglia. Other London depots had different staple traffics. At the Great Northern's King's Cross, the principal shed space embraced some 23,000 square yards, with an additional area of 9,000 square yards for the storage of grain and flour.[128] It was here, around 1850, that the first of London's rail-borne coal depots was established; coal, 'sea-coal' as it was called, had previously been supplied to London by coastal collier from Tyneside.[129] King's Cross also channelled much of the enormous brick traffic for the rebuilding of London.[130] The London and South Western Railway's Nine Elms depot dealt heavily in imported foods, especially

162. The Great Northern Railway's granary at King's Cross, *Illustrated London News*, 1853.

163. The Great Northern Railway's goods shed at King's Cross, *Illustrated London News*, 1853.

from North America and the South African Cape. Fifty trucks of Canadian bacon could arrive in one day; trains of American frozen meat came several times a week, the meat having been taken direcly from refrigerated ships which had docked at Southampton only six hours earlier.[131] Nine Elms, with an arched façade designed by Sir William Tite, was the first London terminus of the railway from Southampton. It had opened in 1838, but had only a very brief existence as a passenger station before being superseded by Waterloo in 1846; henceforth it was used only for goods.[132] Manchester's Liverpool Road station was likewise closed to passengers as early as 1844 and thence became a goods depot. The Great Eastern's Bishopsgate depot had in an earlier existence been the Shoreditch terminus of the old Eastern Counties Railway.[133]

The goods traffic arrangements at Liverpool were considered by some to be even more remarkable than those at London. The London and North Western Railway had six goods depots, as did the Lancashire and Yorkshire. The three companies that between them owned the Cheshire Lines had as many again. Two of the London and North Western's depots were reached by tunnels each 1¼ miles in length, constructed for goods traffic alone.[134] Manchester's London Road station was no less impressive, if in somewhat different ways.[135] The goods depot there was situated beneath the passenger terminus. Its daily tonnage seems to have varied between one and two thousand tons around the turn of the century, roughly double that dealt with at Broad Street in London.[136] Most noticeable was the distinctive diurnal rhythm of the goods traffic. By 8 p.m., with the passenger terminus already beginning to look half asleep, the handling of the outward goods traffic downstairs was at full stretch. Loading lasted until perhaps midnight. Once the trains had been despatched, the station could 'doze off till two or three o'clock, when the goods from every quarter of Great Britain . . . pour in to keep the place alive'. Unloading proceeded until the passenger traffic was in full sway again around 8 a.m.[137] Much of the railways' goods traffic was organized according to this nocturnal rhythm, and had been so since companies began regularly to carry it.[138] Consignments were received for despatch last thing at night, and handed over to the consignee first thing the next morning. In this way, cotton goods could be sold for overseas markets at the Manchester Exchange in the middle of the day. The sold goods were then transferred from the warehouse in Manchester to London Road station that same evening. By early the next morning they had arrived in London, where they were immediately carried by dray to the dockside for shipment.[139]

Goods trains were despatched at night largely because their track timetabling was rendered much easier during periods of slack passenger traffic. Stopping at roadside stations to pick up or detach trucks made goods trains a potential impediment to the operation of scheduled passenger traffic. The exception was perishable goods, such as fish or dairy products – these were marshalled in separate trains which typically ran to express schedules, though still often overnight. By the late nineteenth century, one of them, the famous 'Scotch fish and meat', left Carlisle each evening at 8.51 p.m., timetabled between two fast passenger expresses. It maintained this operational placing until it reached Willesden just outside London.[140] So, as Scottish mails were being delivered through Londoners' letterboxes, the capital's fishmongers and butchers were simultaneously plying Scottish herrings and beef around London's streets.

164. The station at Banbury, Oxfordshire, early twentieth century, showing that some small consignment traffic went by passenger train.

165. The Midland Railway goods depot at Basford, Nottingham, with the company's own delivery vehicles standing outside awaiting use.

One of the startling features of the railways' commodity traffic was its small unit size, the average package weighing in at around three *quarters*, that is less than one hundredweight.[141] Equally startling was its variety. An observer at a goods depot might see tons of grey shirtings alongside a solitary hip-bath, or machinery castings alongside 'a railway rug done up in a strap with a racket and tennis-shoes tied on'.[142] Even though there was a growing tendency in retailing for trade to be done by business houses and department stores, the reverse tendency occurred in the pattern of consumption, because these same houses and stores despatched parcels to outlets or individuals at thousands of different places all over the country. These were goods ordered by post or telegraph one day for delivery the next.[143] In this, the railway retained a common carrier obligation that dated back to the pre-railway era, which helped to prolong the survival of the 'hand-to-mouth' trader. For railway managers, such business became a serious impediment to profitability. In the closing years of the century, increase in traffic receipts appeared to be in inverse correlation with the increase in the number of invoices.[144] Just as the survival of the private owner wagon impeded financial performance in the railways' coal and mineral traffic business, the persistence of the small consignment trade undermined the profitability of its ordinary commodity trade, despite some pricing policies that clearly favoured volume traffics. Within cities and towns, one way that railway companies tried to counter the economic perils of small consignment traffic was by seeking monopolies over road delivery from their goods stations. Some companies were unscrupulous in attempting to secure this trade from a very early date, prompting litigation from existing road carriage firms.[145] Others came to accommodations with road carriers. Pickfords became agents for the London and North Western Railway, and were responsible for the remarkable goods depot at Camden.[146] In the early 1890s, railway companies in London alone owned some 6,000 draught horses for their own collection and delivery vans.[147] It is in this sense that some commentators have claimed that Victorian society was a horse-drawn one[148] – the number of horses used in passenger and freight transport in Britain during the railway age grew from around 250,000 to over a million.[149]

Marx considered the transport industry to be one that sold change of production location.[150] No more clearly was this demonstrated in relation to railways than in the production and distribution of milk. So radical was the railways' impact that the commodity itself came to be called 'railway milk'. The trade was not quick to develop, however. Railway companies made few positive steps to encourage the business. Maintaining the condition of milk conveyed by rail was difficult – initially, there was no means of cooling, nor were preservatives used.[151] The vibrations of early railway vehicles had a homogenizing effect, so that rail-borne milk could much less readily be made into cream.[152] Thus many town-dwellers came to regard railway milk as inferior, 'a poor man's beverage'.[153] By the close of the Victorian era, however, all this had changed, and London's milk demand was being met almost wholly by rail-borne supplies. The quantity imported from the provinces by rail into London rose from an estimated 9.3 million gallons in 1870 to 53.5 million in 1900 and 93.2 million by 1914.[154] In tandem, London's 'milk shed' was extended from a radius of about 10 miles before about 1840 to 20–25 miles in 1860 and 200 miles by 1900.[155] On the Great Western's system, this took in first Berkshire and Wiltshire, then Somerset and, later, Devon and Cornwall. By 1910, the station at St Erth, near St Ives, was despatching 30,000 gallons to Paddington each day.[156] Ultimately, the departure time of the milk train in country districts became the arbiter of milking times. The rhythms of rural life became inextricably part of the new industrialized consciousness.

166. Milk traffic on the Great Central railway's London extension, c. 1900.

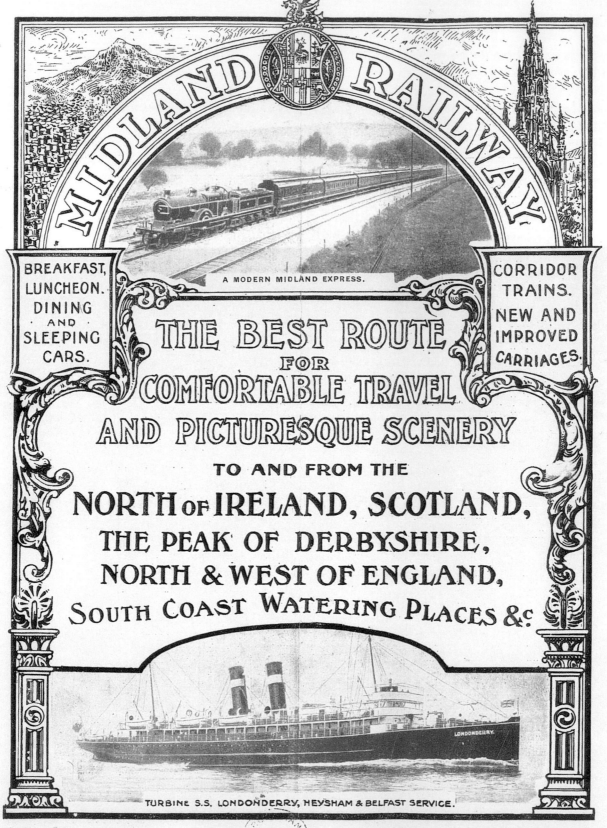

MIDLAND RAILWAY

A MODERN MIDLAND EXPRESS.

BREAKFAST, LUNCHEON. DINING AND SLEEPING CARS.

CORRIDOR TRAINS. NEW AND IMPROVED CARRIAGES.

THE BEST ROUTE
FOR
COMFORTABLE TRAVEL
AND PICTURESQUE SCENERY
TO AND FROM THE
NORTH of IRELAND, SCOTLAND,
THE PEAK OF DERBYSHIRE,
NORTH & WEST OF ENGLAND,
SOUTH COAST WATERING PLACES &c.

TURBINE S.S. LONDONDERRY, HEYSHAM & BELFAST SERVICE.

Derby, February, 1906.

JOHN MATHIESON. General Manager.

TERRITORY

You loved them too: those locos motley gay
That once seemed permanent as their own way? –
The Midland 'lake', the Caledonia blue;
The Brighton 'Stroudleys' in their umber hue;
North Western 'Jumbos', shimmeringly black,
That sped, shrill-whistled, on their 'Premier' track;
. . . .
And in their wake what rainbow splendour ran:
The Bronze-green coaches of the Cambrian;
G.N.S. red and white; North eastern 'plum';
'Salmon' that struck one young observer dumb
At grim old Waterloo . . .[1]

THE COMPARTMENTALIZATION OF SPACE

The social infrastructures which support life and work
under capitalism are not created overnight and require a
certain depth and stability if they are to be effective.
They are also geographically differentiated.[2]

167 (opposite). Midland Railway advertising pamphlet, 1906, showing railway companies and territory.

168. London and North Western Railway multi-lingual timetable, 1895, showing the company in European guise. The space–time convergence of the Victorian railway did not stop at the English Channel.

THE GREAT PARADOX of Britain's railways in the nineteenth century was the way they simultaneously annihilated space *and* compartmentalized it. Geographical space shrank in the face of 'railway velocity', but the institutional agency behind that process, the private railway company, was highly territorial. As the century progressed, the measure and sense of their territoriality intensified – to the extent that, according to one writer, they began to cast strong shadows upon the communities they served.[3] The importance of territory was seen in the progressive round of company amalgamations which gave companies like the North Eastern almost complete domination in the North-East region of England. It was seen in the promotion of new lines, whether they were to defend territory from a potentially troublesome neighbour or to consolidate an existing territorial foothold: the long struggle between the London and South Western and the various broad-gauge companies in the West of England offered a classic illustration. It was seen in the language of railway competition, companies appearing to view themselves as quasi-states: they were constantly engaged in 'battles' and 'feuds', in traffic and price wars, the same interspersed from time to time with working agreements and other 'treaties' or 'unions'.[4] The metaphor of statehood extended to embrace railway employees. Working on the railway was frequently a lifetime occupation. Railwaymen were often styled as company 'servants'. They were bound by a complex set of socio-legal rules but at the same time they benefited from an array of paternalistic provisions. To be a railway employee was to belong to a kind of state.

169. *Dawn near Reading*, watercolour, c. 1870 (artist unknown). A westbound broad-gauge train on the Great Western Railway main line, engineered by Isambard Kingdom Brunel.

170. The Midland Grand Hotel, Euston Road, London, c. 1927. Designed by Sir George Gilbert Scott and completed in 1876, it created the façade to the Midland Railway's London terminus at St Pancras, one of the most impressive examples of high Victorian secular gothic.

It was no accident that, for all the inadequacies of pay and conditions, railway service sometimes inspired fierce loyalties.[5] The metaphor of statehood could be reinforced by the way some companies became associated in the public mind with particular sorts of traffic. Thus the Lancashire and Yorkshire Railway Company was supposedly devoted to cotton, coals and cheap passengers. A variation of this was the way in which, in South Lancashire, the London and North Western was, it was claimed, associated with the Tory Party and the Church, but the Midland Railway with the Liberal Party and 'Chapel'.[6] The idea of statehood invariably brought with it a need for symbolism, for insignia. This found most powerful expression in the liveries of railway companies, lending them almost a tribal or feudal character. The very term 'livery' is indicative of the realm of medieval armies and retinues, as if trains were troop divisions or battalions. One commentator has remarked how a central feature of the frontage of the Midland Railway's St Pancras station was a statue of Britannia, a symbol of English military triumph and national integrity.[7] St Pancras represented the apotheosis of the Midland company's rise to power, providing it with direct access to the metropolis from its territorial base in the Midlands.

The verses by Gilbert Thomas on page 149 vividly capture the symbolic force of railway company liveries.[8] The 'shimmering black' of the North Western 'Jumbos' was no product of poetic licence: Victorian locomotives, even goods engines, were remarkably well turned out. Great Central goods locomotives were

171. F. Moore, *Great Eastern Railway: 'Norfolk coast express'*, c. 1913. This retrospective painting shows the resplendent livery of the Victorian railway.

painted black and lined out in red, even on the underframing. 'Shimmering black' was achieved by the way they were cleaned – after the dust and dirt were washed off, rape oil or tallow was rubbed over the paintwork to provide a protective film, and the final strokes of the cloth left a grained surface in the oil film which enhanced the finish. Wheels, motion and footframing were also carefully cleaned; if any engine was improperly turned out, the cleaner responsible lost a day or more's pay.[9] Where several company territories met, their distinctive liveries created a quasi-military parade. At York, Cambridge, Perth and Carlisle stations, the 'great joint hubs', many colour schemes converged to cast an unforgettable memory, 'the crown and consummation' of dreams.[10] John Betjeman, writing of the company organization on the London underground, claimed that the different railways could also be distinguished by their smells:

> The City and South reeked like a changing-room;
> Its orange engines and old rolling stock,
> Its narrow platforms, undulating tracks,
> Seemed even then historic. Next in age,
> The Central London, with its cut-glass shades
> On draughty stations, had an ozone smell –
> Not seaweed-scented ozone from the sea
> But something chemical from Birmingham . . .[11]

The territorialization of Britain's railways evolved out of the *laissez-faire* policy long pursued by central government in relation to new means of transport.[12] With railways, in particular, a policy of free trade was adopted. Attempts to direct the course of railway expansion to form a national system of communication proved fruitless: 'swayed by motives which it is difficult to fathom, the two Houses, with singular unanimity, agreed . . . to give unrestricted scope to competition'.[13] Parliamentary assent for new lines was provided within a strategic vacuum. There was no system for deciding how railway development could be best directed to service the needs of national defence, to engender trade or, more widely, to meet the interests of the community. The outcome, therefore, was a vast sequence of speculative enterprise. Britain was (initially, at least) bequeathed

> innumerable small lines which were to remain more or less independent and disconnected fragments of a railway system until the more enterprising companies began, on their own initiative, to amalgamate them into through routes of traffic.[14]

In 1844, the average length of individual railroads was only fifteen miles.[15] Where a major trunk line had received Parliamentary sanction and its construction had proceeded through to regular operation, the operating company generally assumed that the stretch of country it served was a reserved area. However, the policy of *laissez-faire* resulted in such companies often finding their 'territory' invaded. Parliament set its face against 'districting' the country in favour of particular companies for fear of monopolistic tendencies.[16] Competition between companies was actively encouraged to serve the best interests of rail users. Among the larger and more established companies, the spectre of uncontrolled competition led them to seek means of protecting their profits. This became the springboard for amalgamation and combination – even Parliament, in select committee in 1853, conceded that competition in fact ended in combination.[17]

172. Inter-company rivalry on the Victorian railway, *Punch*, 1858.

CONFIGURATIONS OF TERRITORY

> . . . the railway system very quickly became a kind of parallelogram of forces in which its very shape was the product not only of the underlying commercial requirements of the economy but of the political tactics and deeper strategy of the protagonists themselves.[18]

It is one thing to recognize the forces propelling the movement to combine, but it is another to determine the particular geographical form that that movement took. How was it that the territorial division of companies came to assume the shape it did? For some companies, it can certainly be argued that their networks mimicked regional economies. The North Eastern Railway grew by the turn of the century to hold a monopoly of the region extending from the Humber estuary north-west to Carlisle and north to Berwick. By 1910, it extended to 1,728 miles of line, comprising 41 formerly separate companies.[19] The process of acquiring such a regional monopoly was twofold. It centred first on the struggle to service the newly discovered Cleveland iron ore deposits south of Middlesbrough. Secondly, and in association with this, the region saw a flurry of attempted invasions by outside companies eager to gain a share of its growing industrial traffic. The outcome was a period of intense railway competition concentrated between 1857 and 1866. At its close, the North Eastern company emerged to boast the most complete monopoly of any district in the United Kingdom.[20]

The Great Eastern Railway was almost as dominant in East Anglia. It consisted of 1,133 miles of line and 26 formerly separate undertakings.[21] Other com-

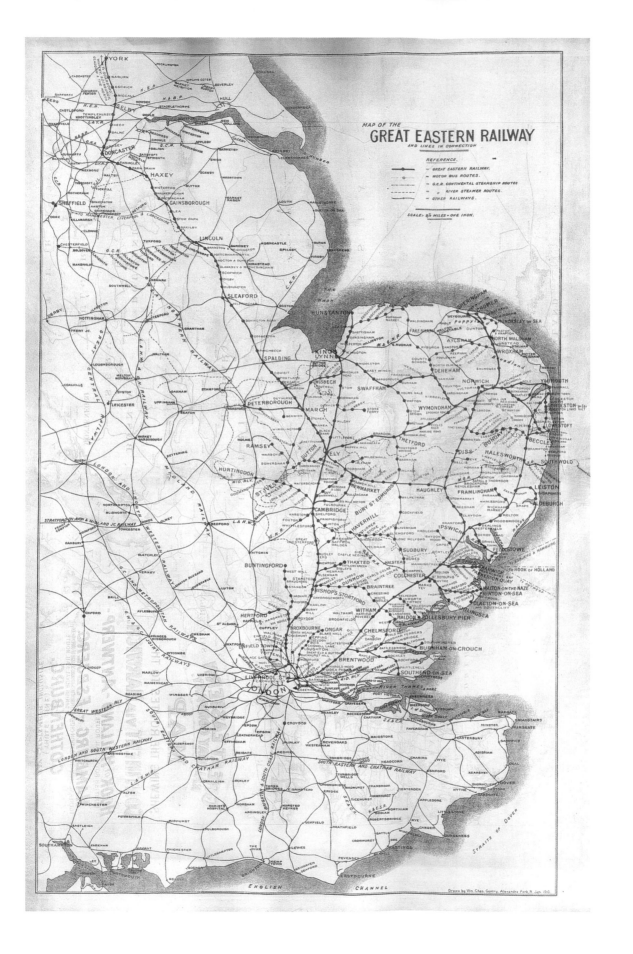

MAP OF THE
GREAT EASTERN RAILWAY
AND LINES IN CONNECTION

REFERENCE.
— GREAT EASTERN RAILWAY.
— MOTOR BUS ROUTES.
— G.E.R. CONTINENTAL STEAMSHIP ROUTES.
— RIVER STEAMER ROUTES.
— OTHER RAILWAYS.

SCALE, 9¾ MILES = ONE INCH.

Drawn by Wm. Chas. Gentry, Alexandra Park, N. Jan. 1910.

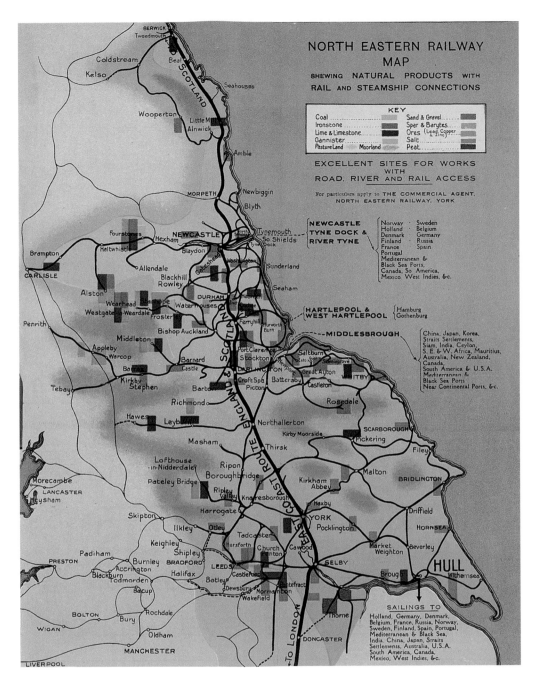

174. Railway map from the North Eastern Railway's *Directory of Manufacturers, Wholesale Importers and Exporters*, 1916. Here was the railway company in imperial guise: the record of 'natural products' follows exactly the style of maps of the British Empire.

panies with similar (if much smaller) regional monopolies were the London, Brighton and South Coast Railway (LBSCR), the South Eastern and Chatham Railway (SECR), the Great North of Scotland Railway (GNSR) and the Glasgow and South Western Railway (GSWR). The power of regional economies in the Victorian era is sometimes insufficiently appreciated: the economy at large was as much a federation of regional economic systems as it was a purposive national realm.[22] A few of these economies were not much more than export sumps, the coal-producing valleys of South Wales perhaps the most remarkable. In other cases, they were seats of specialist economic enterprise locked into an increasingly sharply differentiated exchange economic system. Within such a context, the railway company could become a kind of holding company for the region it served. It acted to maximize not only its own profitability, but also the profitability of local

173 (opposite). Network of the Great Eastern Railway, 1910.

MAP OF THE

LONDON & NORTH WESTERN RAILWAY

AND ITS COMMUNICATIONS.

LONDON AND MANCHESTER	IN	4½ HOURS.
LONDON AND LIVERPOOL	IN	4 HRS AND 20 MINS.
LONDON AND BIRMINGHAM	IN	2½ HOURS.
LONDON AND EDINBURGH	IN	8 HOURS.
LONDON AND GLASGOW	IN	8 HOURS.
LONDON AND CHESTER	IN	4 HOURS.
LONDON AND ABERDEEN	IN	10 HRS. AND 30 MINS.
LONDON AND INVERNESS	IN	13 HRS. 15 MINS.

SLEEPING SALOONS ON THE NIGHT TRAINS.

LIVERPOOL TO

BIRMINGHAM	IN	2 HRS AND 35 MINS
BRISTOL	IN	4 HRS AND 55 MINS.
EDINBURGH	IN	4 HRS AND 45 MINS.
GLASGOW	IN	5 HOURS.
LONDON	IN	4½ HOURS.

PRIVATE COMPARTMENTS, with LAVATORIES, SALOON and FAMILY 1st Class Carriages, RESERVED for Parties, without extra charge.—Separate Compartments for LADIES and for SMOKERS. PRIVATE ELEGANT OMNIBUSES at LIVERPOOL, MANCHESTER, BIRMINGHAM, and LONDON, Euston Station (see other side). LAVATORY CARRIAGES without extra charge for 1st Class Passengers. SLEEPING CARS of an improved description 5s. per Berth in addition to 1st Class Fares. LUNCHEON BASKETS can be obtained at the Refreshment Rooms at the principal Stations (see other side).

SYNOPSIS OF PLACES OF INTEREST REACHED BY THE LONDON & NORTH WESTERN RAILWAY.

175. Map of the London and North Western Railway, from an advertising pamphlet, 1895.

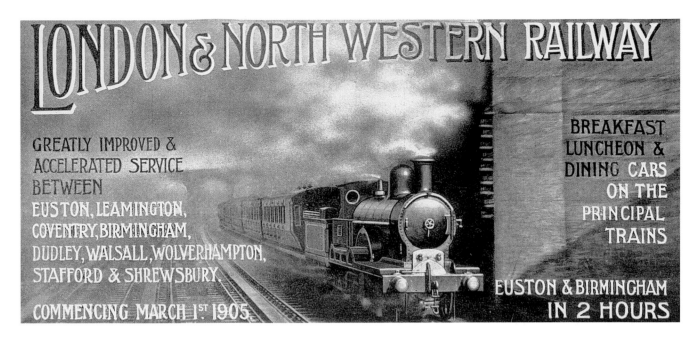

enterprise. Thus the North Eastern Railway has been described as a businessmen's line. Its commercial agents operated under the declared objective of 'aiding manufacturers and promoters in the selection of factory and industrial sites and of putting before them the exceptional advantages offered by the North-Eastern territory'.[23] Its Board of Directors was composed of representatives of the principal industries of the North-East who endorsed railway management strategies and policies that served local industrial need, whether or not these were in the best interests of shareholders.[24] Nor was industry alone important in this regard: the Great Eastern Railway Company became identified with the development of East Anglia's agricultural interests.[25]

Some railway companies did not display networks that accorded with any clear regional entity. The London and North Western Railway linked London with Liverpool, Manchester and Carlisle, with 'offshoots' to the West Riding and North and South Wales, along with feeder lines of varying lengths. This company was basically a trunk route operator. It grew in the way it did in order to secure a co-ordinated operation between the metropolis and the North-West, for goods as well as for passengers. Ackworth compared the North-Western's network with a tree: its suburban lines were roots striking out in all directions into the soil of the metropolis, and the vitalizing sap of traffic flowed to and fro along the trunk, permeating through two or three main branches to the remotest parts.[26] The metaphor is to some extent overworked, in that the company's network configuration does not quite accord with this description. However, the drift is correct.

The Midland Railway Company was a hybrid: it was regionally grounded but also engaged in trunk communication. Ackworth borrowed another metaphor from the biological world to describe its configuration. It was 'a great heart with its life-blood pulsating through countless arteries out from the centre of the body to the furthest extremities.' But whereas real corpuscles are blood-red, those on the Midland were black – that is, coal.[27] The Midland had its origins in the desire of Nottinghamshire and Derbyshire coal-owners to find markets to the south.[28] Thus it comprised a central network focused on the Midland coalfields. Beyond this, it followed broadly the shape of a diagonal cross, the principal axis extending from

176. Modernistic advertising leaflet of the London and North Western Railway, 1905. Once more, the identity of railway company with territory is unambiguous.

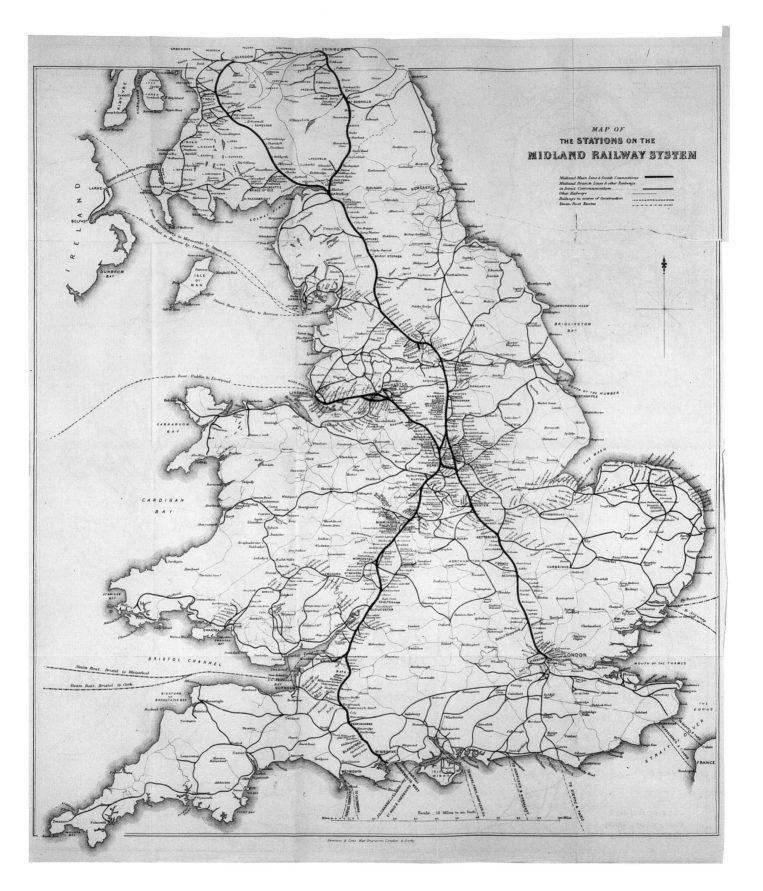

MAP OF
THE STATIONS ON THE
MIDLAND RAILWAY SYSTEM

Midland Main Line & Scotch Connections
Midland Branch Lines & other Railways
in Direct Communication
Other Railways
Railways in course of Construction
Steam Boat Routes

Scale _ 18 Miles to an Inch.

Bemrose & Sons Map Engravers London, & Derby.

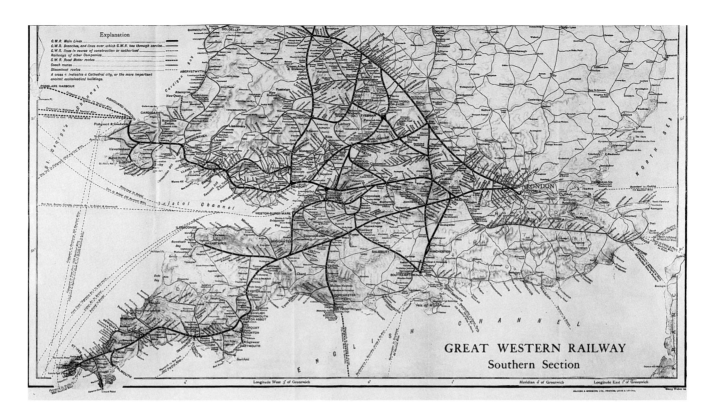

GREAT WESTERN RAILWAY
Southern Section

London to the North-West, the other extending south-west to Bristol and east into Lincolnshire. The parallel drawn between railway systems and blood circulation also featured in contemporary accounts of American railroads. Referring to the San Joaquin Valley, Frank Norris described how from Reno on one side to San Francisco on the other ran a 'plexus of red, a veritable system of blood circulation, complicated, dividing, and reuniting, branching, splitting, extending, throwing out feelers, offshoots, taproots, feeders'. A similar metaphor was used by Emile Zola in *The Human Beast* (1890), when he referred to the array of lines stretching north from Paris as like a huge body lying across the earth.[29]

The largest company in terms of route length was the Great Western; by 1910, it ran to almost 3,000 miles.[30] Its network fanned out from London in a wide arc, taking in North-West England and North Wales at one extremity and Cornwall at the other. This was a sufficiently extensive system to comprise not only distinct regional economies such as South Wales, but also a medley of trunk lines. Its premier route was from London to Bristol, but those to the West of England, to Birmingham and to West Wales also counted on a par with those of other companies. In South Wales, it did not enjoy the kind of regional monopoly that the North Eastern Railway had in its territory, but its competitors there (such as the Taff Vale and Barry Railways) ran operations that were primarily geared to coal export from the South Wales docks; to all intents and purposes, therefore, they were not really regional competitors.

The Great Western might have enjoyed a monopoly in the South-West of England but for the entry of a highly aggressive competitor, the London and South Western Railway. The two fought over access to the two principal towns of Exeter and Plymouth, and they fought over territory in North Cornwall, Devon and Dorset. A glance at the railway map of South-West England depicts the outcome. The pattern of rivalry dated from the mid 1840s when the new London and

178. Station map for the Great Western Railway's southern section, from the company's official guide, 1915. The map shows the company's regular connections as well as its own lines.

177 (opposie). Stations on the Midland Railway system, from the company's official guide, 1915. The map shows not only the Midland's own lines but also its regular connections.

179. A London and South Western Railway express passes Surbiton en route to Plymouth, c. 1900.

180. The Manchester, Sheffield and Lincolnshire Railway's London extension of the 1890s.

Southampton Railway Company succesfully petitioned Parliament to alter its name to the London and South Western, so giving hint of its wider ambitions.[31] Even in 1831, the London and Southampton promoters had suggested a branch leaving their new line at Basing and extending to Bath and Bristol,[32] so pre-dating the earliest moves towards the formation in Bristol of what was later to become the Great Western Railway Company.[33] The London and Southampton's idea of linking the English and Bristol Channels was augmented in the 1840s when the London and South Western Railway turned its eyes to the potential traffic of the industrial north. Its Chairman toyed with a line serving Newbury, Swindon and on to Birmingham, breaking through the broad-gauge barrier of the Great Western.[34] However, the central focus of the sixty-year struggle between these two leading companies was over the south-west peninsula. It is too simple to assume that it was merely a case of a progressive series of westward thrusts, as if they were running some parallel military campaign to annexe or conquer territory. The struggle was complicated by the presence within the south-west of other, free-standing railway concerns (such as the Bodmin and Wadebridge, opened in 1834), as well as by the role played by the battle of the gauges – the Great Western for a long time had derived coherence as a unitary operator in the region not by virtue of ownership but through an identity of interest in the broad gauge. Some of the pre-existing railways may simply have been pawns in the London and South Western's struggles with the Great Western.[35] The Bodmin and Wadebridge, a dilatory venture from its inception, was bought out by the South Western after only ten years. This gave the London and South Western a stake in the territory of North Cornwall, and its board did not hesitate to further its territorial plans. Other South Western pawns were the Exeter and Crediton Railway and the Taw Valley Railway. The strife over the broad gauge in the region has been admirably laid bare in MacDermot's

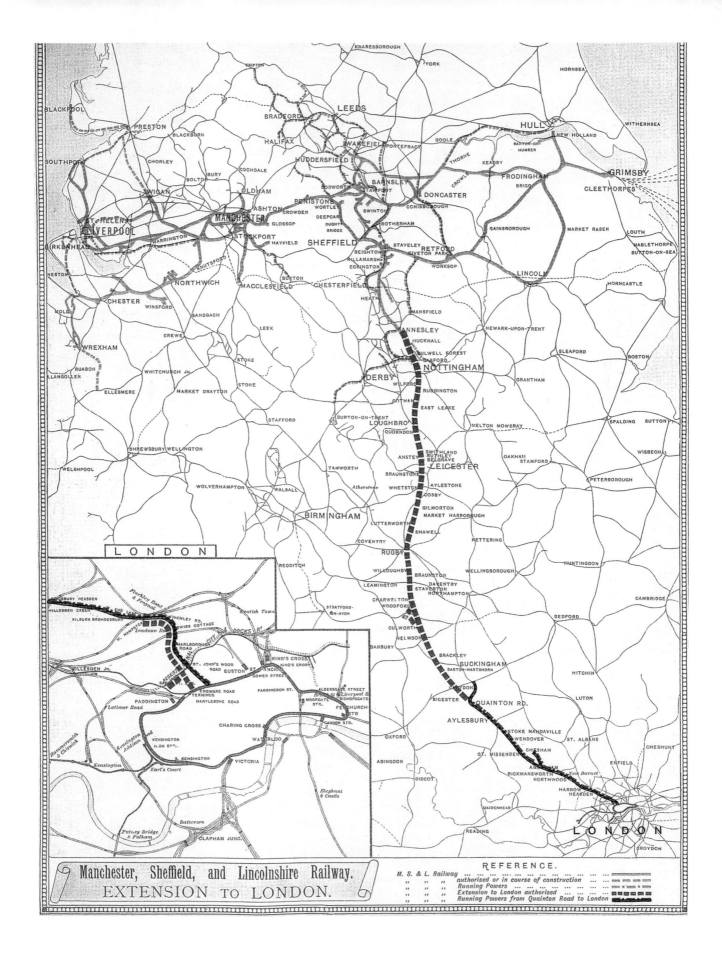

Manchester, Sheffield, and Lincolnshire Railway.
EXTENSION TO LONDON.

LONDON

REFERENCE.

M. S. & L. Railway ....

"   "   "   " authorised or in course of construction ....

"   "   "   " Running Powers ....

"   "   "   " Extension to London authorised ....

"   "   "   " Running Powers from Quainton Road to London

monumental history of the Great Western.[36] It focused first on the territory between Salisbury and Exeter. Later, attention turned to Dorset and Devon and, in particular, the country west of Exeter.[37] The story is seen in microcosm in the case of the Exeter and Crediton line, which was ultimately worked by the South Western from 1862. This line had started off as broad, then it became narrow, then broad again, then mixed gauge under an agreement of 1860. It even lay derelict for four years after its completion in 1847, as the warring factions jockeyed for positions.[38] The tale is one of true Machiavellian intrigue involving company chairmen, directors and leading shareholders. It was an exercise in out-facing, outwitting and outmanoeuvring opponents. The London and South Western and its allies appear to have been the more successful party. Ultimately, however, it was not the railway companies but West Country towns that benefited from this grand competition. Exeter and Plymouth had two express routes to London. Smaller centres like Taunton and Barnstaple ended up with much more elaborate provision than their importance warranted. For the Great Western, much of central and north Devon, part of north Cornwall and most of west Dorset became blank spaces on its South-West railway maps. These were filled by the South Western company. But the particular disposition of these lines had no rhyme or reason other than in the dialectic of spatial competition. None of these districts really had a claim to justify service by one single company.

The company with perhaps the most peculiar of network configurations was the Manchester, Sheffield and Lincolnshire (the MSLR), later to be renamed the Great Central. It started life with a somewhat paltry set of lines between the Mersey and the Humber. It grew to prominence later in the century by virtue of its development not of railway routes but of the Grimsby Docks. One writer described Grimsby as a sort of railway pocket borough, such was the scale of the company's financial stake in the port.[39] However, the dock venture was not the company's primary claim to fame. That came in the last years of the century when its Chairman, Sir Edward Watkin, embarked upon a grand project to take the MSLR into London. The scheme appeared to promise a kind of umbilical cord to economic salvation. Unfortunately, it never was. It acquired the slightly dubious distinction of being the last main-line railway to be constructed in Britain. It was the best engineered, using state-of-the-art expertise and equipment. Yet it was the first to close when railways faded as a transport technology in the mid twentieth century.

TERRITORIAL 'CLEARING'

In the early years of railway development many
companies had found it necessary to settle joint claims
in traffic by agreement.[40]

The territorialization of the Victorian railway system inevitably presented difficulties for those flows of passengers and goods that transgressed company bounds. Intra-regional and metropolitan flows were sometimes quite consonant with such a spatial organization, but problems invariably arose beyond these. From a very early stage, the different companies had to devise a system of cooperation that allowed for the easy transfer of traffic from one set of lines to another. Thus the Railway Clearing House was born in January 1842, in a little house in Drummond

Street close by Euston station.[41] It was modelled on the Bankers' Clearing House and initially embraced just nine companies, all of them narrow-gauge lines. It was regularized by statute in 1850 and by the close of the nineteenth century every company of any significance had become a member of it.[42] Under its statutory authority it was a wholly independent body, governed by delegates selected by the boards of member companies. By around 1900, it had a central staff of over 2,000, along with some 500 'number-takers' distributed around the country. It was handling over twenty million settlements annually, involving clearances of nearly £30 million – some 1.7 per cent of national income.[43]

The scale of the administrative machinery involved in the Clearing House operation almost defies grasp, particularly from our current viewpoint of electronic transactions. The volume of paper and statistics that it generated was vast. If there was one institutional embodiment of the tradition of Gradgrind, it was surely in the Railway Clearing House. Every month, all stations that issued through tickets (tickets that took passengers over other company lines) sent to the Clearing House a list of such issues. The Clearing House administrators then had to ensure that each company was credited with the amount due to it and, ultimately, to strike the balance due.[44] Where carriages as well as passengers passed on to 'foreign rails', a charge of 'demurrage' could become due if the stock was not returned by the foreign company within a fixed period. In goods carriage, the Clearing House operated in much the same way; the main difference was that it was quite common, rather than an exception, for goods wagons to be seen on foreign rails.[45] And, unlike passenger stock, they did not necessarily pass along pre-arranged routes – they could effectively move anywhere in the railway system. The task of monitoring and tracing these movements was a formidable one. Demurrage

181. Advertisement from *The Railway Official Gazette*, 1894, demonstrating the use of 'sheets' on open wagons.

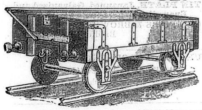

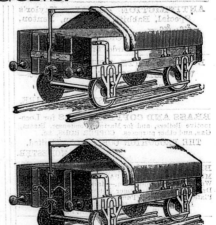

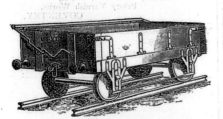

charges naturally became a prominent part of the clearing operation, and ran even to the tarpaulins, or sheets, with which items in open trucks were protected.[46] These sheets were commoner in Britain than on continental lines because of British traders' preference for open wagons. A folding trestle running from one end of the wagon to the other acted like a ridge-pole on which each sheet was secured, to form a sloping surface and prevent water from lodging.[47] The manufacture of the sheets has been described in the following way:

> Widths of jute sacking are stitched together by machines . . . . the mixture with which they are dressed is composed of boiled oil and vegetable black . . . . For the dressing they are laid out on the floor and painted over with huge brooms. Each sheet receives five coats of black . . . . It is then hung up to dry for six weeks or two months, when it is ready for use.[48]

On the Midland Railway alone, some ten thousand new sheets were turned out each year, and nine times that number came back annually for repair and re-dressing. The companies evolved identification markings for their sheets: North Western ones had two red lines, Great Northern white and blue lines running crosswise from corner to corner.[49]

COMMODITY FLOWS AND TERRITORY

> . . . it is the duty of managers of railways to
> develop the resources of their districts to the
> utmost possible extent.[50]

Whatever the facility offered by the Railway Clearing House in assisting through traffic, and despite the measure of consonance or congruence between some company territories and regional economies, it was perhaps an inevitable feature of the compartmentalization of 'railway space' that commodity flows would, over the course of time, come to reflect something of these spatial dispositions. The starkest examples of such a phenomenon were typically on those systems like the London and North Western, the Midland or the Great Western, which were inter-regional in their geographical pattern.[51] The process could be further reinforced by the structure of freight rates, which favoured long-haul over short-haul traffic and volume traffic over small consignments. Competition could also drive down rates, and companies pursued sundry other idiosyncracies of rate policy.

The way in which the territoriality of Victorian railway companies helped configure commodity flows can be seen in the coalfields. In 1866 the Great Western railway carried 2.24 million tons of coal from the South Wales coalfield to depots on its own system,[52] involving an average 'lead' (line-haul) of 76.2 miles.[53] The London area accounted for 11.4 per cent of the total, Birkenhead 8.6 per cent. The single most important share was taken by Swansea (27.9 per cent). Beyond these, the pattern of coal movement was widely diffused, seemingly over a wide spectrum of Great Western territory. The degree to which the geographical extent of the Great Western system determined the spatial character of coal flows is reflected in the diminutive tonnage – only 94,314 tons – transmitted from Great Western to other company lines. There remains, though, the matter of South Wales coal carried by companies other than the Great Western. The only company of any significance was the Taff Vale Railway, which took a remarkable 3.38 million tons in 1867, the bulk of it almost certainly for export or for coastal distribution. The Midland Railway, by contrast, received a tiny 1,637 tons from the South Wales field; the London and North Western only 57,000 tons, and the Cambrian 11,381 tons.[54] One factor contributing to the diffusion of South Wales coal through the Great Western system was its importance in locomotive firing. Local coal was so widely available to companies in the Midlands and the North that the movement of locomotive coal in particular would rarely have assumed any significant proportions. For the many southern companies, however, it was of considerable importance. There are few statistics on it. In 1903, it was recorded that locomotive firing consumed 5.5 per cent of total coal output – no mean figure when translated into a ton-per-mile format.[55]

Analysis of the Midland Railway's carriage of coal from collieries in Leicestershire, in the Erewash valley, and in the mining area north of Derby in 1856 shows a different picture.[56] Although ten years earlier than the Great Western example, an almost identical volume of coal was conveyed (2.2 million tons), a certain reflection of the origins of the Midland company as a coal-owners' line. The company appears to have made full use of its network configuration, yet some 29 per cent of the coal was passed on for carriage over other company lines. A quarter of a million tons went to Peterborough for the Eastern Counties Railway, and another 108,000 to Kew for the South Western and South Eastern Railways. Given the Midland's wide geographical range, well beyond that of many other companies, it is no surprise to find it involved in the supply of coal to non-mining districts. How far other railway companies distributed coal from the same groups of collieries, though, is not apparent from the available statistics.

182, 183. Destinations of coal conveyed by the Great Western Railway from South Wales mines, 1866 (left) and by the Midland Railway from mines in Leicestershire, the Erewash valley and the area north of Derby, 1856 (right).

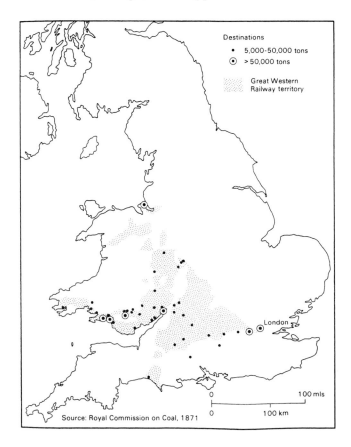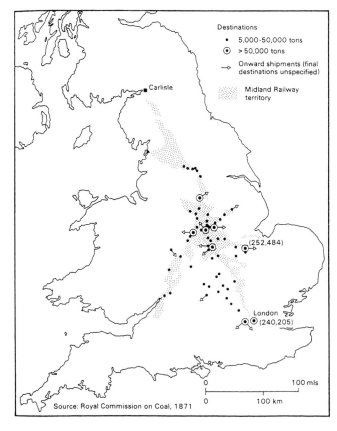

The nature and value of the article to be carried
was obviously one of the criteria to be considered
in fixing rates.[57]

The setting of railway company rates had important implications for contemporary perceptions of territory – especially among industrialists, agriculturalists and the trading community at large, the railways' primary customers. Until the coming of the railways, overland carriage rates had been determined largely by the uniform mileage principle – i.e. rates varied in direct proportion to the distance. Justices' assessments for the land carriage of goods quoted general ton- or hundredweight-per-mile rates between places or within county units. The system was by no means universally observed nor was it exclusive.[58] However, there was an obvious consistency to it, given the small units of operation – most road carriers used wagons with a laden weight of only four or five tons.

On river navigations and on canals, the uniform mileage principle was amended by introducing simple lists of anticipated goods and setting maximum charges for each in the enabling legislation.[59] The rough guiding principle in setting the rates was the value of the goods, thus opening the way for a range of variations on the uniform mileage principle. Further variation was introduced by virtue of the much larger unit loads that could be carried by inland water, making longer-haul traffic cheaper to operate than short-haul. In his estimate of the 'social saving' that accrued from railway carriage, one commentator has concluded that there was considerable variation in inland water rates, both between areas and between commodities.[60]

There can be no doubt about the way many canals and new river cuts transformed perceptions of territory. The canal ventures in south-west Lancashire, beginning in the 1760s, dramatically altered the range of Liverpool's hinterland, especially in the supply of coal.[61] But canals and rivers were not a sufficiently ubiquitous form of transport to have widespread impact on contemporary attitudes. Above all, their traffic was predominantly over short distances, and so deviations from the uniform mileage principle did not have a large geographical area in which to be demonstrated.[62] The railway, by contrast, came close to providing a universal facility of communication by the last decades of the Victorian era. Its traffic was carried over greater distances, bringing deviations from the uniform mileage principle much more clearly into focus. Traders and Chambers of Commerce in particular localities increasingly presented a chorus of complaint about unequal railway charges, especially in relation to mileage, objecting to what became termed 'undue' preference in the setting of rates by companies.[63]

Their primary grievance was that traditional geographical realms were being rudely overturned by the growing deviations from equal mileage rates. They faced a new conception of space – 'relational' or 'railroad' space. A Hull merchant, giving evidence before the Parliamentary investigation of railway rates in 1881, summed up the responses of many in his criticism of the North Eastern Railway Company's preferential treatment of Hartlepool and the Tyne over Hull:

> all the places near the Tyne and Hartlepool which belong, geographically, to those places, are reserved exclusively to them by the action of the North

Eastern Railway, whereas all the places to which we have the advantage, geographically, of access and position, are also opened out on equal terms to the northern ports.[64]

184. Coal train on the Great Northern Railway, 10 December 1905.

In other words, Hull was being deprived of the traditional advantages of its geographical position. Liverpool was also aggrieved. For twenty to thirty years, its Mayor explained to the Parliamentary Committee, there had been a growing feeling that the port was suffering injury from excessive railway charges: 'Liverpool was not being permitted to realize the full force of its geographical position'.[65] Sheffield's Chamber of Commerce complained in a similar manner over the way in which railway rates discriminated against the steel trade.[66] The steel masters did not ask for sympathy for what they regarded as their city's natural disadvantages of geographical position relative to the sources of haematite and pig-iron, but they wanted 'equable rates' on finished steel and incoming raw materials.[67] They claimed to be paying more than five shillings per ton over other steel-making districts for exporting their steel rails, and two to three shillings per ton over other districts in obtaining pig-iron.[68] The steel districts of South Wales, Barrow and Middlesbrough, notwithstanding the quality of Sheffield production, were being assisted, they claimed, to steal a march over the traditional seat of manufacture. A common thread in all these petitions was the destruction of traditional or natural

geographical advantage. The railways helped to create a produced nature, one in which the old absolutes of location were increasingly erased. In the same way that thrusting lines of permanent way, cuttings and embankments, tunnels and viaducts were part of a war with 'rude nature' (to quote Carlyle), the increasing destruction of the uniform mileage principle re-made geographical space.[69] The unlucky traders and townspeople of Merthyr Tydfil probably saw this transformation in its most absurd form. To obtain butter and bacon from Liverpool, they were forced to pay 22s 6d per ton, whereas Cardiff traders, only 24 miles further south, paid only 15s 10d per ton. Thus Merthyr resorted to ordering their supplies to Cardiff, and then bringing them 24 miles back north again.[70] The townsmen of Merthyr, in other words, saw their spatial world turned upside-down.

Of course, there were winners as well as losers in this process. The rate differences that appeared to discriminate against one port or producing area were a bonus for the trade of others. The Mayor of Grimsby, also in evidence before the Parliamentary Committee of 1881, stated that the town's traders were entirely satisfied with their railway services.[71] He argued against a uniform mileage rate, on the grounds that it would 'shut up the trade of some ports entirely'. Grimsby was perhaps exceptionally well placed on account of the Manchester, Sheffield and Lincolnshire Railway's vast investment in its port facilities (see page 162). But the shipowners of Goole benefited over those at Hull from the 'drawbacks' (refunds) that the North Eastern Railway Company allowed them on imported and exported goods – up to 2s 6d per ton.[72] In much the same way, Northumberland's coal-owners benefited because their coal rates to Tyne Dock were cheaper than those their Durham neighbours had to pay to Hull.[73]

The system of preferential rates had a number of explanations – some clear-cut, others arcane. In most cases, companies gave lower rates if large quantities were guaranteed – either as a total per year, or as a minimum size for each consignment.[74] Lower rates were granted on imported traffic because companies often anticipated a return trade (flour for grain, for instance).[75] The fact that import/export traffic was usually high in volume further justified the lower charges: they were an obvious traffic manager's model. Some rate preferences were explained by competition – where another railway company had a shorter line between two points, or where an alternative means of transport was available, such as coaster.[76]

Other reasons for preferential rates, more complex and not nearly so easily delineated, gave rise to claims in the trading community of 'undue' preference. Generally, companies felt an obligation to assist the trade of the region they served. The North Eastern Railway had a clear identity of interest with a discrete economic region – its managers and directors would have been foolish to view their business activity differently. The Midland Railway, the North Staffordshire Railway, and the London and North Western Railway all openly declared similar objectives.[77] However, the setting of preferential rates went further than this. It involved pursuit of a 'policy of bringing different supply areas into competition at a given market, and conversely, a given trade was spread between different ports'.[78] A manager on the London and North Western Railway actually stated to the Royal Commission on Railways in 1867 that the objective of his company was to 'lower the natural inequalities existing between one place and another'.[79] Again we see that the 'production' of nature was a declared intention of those who operated the railways. This policy was not necessarily operated only within single company domains or where several companies developed working agreements – it also engaged companies with lines stretching far beyond their home areas. Issues of profit were naturally implicated in such decisions, but not necessarily in a specific sense – it was impossible within the accounting frameworks of Victorian railway companies to discover with any precision what was the true cost of carriage of any

186. A 'sea of coal' at Aintree yard, near Liverpool, 1911.

one consignment.[80] The policy reflected a more general belief, powered by the prevailing political economy of the day, in the value of competition.[81] One North-Eastern mine-owner searched out distant markets when coal demand was depressed, but sold locally when it was more buoyant,[82] reminding us again of the degree to which Victorian railways were embedded in the contemporary workings of capital. Over and again, complaints of undue preference were examined by Parliament and found wanting. To have adopted the uniform mileage principle would have meant the discontinuance of much long-distance traffic and of competitive services.[83] It has even been suggested that the companies' behaviour was not inconsistent with their having something of the nature of public utilities.[84]

Preferential rates also altered relationships of territory in less direct ways, through the different classes of rate devised for different types of goods. Commodities were broadly divided into six classes, according to their value. 'Goods and minerals' were in the first class and were charged the lowest rates, while items of low weight but high value ('small parcels') were in the highest.[85] The system, basically the creation of the Railway Clearing House, was progressively refined over the years, and under legislation of 1891 and 1892 it gained statutory authority.[86] Within each of the six classes, there were further classifications. For example, the fifth – perishable merchandise – was subdivided into three. The first subdivision was for milk only; the second covered butter, cream, eggs, certain kinds of fish, hot-house fruit and dead poultry and game; the third covered ice, and sundry other types of fruit and fish not covered in the second.

The first-class rate, for goods and minerals, had the most elaborate sub-classification, comprising eight different divisions. Coal and iron were in the first, cigars and cigarettes in the last. The range showed a graduation from cheap, heavy articles that were consigned in large quantities to lighter, more valuable items requiring more space and more care in handling.[87] The upshot of this pricing scheme was naturally to favour areas of primary production like mining over manufacturing districts. It was even suggested that the cheapest classes of goods were sometimes carried at a loss.[88] This was in all likelihood true – for example, where different collieries were grouped together, via inter-company agreements, and charged equal rates to nearby ports,[89] some of the companies making such concessions must have been doing so at or below the margin of profit. The manufacturing sector that claimed to be among those worst served by the Clearing House classification was the chemical industry. One proprietor complained to the Parliamentary Committee of 1881 not only of chronic deviations from the uniform mileage principle, but of the way that, because many of the materials used in the industry post-dated most Railway Acts, companies had chosen arbitrarily and unjustifiably to place them in the highest class.[90]

Only rarely did traders or the business community in general try to challenge the railway companies at their own game, but this is exactly what the commercial and civic leaders of Hull did in the 1880s. In an effort to break the monopolistic hold on its hinterland enjoyed by the North Eastern Railway Company for over a quarter of a century, the Hull and Barnsley Railway and Dock Company was floated with an initial capital in 1880 of £4 million.[91] One of its primary targets was the coal trade of South Yorkshire, and by 1911 it had achieved a substantial share of the district's output.[92] The company, however, was never financially sound. Its survival ultimately rested on its coming to terms with the North Eastern Railway, the company it had hoped to outflank.[93]

During the 1880s and '90s, a benevolent British
Government . . . decided upon a solution to the problem
of poverty in Ireland . . . . building railways in the
remoter parts.[94]

By the closing decades of the Victorian age, it was an unlucky territory or district
that did not benefit from the facility of railway communication, even if, as among
Hull traders, there was serious disquiet about railway rates. However, in some
parts of the country, a combination of difficult terrain, poor commercial prospects
and diminutive populations made railway construction much more problematic –
in the north and west of Ireland, above all. In areas such as these, so-called 'light
railways' came into their own. In Ireland, they were mostly constructed under the
Tramways (Ireland) Acts between 1860 and 1900. By the close of the Victorian era
there were eighteen such lines, extending over 562 miles, using a gauge of three
feet.[95] In mainland Britain, the earliest light railway for public use, opened in 1836,
was the 1 ft 11½ in gauge Ffestiniog line, which linked the slate quarries of the
mountains of North Wales with Portmadoc.[96] 'Light railways' proper, however,
were born under the Light Railways Act of 1896; one of the best-known was the
24-mile Kent and East Sussex line, opened in 1900.[97] Their great merit was the
relatively low cost of their construction and operation, together with relatively
simple rules of working. In engineering terms, they could accommodate gradients
of up to 1 in 40, and curves laid out to a minimum radius of 150 feet. This made
them highly adaptable compared with standard-gauge (4 ft 8½ in) projects.[98]
However, it was rare for such lines to fulfil the hopes of their promoters. Many
were financially precarious from the start, even with heavy public funding. The
majority enjoyed only very short lives, and road transport eventually confirmed
their extinction.

187. Station at Duffws on
the Ffestiniog Railway, late
1880s.

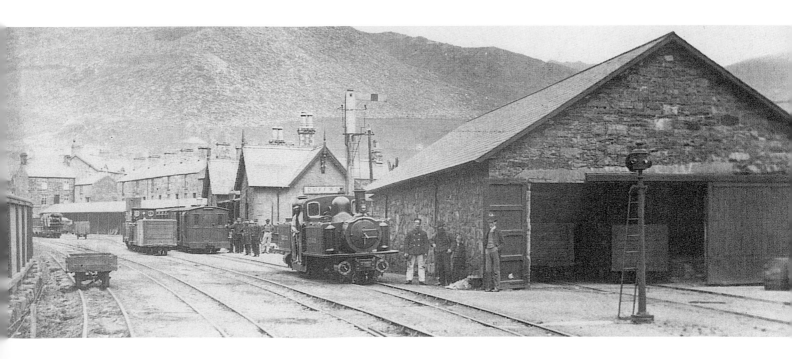

6

LABOUR

THE RAILWAY NAVVIES

The comparatively brief time assigned for the
completion of this stupendous work, rendered the whole
operation one of extraordinary character. Numerous
gangs of labourers of muscular strength, resembling
races of *Athletae*, covered the whole extent of the line.
By day and night they struggled, without relaxing, at
the incessant toil . . .

. . . by night the hill literally swarmed with moving
bodies, lighted to their work by torches flickering from
side to side, and from place to place. Creaking cranes,
dragging up by ropes and pulleys the laden barrows with
their guides, and again slowly curbing their descent
down the almost perpendicular banks.[1]

ONE OF THE GREAT PARADOXES of the railway age was the way the mechanical power of steam was set alongside the muscle power of the navvy. While Britain led the world in the application of steam power to locomotion, the railways themselves were made by navvies. At the height of the second Mania, there were 200,000 of them at work.[2] In the space of a few decades, this body of men 'accomplished feats of construction which dwarfed the building of the pyramids in the ancient world'.[3] They laboured with picks, shovels, wheelbarrows and gunpowder. The spoils of their excavations were mostly drawn away in wagons led by horses, not by steam engines. Not until much later did steam excavators begin to ease the heavy labour of earth-moving, and contractors' engines haul away the spoil along makeshift tracks. Only when the Manchester, Sheffield and Lincolnshire Railway (later, the Great Central) launched its new route to London in the 1890s did steam excavators become commonplace,[4] with the six contractors who built the line using 39 between them.[5] Steam *did* figure from a very early stage, however, in pumping, notably in association with tunnelling works. At Kilsby, on the London and Birmingham Railway, where a planned 1½-mile tunnel met a huge bed of quicksand, 13 steam pumping engines were installed in the mid 1830s, working at the rate of 1,800 gallons a minute.[6]

If the methods of railway construction were curiously incompatible with what was otherwise the age of the machine, the rough society of the navvy was well in accord with the turmoil that characterized the various social orders in the 1830s and 1840s. For some observers, navvies appeared to form part of a spectrum of radicalized, sometimes revolutionary, disaffected groups which became a hallmark of the period, across Europe as well as in Britain. The reality, however, was rather

188. William Mackenzie, lithograph, 1841, depicting navvies cutting their way through solid rock at Bishopton on the railway from Glasgow to Greenock, completed in 1841.

PUMPS FOR DRAINING THE KILSBY TUNNEL

189. J. C. Bourne, lithograph, 1839, of the pumps installed for draining the 'subterranean waters' of Kilsby tunnel during its construction in 1837.

different. Some navvies had trades to their names; many had once been common labourers; some came from the localities where construction was in progress. A few were undoubtedly criminals, who found the anonymity of the navvies' existence a welcome cover from arrest and prosecution. Others, though, belonged to the same gangs that had built roads and canals. The word navvy, short for navigator, initially derived from canal-building, but there is some doubt as to whether railway labourers used the term to describe themselves.[7] It goes without saying that there were political agitators among the navvies who laboured in their thousands in the 1840s and later, but it was the men's social not their political behaviour that was at the root of contemporary concern and distaste. By the standards of the day navvies were well paid, even if they were subjected to the abuses of the truck system – the practice of paying wages in goods or in vouchers which could be exchanged only at a contractor's own shop. It was their propensity to fighting, rioting and bad living, along with the barbarity of many of their shanties and encampments, that so offended. The often itinerant nature of their labour, its harshness, and the ever-present dangers of injury or death, made for a very rough and unfamiliar sort of society – one, moreover, that was visited on unsuspecting realms, rural areas hitherto insulated from the excesses of industrialism. Among the mill-towns of Lancashire, the social evils of factory production had, by the 1840s, become an all-too-familiar sight, and increasingly drew comment from social reformers and radicals. The navvies, especially those without trades, were no less proletarian than their mill counterparts; indeed, there was arguably greater concentration of capital in railway contracting than in cotton spinning. The difference with the navvies was their inherent mobility as a labour group, and the way their life and their labour were fused. Some navvies found temporary lodgings, but most lived on the job. In effect, they became rather like an army of pioneers, but one bereft of any central religious or social ideal. Encamped in open country, they were akin to new colonists, but often of a barbaric kind – they might as well have been transported convicts in Van Dieman's Land.[8]

The compound of sin that, it was claimed, the navvies brought with them was best articulated by the clergy. In the eyes of the church, the navvies were second to none for godlessness. Moreover, their brute strength and their devil-may-care attitude to danger appeared to cast them as almost inhuman, at a time when Christian teachings were under attack from the growth of a natural science that was soon to proclaim man's descent from the apes. Reputedly 'they ate and drank more than any other men: two pounds of meat, two pounds of bread and five quarts of ale a day'.[9] Most of their earnings appeared to go on alcohol and their drunken revelries, including fighting and rioting, became a terror to ordinary folk. One early historian of the railway age summed up many public reactions when he wrote how painful it was 'to find that the triumphs which the human intellect has achieved should be so intimately associated with the moral degradation of so large a section of the community'.[10] Another remarked how navvies lived only for the present, caring nothing for the past and indifferent to the future; they spoke of God only to wonder why he had made some men rich and others poor.[11]

Their living conditions and unwholesome society were an early concern to Parliament, which set up a Select Committee in 1846 to enquire into them.[12] From the report and minutes of the evidence, it is plain that the navvies had rapidly been accommodated into 'the condition of England question'.[13] As a group, they formed yet another victim of the social evils of industrial capitalism that so exercised

190. J. C. Bourne, men and horses at work on the construction of the London and Birmingham Railway, c. 1837.

191. David Hill, cutting near Proven Mill Bridge on the opening day of the Glasgow and Garnkirk Railway, 27 September 1831, lithograph, 1832. On the right, the thatched hovels of the navvies who built the line afford a curious backdrop.

contemporary social commentators like Chadwick and Carlyle. However, a number of modern analysts disagree with the opinions of contemporary social observers; basing part of their work on the returns of Census enumerators, particularly from 1851 onwards, they have drawn a picture of a labour group much more integrated with the local economy and much more at ease within its society.[14] It is possible that, by the later decades of the century, the economy and society of navvies had become better integrated with the localities in which they worked, but such revisionism carries serious dangers. The commentary of contemporaries, of 'respectable persons', affords a vital record of how the navvy was perceived given the prevailing attitudes of the day, particularly during the critical decades of the 1830s and 1840s. If we are to uncover the experience of the railway, it is these kinds of clues to outward sympathies and underlying values that must remain at the forefront of interpretation.

The Parliamentary Select Committee's report and minutes ran to well over two hundred pages. They described the railway labourers as being

> brought hastily together in large bodies; no time is given for that gradual growth of accommodation which would naturally accompany the gradual growth of numbers; they are therefore crowded into unwholesome dwellings, while scarcely any provision is made for their comfort or decency of living; they are released from the useful influences of domestic ties, and the habits of their former routine of life . . .[15]

In elaborate and repetitive manner, they document the evils of the truck or 'tommy' shops among navvy encampments, the irregular and unreliable systems of paying the men, the undue prevalence of accidents involving serious injury and sometimes death, the squalid habitations and the wider moral depravities that appeared in many eyes to set navvies as a race apart. Worst of all, they were apparently devoid of any religious belief, neither attending worship on Sundays nor showing any interest in the scriptures.

The Sheriff of Edinburgh described in detail the nature of the navvy encampments on the Hawick line of railway.[16] The men's huts were built of wood and turf. Each was twenty feet by twelve, divided into two with a fireplace on each side, and provided accommodation for up to thirty men, often with two or three to a bed. On the South Devon line, according to a local clergyman who was engaged to attend to the navvies' religious education, dwellings were yet more primitive. Rafters were run on to a high hedge or bank and then a front and sides were made with turf; invariably, these hovels were damp, foetid and easily infested. Men could pay three shillings a week for them. The committee of enquiry saw parallels between the housing of railway labourers and the quartering of an army. In the latter case, it was remarked, the State took care that the men were properly quartered, but the railway contractor was under no similar inducement.[17] When the contractor Samuel Morton Peto gave evidence that he built barracks for his men in districts where lodgings were unobtainable, he was demonstrating a rare practice.[18] As a comparison, the total effective force of the army, navy and ordnance in the mid 1840s was around 160,000,[19] so the 'armies' of navvies were easily the greater force and arguably merited the kind of welfare that Peto offered. However, no legislation to this effect followed the enquiry, Parliament appearing to

192. J. C. Bourne, stone-masons at work on the London and Birmingham Railway, c. 1837.

think that remedies were best left in the hands of the railway companies.

The social conditions of the navvy cannot be understood apart from the frenetic pace of capitalist expansion that characterized the mid 1840s, as well as some later years. The Select Committee was much less alive to this underlying mechanism than it was to documenting social ills. However, several depositions made plain the degree to which construction work was 'urged unduly forward'. The London and Birmingham Railway had men working night and day on the line around Northampton, and the company was forced to erect temporary huts to retain them on the job.[20] Conditions appear to have been so bad that the local agricultural labourers refused to be induced into what they termed the 'degradation of working upon the works'. Allowing longer time scales for construction would have required fewer men, would have been 'cheaper and less demoralizing'. The harsh reality, though, was that most companies sought to open lines as quickly as possible, and many paid 50 per cent more to speed the work.

> In great railway works the interest upon 600,000 or 700,000 [pounds] is so great when it is spread over a number of years, and the company sacrifice that interest until the line comes into operation, and they bind their contractors to knock off the work quickly to save the enormous amounts of interest.[21]

The navvies formed the base layer of what became a remarkable hierarchy of labour organization. Although the railways were ostensibly built by contractors like Thomas Brassey, much of the actual work was organized through sub-contractors. The main contractor first appointed agents for each section of line. Each agent in turn let out the work in sub-contracts, generally for specific projects such as masonry works or earthworks. The sub-contractor then took on a ganger – a minor class of contractor, with a little capital, who superintended and laboured at the same time. It was the gangers who then engaged the navvies. The navvies worked either at a fixed daily rate or on piece work, or else organized themselves into a 'butty-gang' in which fixed-price bargains were made with the gangers. Sometimes the main contractor chose a more direct method of labour organization and employed gangers directly, in which case the navvies effectively became employees of the main contractor. Samuel Morton Peto, who ranked alongside Brassey in the scale of his commitments as a railway builder, at times operated in this manner. In May 1846, he had about 9,000 men in his employ, of whom perhaps two-thirds were directly engaged. The great merit of sub-contracting was its inherent flexibility, in terms of capital as well as labour. The exceptional haste with which railway companies were floated and the associated pressure to speed their construction made such a flexible mode of production almost inevitable. It was a vital requirement to be able to increase or decrease the labour force at will. Moreover, the primitive nature of estimating and accounting, especially in the early years, added to the flexibility of the systems. The task of construction was also fraught with risk. Heavy rains could turn newly made embankments into quagmires. Tunnelling could be delayed for days by unstable strata. As a result, contractors' estimates were frequently very wide of the mark and often ended in bankruptcy. Ten of the thirty main contractors who undertook to build the London and Birmingham Railway failed completely.[22] It was reckoned that no contractor could estimate his costs closer than to within 25 per cent.[23] Inevitably, therefore, there was a high turnover among contractors.

The contractors' difficulties were often compounded by the state of the labour market. In peak times of railway-building, bricklayers, masons or even just men with picks and shovels were not readily found. Wages rose, and men who became dissatisfied with their conditions could easily move to another construction site. According to calculations made by one of Thomas Brassey's staff, in 1843 pickmen were commanding 15 shillings a week, but by 1846 the figure had risen to 24 shillings in the face of burgeoning labour demands.[24] Nor were contractors

194. Samuel Morton Peto (1809–89), arguably one of the most socially enlightened of leading railway contractors.

195. Steam excavator in use on construction of the Manchester, Sheffield and Lincolnshire Railway's London extension near Leicester, mid 1890s.

insulated from the wider workings of the capital market. Some of the biggest contractors accepted payments from new railway companies in the form of shares or mortgages rather than in hard cash. In a few cases, contractors even built lines at their own expense in the expectation of later pecuniary reward. Railway shares, however, were volatile. Commercial panics like that of 1847 seriously weakened liquidity. In 1866, following the collapse of the City finance house of Overend & Gurney, even Peto failed as railway shares fell to a third of their value in a single day.[25]

The last major construction feat of the navvies, unassisted by mechanical apparatus, was the Midland Railway's new route to Scotland in the first half of the 1870s. The famous Settle–Carlisle line remains one of the most remarkably engineered railway routes in Britain. The navvies who laboured upon it (over 30,000 all told) had to contend with torrential rain, extreme cold, bog and boulder clay, not to mention epidemic disease.[26] The navvy encampments showed precious little change from their counterparts of thirty years before. Lawlessness, rioting and theft were commonplace. The men's capacity for drink was undiminished. Nevertheless, a reporter for the *Daily News* found the heave of their shovels like clockwork, the perfection of animal vigour.[27] The greasy clay melted away in the face of their muscular strength.[28] Twenty-five years later, when the Great Central main line was in the making, the navvies who worked on it were captured on film.[29] The pictures show an altogether more civilized band of workers, but much of the old camaradie seems to have faded.[30] The life of the navvies had become a legend.

196. Navvy hut at Calvert on the Manchester, Sheffield and Lincolnshire Railway's London extension, mid 1890s. The squalor of the navvy quarters of fifty years before is nowhere to be seen.

RAILWAY SERVICE

He knowed Toodle, he said, well. Belonged to the
Railroad, didn't he? 'Yes, Sir, yes!' cried Susan Nipper
from the coach window. Where did he live now? hastily
inquired Walter. He lived in the Company's own
Buildings, second turning to the right, down the yard,
cross over and take the second on the right again. It was
number eleven; they couldn't mistake it; but if they did,
they had only to ask for Toodle, Engine Fireman . . .[31]

Charles Dickens's portrait of Mr Toodle, husband of Paul Dombey's nurse, encapsulates many of the essential features of railway service. Toodle was a stoker by trade; as a very young man, he had worked in mining. His vision of the future was unambiguous: 'I'm a-going on one of these railroads when they comes into full play,' he proclaimed to Mr Dombey when his wife was engaged to look after young Paul. He also declared his ambition to read: 'one of my little boys is going to learn me.'[32] Toodle was not long in achieving his goals. He became a fireman for the London and Birmingham Railway, on the line that had wrought its path of creative destruction through the very district in which he and his family lived, Staggs Gardens in Camden Town. He 'belonged' to the railroad and resided in its 'own buildings'. Later, when Mr Dombey travels from Euston to Leamington, Toodle turns out to be the fireman on the train and introduces himself to Dombey and Major Bagstock as they walk up and down the platform. Dressed in a 'canvass suit abundantly besmeared with coal-dust and oil,' Toodle was, as Dickens describes,

197. Driver and fireman on a locomotive of the London and North Western Railway, 1860s.

198. London and North Western Railway guard, *Fore's Contrasts*, 1852.

'professionally clothed'. When Dombey mistakes Toodle's approach for a request for money, he receives a quick riposte: 'No, Sir . . . we're a-doin pretty well, Sir.'[33]

By the close of the Victorian age, railway employment had reached over 621,000,[34] nearly 5 per cent of the working population. As early as 1870, it had become the sixth largest occupational category in the country.[35] This was not a lumpen proletariat in the fashion of the cotton mills of Lancashire: to be on the railways was to be enrolled in a very particular kind of service. Railwaymen wore uniform. Potential recruits had to satisfy quite stringent tests of education and behaviour. All were bound by a quasi-military system of discipline. For the great armies of the under- and unemployed in the countryside, railway work had an unmistakeable lure – 'from barn and byre, field and fold they were recruited'.[36] It was a vocation almost exclusively for men: at the 1851 Census, there were just 54 female workers recorded for the whole industry.[37] As late as 1891, *Chambers's Journal* remarked that female railway clerks, very common on the Continent, just did not exist in Britain.[38]

The commencing wage for a porter of 16 to 18 shillings a week in the 1840s easily outstripped that of the average farm labourer.[39] Higher grades were rewarded with higher wages, and thus railway employment quite easily vied with factory, forge and mine. Toodle, 'a-doin pretty well' firing engines on the London and Birmingham Railway, was probably earning up to five shillings a day.[40] In addition, he had a clothing allowance, housing and perhaps other perks. Clothing allowances could be remarkably generous – on the Great Western railway in 1852, the company provided its passenger guards with one great coat, one frock coat, two waistcoats, two pairs of trousers, two pairs of boots and a cap yearly.[41] On the London and Greenwich Railway, a monthly bonus was paid to engine crews who could reduce the amount of coke consumed in fireboxes.[42]

A particular attraction of railway employment was its security and the chance of betterment. In other industrial sectors, fluctuations in trade were accommodated by laying labour off in slumps and taking it on in boom periods. However, on the railways it was difficult to regulate labour relative to fluctuations in the volume of trade and traffic. Railways were a service, not a product-making sector, relatively few personnel could be dispensed with in times of depression. This relative permanence of employment was underscored in the way that wage increments were typically based on length of service. Supplementary benefits such as housing also indicated that companies expected employees to remain with them. On the establishment of the London and Birmingham Railway, potential recruits were required to provide extensive information about themselves and their families, including names of previous employers and length of service.[43] By the 1890s, *Chambers's Journal* observed that prospective booking clerks were typically required to pass an examination, to appear before the Board of Directors and to provide testimonials. Even then, they were merely registered; actual employment waited upon a vacancy.[44] On the London and North Western, the examination on entry was supplemented by another, taken after two years service, to test the clerk's knowledge of shorthand, railway geography and the railway work on which he had been engaged. If the clerk's salary was to advance beyond £50 per annum, he had to

199. Mobile platform refreshment buffet at Derby station on the Midland Railway, 1908.

submit to yet another examination, involving further testing in shorthand as well as in subjects like block- or train-working.[45] Use of the term 'railway geography' echoed the satirical commentary of *Punch* of the 1840s.[46] Here, though, it reflected the territorialization of railway companies and the critical part that their personnel played in facilitating commodity movement from one place to another.

Promotion prospects on the railways were clearly augmented by the expanding nature of the industry. New lines offered new opportunities to employees prepared to move. Alongside this, most companies awarded promotion for faithful and efficient execution of duty. One of the largest fields for promotion was portering.[47] To become a porter required no trade or definite occupation; it was necessary merely to able to read and write and to demonstrate good character.[48] Promoted porters most commonly became guards, but some became clerks or signalmen. In the locomotive grade, the promotion ladder was more circumscribed. Initially, a man who wanted to become an engine-driver was required to serve some years in the locomotive works of the company, learning all the parts and fittings of an engine. He was then eligible for a post as fireman, where he could remain for a long time. Upon being appointed a driver, he would be started on slow goods trains; later, if he showed competence, he could rise to take charge of passenger trains.[49] On the London and North Western railway in the 1850s, there were five separate classes of engine-driver, ranging in wages from 5s 6d to eight shillings a day.[50] The responsibilities of enginemen were vividly described by Sir Francis Head in 1850:

> Even in bright sunshine to stand – like the figure-head of a ship – foremost on a train of enormous weight, which, with fearful momentum, is rushing forward faster than any racehorse can gallop, require a cool head and a calm heart; but to proceed at this pace in dark or foggy tunnels, along embankments, and through deep cuttings, where it is impossible to foresee any obstruction, is an amount of responsibility which scarcely any other situation in life can exceed.[51]

For agricultural labourers used to poor pay, unreliable work and rigid social stratification, employment on the railway offered access to a different world. Even for those already used to industrial employment, the benefits were clear – Daniel Gooch had no difficulty in recruiting enginemen and firemen from the north of England for working the Great Western Railway in its first years.[52]

200. Station staff at Goring, near Reading, on the Great Western Railway, c. 1892.

201. Porters on the South Eastern Railway.

Alongside the attractions of railway labour must be set the fact that it was a highly disciplined industry.

> The peculiar nature of railway discipline arose mainly from the requirements of safety, the necessity of strict observance of time and the fact that all kinds of unskilled men were responsible for the safety of persons and property.[53]

The enabling Acts for particular lines of railway provided the initial basis for company disciplinary codes, and brought them under Parliamentary sanction. The General Acts of 1840 and 1842, which set out to regulate railways, enforced them.[54] Thus men guilty of serious misconduct could be arraigned before a magistrate and summary justice delivered. The accused could even be committed for trial at Quarter Sessions, although it was more common for the companies themselves to administer disciplinary procedures. Typically, those found guilty were dismissed the service. More minor offences brought fines, following the pattern that had long prevailed in factories. Employees could also be cautioned. Among engine-drivers, disciplinary offences included being absent without leave, causing minor damage by careless driving, and running short of water.[55]

The overall framework of railway discipline and regulation was largely derived from the military, and it was probably no accident that ex-military men quickly found positions of responsibility on the railways. At its opening in 1830, the Liverpool and Manchester Railway Company was following military practice in issuing 'orders of the day'.[56] The elaborate hierarchy of grades constructed by railway companies also reflected the military model. In turn, in order to oversee the maintenance of discipline, companies instituted police establishments. Thomas Roscoe, in his 1839 guide to travelling the London and Birmingham Railway, described the policemen stationed along the railway. They were there to prevent intrusion, to keep the road free of obstruction, and to make signals as the trains

202. Railwaymen with broad-gauge engine and rolling stock pose for a photographer at Abingdon, Oxfordshire, c. 1863.

passed, using red and white flags by day and lamps after dark (somewhat perversely, green was used for caution and white for 'line clear').[57] Their positioning varied according to local circumstances, but was typically at between one- and three-mile intervals.[58] The early Great Western railway police were all sworn constables. Modelled on the Metropolitan Police of the time, even to the similarity of their uniform, they were either posted at stations or patrolled sections of line. Fundamentally, their task was to preserve orders, but they also undertook operational duties.[59] Railwaymen's duties were set out in the company rule-book (known colloquially as the Bible, even if its exceptional detail more resembled the Koran).[60] This was a powerful example of the railway's reliance upon the printed word; the industry became increasingly dominated by paper, whether in the form of posted notices about train operation or in the clerical procedures of the ticket or the parcels office. At the Newcastle Central parcels office in 1899, clerks despatched or received two or three hundred parcels in half an hour.[61] Each parcel required a waybill, of which a copy was retained to make cash-book entries. Lists were then compiled of the amounts due from all the stations to which parcels had been sent, and these were amalgamated once a month and sent for audit. To be recruited as a clerk, therefore, required reasonable standards of intelligence, numeracy and literacy, not to mention the 'smartness, alacrity, energy and zeal' that some companies also expected.[62] This was why boards of directors deliberated on many appointments themselves, and why the Railway Clerks' Association was keen to counter those who made disparaging remarks about the 'rank and file' or 'routine' nature of the working life of a railway clerk.[63]

That the railway industry was highly authoritarian goes almost without saying. One corollary was that it had the potential to inspire loyalty and a sense of achievement. Uniforms were clearly part of this, and it would have been a strange young recruit who did not find some pride in the green plush clothing and glazed top hat that, for instance, the Great Western gave even its porters in the 1840s.[64] The London and South Western initially attired its guards in scarlet coats, later

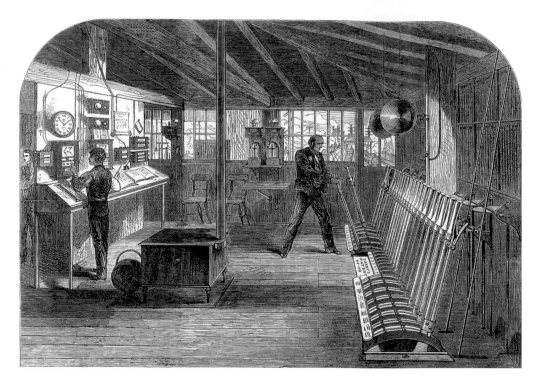

205. The signalman's
realm: the box at London
Bridge station on the South
Eastern Railway, *Illustrated
London News*.

replaced with blue piped in scarlet.[65] They must have cut impressive figures. Working on the railway directly connected ordinary men with what was undeniably the wonder of the age. Dickens captured some sense of this in his portrayal of Toodle's obvious pride in being a railway fireman. The railway in the 1830s and 1840s was a remarkable spectacle, almost everywhere open to public view – to be associated with it gave ordinary men a sense of purpose and of being implicated in modernity.

Loyalty became a powerful feature in the hierarchy of grades in the railway. The elaborate division of labour engendered tribalism among railwaymen. The industry became a series of 'bailiwicks' – signalmen, engine-drivers and passenger guards, to name just three groups, each evolved their own distinctive working traditions and cultural practices, even language.[66] The language of the 'bailiwick' was a 'working organic language which crackles with wit and social criticism'.[67] It was neither the language of the gutter nor the language of railway jargon; rather, it reflected a kind of industrial kinship. Some engine-drivers were allocated their 'own' engines so that there occurred a kind of fusion of man and machine, and many companies offered drivers premiums for fuel saving. On the London and North Western in the mid 1890s, this amounted to two shillings for each pound of coal less than the standard use per mile; firemen were allowed eightpence per pound.[68] On the Great Western, drivers often got bonuses of ten pounds a year for economy in the use of coal and for general good conduct.[69] Signalmen and stationmasters, if they occupied the same box or station for any length of time, could develop a sense of personal possession, which could breed jealousies. These seem to have become most marked among enginemen: 'The men of the city and town sheds, who usually worked long-distance trains, had a friendly contempt for their colleagues who operated "out in the sticks".' The same writer claimed that men born on the millstone grit were always more abrasive than their counterparts in the chalk and clay areas. On granite, fen or coastal areas, however, engine-drivers always considered themselves separate, as well as distinct from other railway workers.[70] The basis of these claims is not clear; it is, of course, possible that such natural identities were, more correctly, functions of company territorial identities which did sometimes have a basis in natural regions. Even so, the potential clearly existed for an almost kaleidoscopic divison of railway labour, one that was endogenously as well as exogenously forged. This was certainly one reason why combination among railway workers was so slow in coming – there was no permanent trade union among railwaymen until 1871.[71] In effect, the companies had created a structure of industrial organization that illustrated very forcibly the principle of divide and rule. Railwaymen themselves somewhat unwittingly reinforced this by their sectionalist outlook.

The control exercised by railway companies over their staff was often reinforced through educational measures. Many set up educational institutes for their junior members. At Crewe, the Mechanic's Institute dates from 1844–5. Its object was to provide a theoretical supplement to the practical knowledge gained in the Crewe works, but it also offered art, literary and commercial classes.[72] The Great Eastern established a Mechanic's Institute in 1851 at Stratford New Town in east London.[73] On the Midland Railway, a similar centre was founded at Derby, also in 1851.[74] By the last decades of the nineteenth century, most railway works

enjoyed similar provisions, some companies also forging combinations with outside educational authorities.[75]

The educational influence that the railways exercised could be extended to embrace the families and social lives of their staff, reflecting the paternalistic traits of earlier eras. From the 1830s, some companies showed an interest in educating the children of railwaymen. By 1840, the London and Birmingham Railway had set up a school at its Wolverton works site. Crewe had a company school by 1843, Swindon by 1844, Ashford and Woodhead by 1848 (respectively for the Grand Junction, Great Western, South Eastern, and Manchester, Sheffield and Lincolnshire companies). Where there were not enough children of railway servants to found separate schools, companies supported denominational schools through donation and subscription.[76] Revenue from Sunday trains was used to support schools, which helped to temper objections from shareholders about spending commercial profits on educational support.[77]

Company policy on schooling was intricately linked, in most cases, to policy on religious observance. In 1843, the directors of the Great Western Railway had urged their shareholders to make individual contributions to provide 'the means of

206, 207. Wolverton, Buckinghamshire, the creation of the London and North Western Railway. Left: a view taken in the late 1860s, showing St George's Church, the Science and Art Institute, a lodging house and, in the far distance, the Creed Street schools. Above: the Science and Art Institute as extended in the later nineteenth century.

208. Edward Snell, watercolour, 1849, showing a bird's eye view of Swindon railway works and settlement.

209. *The Railway Signal*, the monthly journal of the Railway Mission.

religious instruction and worship for men and their families'. A year earlier, one of the directors had bequeathed £500 towards the erection of a church and school at the company's works at Swindon. Some shareholders were lukewarm in their support, and others objected. But so succesful was the subscription call that by 1845 church and school at Swindon were in being.[78] Churches were also erected in other railway towns, namely at Wolverton, Crewe, Doncaster and Stantonbury,[79] and companies also provided monies to help maintain existing churches and to build new ones.

Unravelling the precise motives behind policies of educational and spiritual guidance is not easy. In some aspects, it was probably highly utilitarian. Railway work, for example, was often a family occupation, sons following fathers and railway families often inter-marrying.[80] Schooling thus became an obvious means by which a pliant and suitably educated labour force could be nurtured. Encouraging the facility for Sunday worship might equally be seen as a logical means of checking the strength of the movement against trains being run on Sundays, quite apart from using Sunday trains to support railway schools. Perhaps there was a measure of Christian feeling in the decisions of some company directors to support religion, but from the London and Birmingham's half-yearly meeting of August 1840 the practice appears to have been tied to a more secular notion of exalting the company's character.[81] More widely, the hours of work for the majority of railwaymen made attendance at divine worship on Sundays extremely difficult, or even impossible; at the least, it could mean giving up precious leisure or sleeping time.

Companies also gave support to temperance work on the railways, with self-interest appearing much to the fore. The temperance movement received practical encouragement from railway directors and chief officers, who carried on 'an active propaganda'.[82] Among the different temperance organizations, the Railway

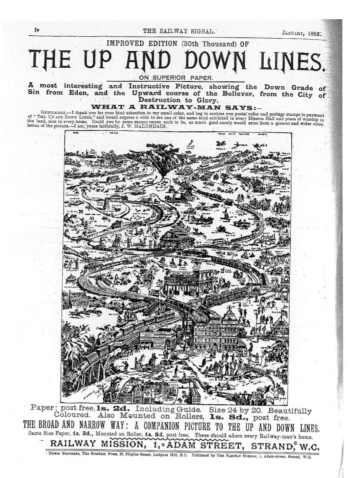

Mission had its own monthly publication, the *Railway Signal*. Styled as a journal of evangelistic and temperance work, it offered 'total abstinence cards' to its readers, as well as a medley of biblical texts. Some of these were incorporated into elaborate posters which used the railway as instructing metaphor – 'up' lines took members from the City of Destruction to Glory, 'down' lines from Eden to Hell.[83] By the 1890s, there were Mission branches in places as far apart as Peebles, Dowlais, Lowestoft and Tunbridge Wells.[84] Here, exhausted railwaymen supposedly found salvation, happy in the knowledge that their superiors looked favourably upon such visible demonstrations of sobriety.

The social concerns of railway companies extended beyond education and religion to embrace incapacity through sickness, disability through injury while at work and, more critically, the impact upon his family of a railwayman's death through accident. As early as 1840, the London and Birmingham Railway's directors offered compensation for accidents without conceding any legal liability.[85] Subsequently, most companies awarded accident pay of some form and, in particular cases, lump sum payments or other help with surgeons' or doctors' fees.[86] The frequency with which railwaymen needed surgical treatment prompted companies to make annual donations to hospitals and infirmaries. By 1872, the London and North Western was paying £443 per annum to a total of 47 such institutions.[87] Sickness benefit, generally, was met by a combination of company provision and friendly society funds.[88] The friendly societies were often organized and subsidized by companies, and membership of them was frequently compulsory

211. A. F. Tait, lithograph, 1848, of platelayers working at Crewe station.

for railwaymen. The Great Western founded a Provident Society as early as 1838. By 1871, this offered sick pay of between 12 shillings and a pound a week, along with death and superannuation benefits; members contributed between 8*d* and 1*s* 4*d* per week and the company provided a subsidy of £1,000 per annum.[89] The Great Western also had a widows' and orphans' fund, to which it made contributions; Queen Victoria became its patroness and its secretary regularly sent out letters to potential benefactors.[90] In actuarial terms, these kinds of funds were typically rather suspect and, in due course, they became the subject of government scrutiny.[91] In addition, subsidy by the railway companies almost inevitably invited a certain laxity in administration. Sickness benefit was very uneven across the grades of occupation. The platelayer, for example, was not eligible for membership of a number of schemes and, since his was hazardous work, insurance against accidents could be obtained only at prohibitive premiums.[92] For clerical workers, including station-masters, it was generally the companies rather than the friendly societies that provided sickness benefit, with the sums awarded related to pay.[93] This same group also benefited from company provision for superannuation. The preferential treatment accorded this particular occupational group was clearly a reflection of the long average length of service that was common within it. The Railway Clearing House itself set up various benefit schemes to which railway companies had full access.[94] The superannuation fund, established in 1873, had just short of 2,000 members by its second year of operation and nine railway companies had joined; it offered a pension rate of 25 per cent of salary after ten years' membership, rising to a maximum of 67 per cent with 45 years' membership. However, compared with the great mass of railway employees, these membership figures were paltry, and the Clearing House was disappointed with the poor take-up; much the same applied to a sickness fund established in 1860.[95] By contrast, among the principal railway friendly societies, the Railway Benevolent Institution, founded in 1858, had some 157,000 subscribers by 1910.[96]

212. Advertisement for the Railway Permanent Benefit Building Society.

It is not easy to pass summary judgement on these various benefits. Friendly societies, for example, had long been a fact of life for ordinary working men. By 1850, they had around 1½ million members; by 1880, this figure had risen to 2.2 million, or 30 per cent of the adult male population.[97] Critics of railway friendly societies point to the continuing presence of distress among railwaymen and their families throughout the period. But other employment sectors experienced distress just as serious, mining among them. Companies' part-reliance on friendly societies was castigated in some quarters as a dereliction of duty.[98] In effect, railwaymen were often responsible for compensating themselves for sickness or for injury that they sustained while working. In this way, according to the *Pall Mall Gazette* of 1866, 'the dividends of the shareholders are kept up, and the widows of mangled porters and stokers have a pension from a fund provided by the porters and stokers themselves'.[99] The General Railway Workers' Union commented on the shocking death and injury record of the London and North Western Railway:

> In spite of these appalling figures, the L & NW make a great deal of their philanthropic regard for the men they employ. Especially do they delight in declaring that their Insurance Fund is a purely philanthropic institution. Of course, Railwaymen know differently. They know perfectly well that it is a means for shackling their freedom and restricting the liberty of the employees.[100]

Such stinging verdicts were echoed, sometimes yet more trenchantly, in accounts of the long hours that railwaymen were frequently required to work. Marx cited the case of an engine fireman who in the mid 1860s undertook an 88-hour week, including one duty spell of 29 hours.[101] More generally, railwaymen were being required to work 14, 18 and 20 hours. Inevitably, some suffered exhaustion: 'their brains stopped thinking, their eyes stopped seeing'.[102] Even that distinguished medical journal, *The Lancet*, was prompted in 1862 to press for reform of the working hours of railway servants.[103] Excessive periods of duty led to a rising number of accidents for which railwaymen could be held personally responsible in the law courts. During the last two decades of the century, there were four to five hundred railwaymen killed annually and some five to six times that figure injured.[104] In 1890, the London and North Western Railway alone recorded 74 deaths and 925 injuries.[105] An anonymous correspondent to the *Railway Service Gazette* recorded that he was obliged to work 10, 12 and sometimes 14 hours per day. In effect, there was no limit to the hours the company could seek to extract from him, since the rules decreed that 'every servant must devote himself exclusively to the service of the company, attend during appointed hours, reside and do duty where and when required, Sundays included'.[106] Excessive hours had been normal since the first lines were laid: in 1842, the inspectors of the Railway Department of the Board of Trade repeatedly remarked upon the safety implications.[107] A disastrous head-on collision at Radstock in 1876, on the Somerset and Dorset Company's new extension to Bath, revealed a telegraph clerk who worked from 6.30 a.m. to 9.30 p.m., a station master who worked from 5.30 a.m. to 6.30 p.m. and a boy assistant who was on duty from 8 a.m. to 10 p.m. All were grossly overworked and shouldered astonishing responsibilities, according to the investigating officer.[108] Engine-drivers suffered equal exploitation: for many years, agreed rostering arrangements were non-existent,[109] drivers had no defined rest-

213. Handbill advertising a railwaymen's meeting in Liverpool, 1892. The organisers clearly sought to engineer a powerful sense of theatre: railwaymen were invited to attend in their uniforms and there were several brass bands.

periods, and they had to be permanently on call. Thus duty turns could be a few hours one day and twenty the next. Few employment sectors bore comparison.

Railwaymen mounted a long campaign for shorter and more regular working hours, beginning in earnest in the 1860s and intensifying after the financial collapse of 1866 when many companies found themselves over-extended. A Railway Clerks Association was formed in 1865, and other grades soon followed.[110] Initially, they met with some success. Between 1872 and 1874 new agreements reduced working hours and increased wages – goods guards, for example,

> obtained sixty hours in lieu of eighty-four hours as the limit of the regular week's work, their rates of wages were increased, and they received just payment for overtime, while Sunday ceased to be counted as part of the ordinary week.[111]

However, these efforts encountered severe opposition from many companies; when trade conditions became less favourable, as was the case in the late 1870s, many of the earlier concessions were withdrawn.[112] The struggle continued against the background of the Second Reform Bill of 1867 which gave most railwaymen the right to vote, and a damning Parliamentary enquiry in the early 1890s.[113] In May 1880, a demonstration in Exeter Hall brought together 5,000 railwaymen with the object of promoting the Nine Hours movement.[114]

Excessive hours were clearly part of the means that companies used to maintain and enhance profits. But they were also a function of the real difficulties experienced in running and manning lines. The clock was the enemy, not just of railwaymen, but of the companies too. Lateness and unreliability in train services affected public confidence and usage and, in the worst cases, led to accidents. The Eastern Counties Railway, legendary for poor timekeeping and disorganization, became the butt of the comic and satirical press. For most companies, railway operation presented a largely novel problem of manpower organization – not just regarding labour discipline, but in the more mundane business of ensuring that labour was in the right place at the right time, whether it was enginemen to drive trains, or shunters to sort rolling stock. As railway lines proliferated and as company networks grew, a formidable task of coordination emerged. By and large, the travelling public was oblivious of the labyrinthine organization required to ensure that trains actually ran.

One way companies organized their manpower was to require railwaymen temporarily to live away from home. This applied most to enginemen and firemen, but few traffic grades were unaffected. Initially, most lodgings were in private houses, but by the last decades of the century some companies had begun building their own hostels. By 1891, the London and North Western provided accommodation in most of the cities and larger towns on its route system.[115] Where railway 'barracks' were not available, companies gave lodging allowances: the Great Western, for instance, gave 2s 6d to drivers for the first night away and 1s 6d for subsequent nights. Firemen were treated in a similar manner.[116] Lodging away from home clearly interfered with family life and was often unpopular. In the twentieth century, it became a bone of contention among railwaymen and precipitated strike action by the unions. In the Victorian era, though, it is hard to imagine how companies could have operated otherwise. So-called 'double-homing' (what sociologists today call 'multiple life-domains') became an unavoidable aspect of many railwaymen's lives.

A different sort of space mobility was visited upon station grades. Station-masters and clerks were moved most frequently, often in relation to promotion. On the London, Brighton and South Coast Railway between 1865 and 1869, roughly one in ten station-masters moved his place of work, and roughly one in five clerks.[117] On the Midland Railway, a young man from Bedfordshire called George Simmons obtained his first employment as a porter at Coalville in Leicestershire in May 1875. Over the ensuing 44 years, until his retirement in 1919, his career with the Midland company took in nine different geographical locations, spread across the breadth of midland and northern England.[118] In this sense, joining the railway company was a decision that dictated a course for life. It was a pattern repeated over and again, in varying measure, on every other railway company system.

Some commentators have seen the labour organization of Victorian railway companies as a foretaste of the scientific management strategies of the later twentieth century.[119] One of the clearest similarities is a highly differentiated internal labour structure. But equally significant is the facility created within the different labour divisions for the development of a sense of autonomy and self-identity. However, if it was such a managerial structure, it clearly failed in its wider purpose – as witnessed by increasingly widespread labour unrest which became a feature of the industry in the last years of the century, not to mention the articulation of that unrest within the framework of national trades unions. For critics of such interpretations, there remains no escape from the fact that railway labour had as many social-psychological dimensions as material ones, although there were senses in which it added new dimensions to the meaning of work. This was no factory-style labour system in the classic tradition of industrial capitalism, even if it could still sometimes visit upon its employees similar measures of exploitation.

214, 215. The Great Eastern Railway's hostel for train crews at Stratford, East London, c. 1911. The partitions off the corridor (above) hid sleeping cubicles.

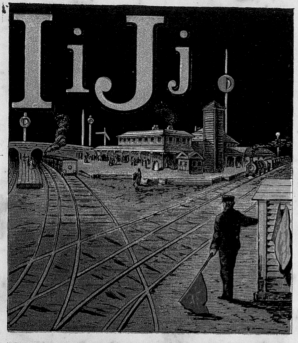

7

EDUCATION AND SOCIAL REPRODUCTION

Education was to be set up as an autonomous
practice, spread over the entire surface of society,
with a distinct purpose.[1]

ONE OF THE GREAT CRUSADES of Victorian society was the desire to educate its younger generations. Features of the British educational system today reflect the system that was developed in the mid nineteenth century. Amid the social turmoil of the 1830s and 1840s, the propertied classes saw it as a paramount necessity to diffuse knowledge among the lower orders. Not to do so, according to Dr James Kay in 1832, would be to invite an explosive violence in which the very fabric of society might be destroyed.[2] The birth of a universal system of education, however, proved a highly contested one, especially where the respective roles of Church and State were concerned.[3] One of its critical constituents became a system of nationwide school inspectors, and by 1860 the Education Department in London was employing sixty men for the task. That year they visited over 10,000 schools, a prodigious feat for so small a band of civil servants.[4] What contributed to this remarkable productivity was the facility afforded by the expanding railway system to travel the length and breadth of the country.[5] So, just as the railway offered to the governments of the 1840s a means to move troops around to quell social disturbance, it also enabled school inspectors simultaneously to instill a different and more subtle kind of social order.

One of the hallmarks of any educational regime is the imprinting in young minds of certain intellectual and moral traits necessary to sustain the social formations within which they are born. In Victorian Britain, this requirement was met through the harsh discipline of the schoolroom, rote learning and the prominence of religious instruction. Intellectual development naturally relied more on the nature of the subject material, whether it was the examples used in arithmetic calculation or the social narratives used in teaching pupils to read or write. Recovering the particular format of this subject matter is difficult. Most ordinary schools had no textbooks in any conventional sense. One must therefore look at children's literature more widely to begin to apprehend the measure of the engagement of the railway in the educational field. Inevitably, this predisposes enquiry to the realm of the middle classes. But since this was the fastest-growing of the social formations of the Victorian era and the one to which upwardly mobile working-class groups aspired, it is perhaps less limiting than might at first be supposed.

216 (opposite). Page from *Warne's Railway ABC*, c. 1865.

217. The railway as featured in a set of 96 multiplication cards in rhyme, c. 1850. The idea of 'conquest' repeated a pattern found in many descriptive accounts of the railway expansion of the 1830s.

4 times 8 | **are 32.**
A conquest gained | by Britons true

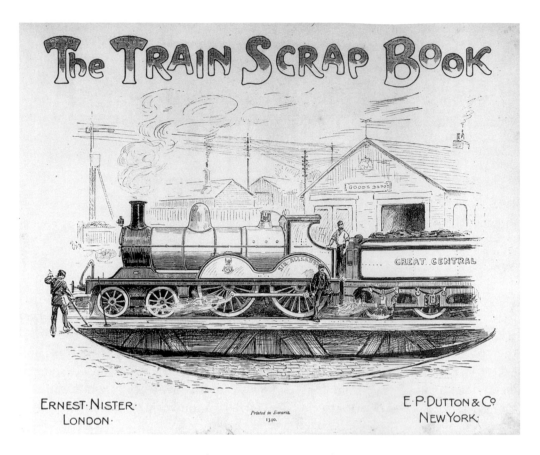

'EDUCATING WILLY'

Willy at that instant heard a great rumbling noise, and,
turning round, he saw a strange-looking carriage full
of fire inside, and, as it rolled on, it made a terrible
whizzing noise, and a great deal of white smoke came
out of it. Willy thought it was on fire . . .[6]

This passage is from a children's story-book published in 1847, which appears to
have had a two-fold purpose: first, to help quell the common fears and anxieties
about the early railway; secondly, to convey something of its scientific wonder,
including instruction in the basic principles of steam locomotion.

The railway entered the realm of children's literature with remarkable speed.
But just as stories set in the space age figured in children's comics of the 1950s,[7] it
is no surprise that the wonder of the age of the 1840s was quickly adapted in
rather similar ways. Writers and publishers were quick to set the novelty of the
railway within the realms of ordinary educational practice. Thomas Dean & Son
issued a 'railway alphabet' in the mid 1840s, probably the first of its kind;[8] the
formula was re-used by different publishers throughout the Victorian period. The
choice of alphabet words was both fascinating and banal. 'F' was for fog, which
was hardly railway-specific. 'A' was for arch – according to the picture on the card,
the great triumphal arch at Euston. 'J' was for journey, 'so pleasant to take, by
which all their money the Company make'. 'U' was for urchin, 'so simple and
small, who cannot make out how the train goes at all'. It is very likely that such
railway alphabets were for the most part seen by children who already knew their
ABC. Thus their function was more to teach children about railways than to use

railways to teach them their letters. Even so, the exercise is a revealing one. The identity of the railway company with capital in the example quoted above is unambiguously portrayed. That there were many who experienced great difficulty in comprehending the sight of a railway engine is also made fully apparent. In later railway alphabets, the selection of words changes somewhat, as the extraordinary character of the railway faded. Thus in *The Railway ABC* published by Frederick Warne around 1865 (illustrated on page 194) the focus is more upon the various tasks perfomed by company personnel.[9] The letter 'J' was for junction, where a solitary pointsman stood outside his stand with red flag at the ready. 'K' stood for key, 'which the guard retains, lest men should leap out of moving trains'. The letter 'L' stood for lamp, the accompanying illustration depicting a railway porter preparing lamps for use on a journey. 'M' was for mail, and was pictured by a General Post Office railway van and its on-board officials. Another alphabet of around 1879, published by George Routledge & Sons, used the word 'excursion' to represent the letter 'X' (using 'ex-' in this way became common in late Victorian children's alphabets, whereas earlier ones had avoided the problem by omitting the letter altogether). The same alphabet identified the letters 'Q' and 'R' with quick and run, with a picture of a passenger and attendant porter hurrying to catch a train on the point of departure.[10] In both Dean's and Warne's earlier alphabets, 'Q' had stood for Queen (referring to the young Queen Victoria's early patronage of the railway) and 'R' for rail; by the late 1870s, however, the increasingly familiar life of haste had become the appropriate exemplar.

219. Cards from Thomas Dean and Son's *Cousin Chatterbox's Railway alphabet*, c. 1845.

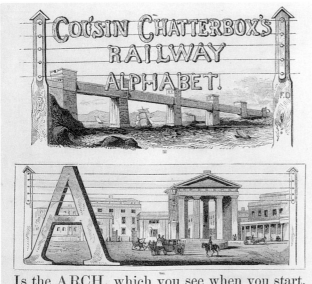

Is the ARCH, which you see when you start,
That people pass under before they depart.

Is a BUFFER, with pads so complete,
It saves you from jolts when the carriages meet.

Is the STATION, with bustle and din,
Where some folks get out, and others get in.

Is the TUNNEL, that's under the ground,
Here the whistle is heard with a very long sound.

Is the URCHIN, so simple and small,
Who cannot make out how the train goes at all.
V is the VIADUCT crossing the road,
Where the river beneath it is oft overflowed.

The railway ABC was obviously one way in which children could be introduced to the distinctive vocabulary of the railway. Most, for instance, feature a station for the letter 'S'. In Dean's alphabet of 1845, this was characterized by 'bustle and din', where 'some folks get out and others get in'.[11] The word 'station' had been unknown on the Stockton and Darlington line when it opened in 1825; some other early railways used the French word 'depot'.[12] Francis Whishaw included 'station' in the glossary of his *Analysis of Railways*, but allied it with 'depot' in cases where there were warehouses attached.[13] By the 1840s, 'station' apparently had an almost universal currency;[14] even so, its novelty remained. Some children's books dealt explicitly with the railway's new language, offering explanations of words like 'terminus' and 'train'.[15] 'Train' had its origins in the phrase 'train of wagons' or 'train of carriages',[16] with 'a steam engine attached to draw them along the line of railway';[17] subsequently, the word came to be used on its own, or else juxtaposed with 'railway'. Passenger class distinctions were also noted in the existence of separate carriages for different class groups.[18]

There were many other kinds of alphabets for Victorian children, and in some of these the railway also made an appearance. *Master Punch's Comic Alphabet* of around 1842 illustrated the letter 'E' with engine – 'a won-der-ful Engine, that runs upon a rail'.[19] The illustration was in classic *Punch* style, but it is not clear what was being satirized. In the early 1850s, *The New London Alphabet in Rhyme* offered for 'N' the 'counterfeit' example of the new station at King's Cross:

220. Page from *Master Punch's Comic Alphabet*, c. 1842.

> N's the great Northern Station, the newest of all.
> If northward you'd travel, 'tis here you should call.[20]

At the head of the page is an engraving of Lewis Cubitt's powerful design for the station, the arrival and departure trainsheds projected right through to the frontal exterior in a way uncharacteristic compared with many previous treatments.

The economic functions of the railway occasionally figured in children's literature. Griffith & Farran published *The History of the Quartern Loaf* in 1860, one of its pages showing a railway train taking flour to London.[21] The same publisher also produced histories of tea, sugar, coal, cotton and gold but, curiously, the railway does not feature in any of those, even though coal was easily the railway's staple traffic.[22] The verses are nevertheless instructive in other ways. The flour 'sold to the London man' is illustrative of the concentration of capital in commodity trading. The metaphor of flight appears again, as well as the life of haste with which the railway became so associated.

The story of railways told by the Religious Tract Society, in the form of a conversation piece between father and son, also returned to the metaphor of flight.[23] The child, responding to the knowledge that Stephenson's 'Rocket' ran at an average speed of 28–30 miles an hour, remarked how it was 'almost like flying', and wondered whether they will not 'go on discovering, till we shall fly'.[24] When the father takes his son on a railway journey, he observes how the train starts 'quite in time' and states that 'where time is an object, railway travelling is a great improvement'. Further, 'a saving of time, to a man who knows how to improve it, is a saving of money'.[25] A declaration that better encapsulates the age would be hard to find – it could almost be straight out of Marx's critique of capitalist political economy. Even more revealing, it is contained within a children's storybook; moreover, one issued under a religious imprint. The religious label becomes intelligible when the father likens the railway journey to life's journey, with the

This is the flying Railway Train
Hasting away with might and main;
For the flour has been sold to a London man,
Who wants it for baking as soon as he can,
To make the Quartern Loaf with.

221. The railway as featured in the *History of the Quartern Loaf*, 1860.

stations as the different phases of life, and ascents or gradients the symbols of life's adversities.[26] This metaphor was widely adapted and evangelized by temperance groups.[27]

For children, as much as for adults, the view from the railway carriage and the sensations of railway travel were coloured by not a little incomprehension. When 'Willy' travelled on the railway in the 1840s, he saw from his carriage window 'houses and trees and fields, looking as if they were moving'. Sheep appeared the size of lambs and houses looked like the 'baby houses' found in toy-shops.[28] The author was endeavouring to record the difficulty people had in appreciating how fast they were actually travelling, especially when it became common for all passengers to be in enclosed carriages. There was also a problem in the experience of perspective, in registering that objects grew smaller as they became more distant from the observer and bigger as they grew nearer. The unaccustomed speed of railway travel enormously extended the purview within which perspective became significant, and it was further enhanced by the elevated vantage points of the permanent way. Robert Ballantyne, in a railway tale for children, described how those who travelled in carriages at 60 miles per hour formed only the faintest conception of the pace that they were going. To realize it to the full, one needed to stand on the engine. From the carriage window 'houses, fields, trees, cattle, human beings go by in wild confusion – they appear only to vanish'.[29]

Predictably, much Victorian children's literature addressed the technology of the age. One offering encapsulated the genre. In *Three Useful Giants: wind, water and steam* (published by Thomas Dean & Son), steam was described as follows:

Without his aid to cook our meat,
 Queer dinners we should see;
Nor could we have the kettle boiled
 For breakfast or for tea.

This giant he has eyes of flame,
 And cheeks of ruddy glow,
The mother is as pale and cold
 As either ice or snow

But he, my son, hot, fierce, and bold,
 There's nothing can restrain,
But iron prisons, hoops, and bars,
 When he his way would gain.

But when restrained obedient, then,
 He'll to his masters be,
Performing every task they set,
 Though he'll not work when free.[30]

In the *Young Student's Holiday Book*, probably written around 1870, railway building is described:

> An iron railway is constructed by first cutting a way through the country towards the place at which it is to terminate; but as no country is completely level, and as it is requisite that a railroad should be nearly as level as possible, hills must be cut through, and archways formed over valleys . . .

The extract went on to explain how, once these tasks were complete,

> . . . straight bars of iron are laid along the whole length of way made for them, in lines parallel to each other, which form a track on which the wheels travel. In most roads two lines are used, – one for going, and one for returning.[31]

This is remarkably similar in language and expression to descriptions of the railways dating from the 1830s – even thirty years on, the novelty of the permanent way appeared to be undiminished, perhaps because railway companies were still breaking new territory. The principle of vehicles being guided by fixed tracks (part of the railway's 'machine ensemble') also remains a prominent image, although it must have become less striking as tramways proliferated in the cities of the late Victorian age.

In *Stories of Inventions* (1887), the author reminded his child readers of the great doubts that had prevailed about the use of steam locomotives rather than horses on railways. Although colliery railways were using them years before they were tried on the Stockton–Darlington line, 'seeing was not believing'. Popular scepticism had been so strong at Newcastle, despite the great opportunities there for observing locomotive haulage, that in 1824 a scheme was floated for a canal linking Newcastle with Carlisle. Popular, and some informed, opinion was generally against the 'new-fangled' invention.[32] Nevertheless, the opening day of the Stockton and Darlington Railway, 27 September 1825,

222. Railways 'then' and 'now', from Dean and Son's *Victoria Toy Book*, c. 1890.

THEN

Now.

was kept throughout the district as a holiday; and horses, gigs, carts, and other vehicles, filled with people, stood along the railway, as well as crowds of persons on foot, waiting to see the train pass.[33]

Such a scale of interest was not unqualified enthusiasm, but rather a fascination with the spectacle of steam locomotion, including all the accompanying doubts and terrors. The author of *Sergeant Bell and his raree show* talked of the Manchester and Liverpool Railroad as 'having made so much noise in the world', claiming that in Germany and elsewhere abroad 'nothing is asked of Englishmen, but about the Thames Tunnel and the Manchester Railroad'.[34]

In *Discoveries and Inventions of the Nineteenth Century* (1876), the child reader was introduced to the idea of railways underground – namely, the Metropolitan Railways. While most stations had 'roofs of the ordinary kind, open to the sky', two stations were completely underground, with roofs 'formed by the arches of brickwork immediately below the streets'. These were the stations at Gower Street and Baker Street. Although underground, they needed little in the way of artificial light by day – they were 'illuminated' by lateral openings through the springing of the roof arches, which were lined with white glazed tiles and covered in with glass. The combined result was to transmit and diffuse daylight in a most ingenious manner.[35] Artists and print-makers were quick to offer depictions of this novel phenomemon. Towards the end of the century, the 'tube' railway

223 (below). *The Twopenny Tube,* from Nister's *Train Scrap Book,* c. 1900.

224 (bottom). Samuel Hodson, Baker Street station on London's Metropolitan Railway, watercolour, c. 1865. Note the method for allowing daylight on to the platform areas.

appeared in London, and *The Train Scrap Book* for children of the early 1900s included a fine line drawing of the famous 'Twopenny Tube'.[36]

Following the prodigious feats of the various railway companies in carrying people to the Great Exhibition in London in 1851, the vogue of 'sight-seeing', particularly among middle-class families, became progressively more established. Not long after the Crystal Palace extravaganza, March's *Library of Instruction and Amusement* issued *The Birth Day Present*.[37] This included an account of a trip by train to the 'London sights', namely St Paul's, the shipping ('so noble with banners unfurled') and the shops ('with fronts of plate glass framed in marble and gold'). *Annie and Jack in London*, number 77 in George Routledge & Sons' series of sixpenny toy books, was another, later sight-seeing story. A revealing feature is the sentiment of one of the children on the up journey:

> And though they had not a long journey to go,
> The train seemed to Annie uncommonly slow.[38]

Whether this is the view of the child or of the adult writer does little to diminish the force of the observation that, by the later 1860s, people could conceivably think of railway travel as slow. The same notion appears in *Aunt Louisa's holiday guest*:

> Home for the Holidays, here we go;
> Bless me, the train is exceedingly slow.[39]

225. Illustration from *Aunt Louisa's Holiday Guest*, c. 1870. A group of schoolboys urge the engineer to hurry them home for the holidays.

BOARD GAMES AND JIG-SAW PUZZLES

> . . . games also became part of the industrial and social
> life of entire nations, reflecting changing ideas and
> ideals, particularly during periods of major upheaval.[40]

Educating Willy was not confined to the realm of alphabets or books. Another medium was the board game. One early example was *Wallis's Locomotive Game of Railroad Adventures*, published about 1840.[41] Printed on linen and folded in the format of a map, the game had forty-eight picture squares, arranged in double-banked manner around the sides. They depicted railway engines, carriages and wagons; station frontages, including the Euston Arch; engines in snowdrifts; engines off the rails, and passengers losing their hats while at speed in open carriages. Many appear to have been copied, in both format and subject, from contemporary prints. Players drew counters to play, which allowed the usual options of advancing, being sent back or missing a turn. A player won by reaching the central square, which was embellished with a picture of Britannia.

Wallis produced another railway game around the same time, which was a modification of one produced in 1794. *Wallis's New Railway Game, or Tour through England and Wales* consisted of a coloured county map, with railway lines overlaid in black.[42] The game was played with a 'totum' not a dice (a device that was apparently introduced to avoid bringing an obvious symbol of gaming into decent-living households[43]). Players used a 'pyramid' or 'traveller' as position marker (not a train, interestingly), and position points were town-based – some with railway stations, some without. London, number 117, was the goal. Although

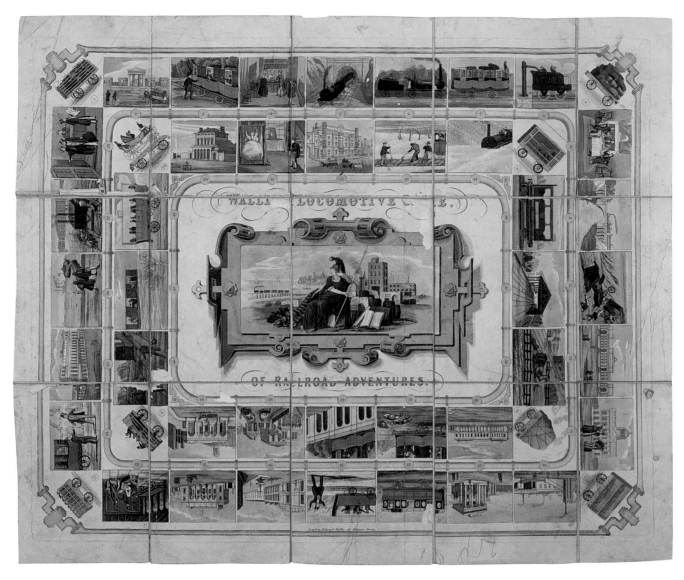

226. Wallis's locomotive
game, 1840.

clearly intended for adults as well as for children, the educational power of such a
game was plain. The key provided topographical, historical and other details for
each of the 117 towns. At Cambridge, the 'traveller' was penalized two turns to
visit the colleges. At Gloucester, he or she stayed over one turn 'to view the cathedral, the ship canal, and extensive improvements'. But at Birmingham, 'celebrated
throughout the world for its manufactures', as the key recorded, the player did not
delay, but jumped forward 27 points. 'Railway here, go on to 83', the text stated,
providing a dramatic symbol of the time–space compression instituted by the
railway and of the speed with which such transformations registered within the
popular realm. The game's subtitle was instructive in this respect. As a 'Tour
through England and Wales', it was clearly as much a topographical excursion as
a game of chance, and such landscape forays were enormously enhanced by the
facility of the railway, as a growing number of railway travel books testified. One
early example of the genre was T. Roscoe's *Home and Country Scenes on each side
of the line of the London and Birmingham and Grand Junction Railways*, apparently a compendium volume of two separate guides that Roscoe had originally
produced for the two railways. [44]

Race games like Wallis's had their origins in the middle of the eighteenth century, when they were used to teach history, elementary mathematics, mythology and astronomy. Race games for amusement, however, appear to have become widely available only in the 1830s.[45] One published by William Spooner in 1848, *The Cottage of Content*, had 'Right Roads and Wrong Ways', including a 'Rattle away Road' which depicted a railway train, the same train also appearing on the game's outer cover.[46]

One railway board game, published towards the end of the nineteenth century, reaffirmed the educational purpose that was attached to some of its eighteenth-century predecessors. *Binko's Registered Railway Game* showed a county map of England upon which were imprinted the principal lines and stations. Its rule-book was prefaced:

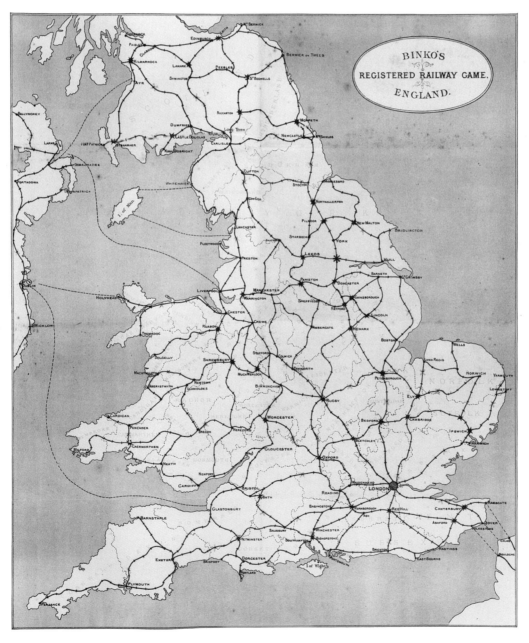

227. Binko's railway game, late nineteenth century.

the present system for teaching geography in schools is not sufficiently practi-cal, so much so that a number of children are in doubt concerning the top-ography of their own native land. A great part of the above is explained by the study of geography being distasteful to a number of pupils, who prefer more interesting subjects.[47]

This game was intended to give teachers an easy method of instructing pupils in geography. Players began by choosing their intended destination and moving loco-motive markers upon the throw of a dice, encountering the usual penalty and bonus positions on the board. Whether Binko's product was ever used in schools is hard to tell, but its existence is at least suggestive of the identity of the railway with an extending knowledge of geographical space, a tendency that became apparent from the first decades of the railway era. Another railway race game of the same period, *The New Game of the Royal Mail or London to Edinburgh by the* LNWR (published by John Jaques), contained little that was educational,[48] It probably reflected the intense rivalry that developed between leading companies in the provision of train services between London and Scotland towards the close of the century.[49] The board was in the form of a strip-map showing the railway line from London to Edinburgh, with topographical and other details marked alongside it.

228. Wallis jigsaw puzzle, 1860 version of the original game of c. 1840, depicting the London and Birming-ham and Liverpool and Manchester Railways in panorama.

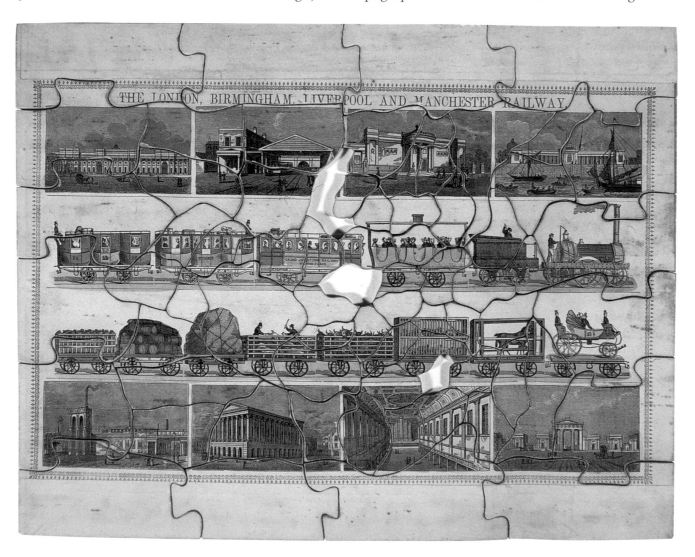

Engines were used as markers and a dice employed. Penalties involved foregoing a turn to visit the local sights – in one case Harrow's schools, in another the coal mines around Wigan.

Jig-saw puzzles provided another medium through which the spectacle of the railway could be readily depicted. The Liverpool and Manchester Railway was commemorated in a puzzle published by Wallis's late in 1830. It comprised a hand-coloured engraving in which the engine 'Northumbrian' pulls a train of carriages and trucks laden with passengers. The puzzle recorded the line's length (31 miles), the average journey time (an hour and a quarter), the line's cost and its day of opening.[50] When Charles Dickens, in *Dombey and Son* (1848), wrote of the upheavals in Camden Town connected with the works of the London and Birmingham Railway,[51] he also remarked how the railway spawned all manner of commemorative pieces. Among these would probably have been another Wallis jig-saw puzzle, in which the London and Birmingham Railway was shown in panorama with the Liverpool and Manchester. The design, a wood engraving that featured railway buildings as well as trains,[52] appears to have had quite a long currency – it reappeared under the imprint of William Peacock about 1860, featuring a map of England and Wales on the reverse, yet another symbol of the railway's conquest of space.[53] A similar double-sided puzzle was made by J. W. Barfoot around 1850.[54] Entitled 'Railway Scenes', the design formed a curious collage, with a miniature of James Watt at the top centre, a vignette of the Newcastle high-level railway bridge at the top left, with a train and crowd of waiting passengers as the main subject in the lower half. The prices of these puzzles varied from about 1s 6d to as much as seven shillings depending on size,[55] clearly putting them within reach only of the middle classes. Cheaper, more simply made items were also produced, many from Holland, but none appears to have survived.[56]

SHEET MUSIC

Oh! My Johnny is the driver of a big *Engine*,
On the Railway line, oh! he looks so fine,
And on Pancake day he's to be mine,
Is Johnny the Engine driver.[57]

Among the middle classes of Victorian Britain, the piano forte occupied a central position in the society of the family. Just as the books and games of the period were quick to record the 'railway wonder', so too did the scores of popular music. Predictably, perhaps, the initial object of such compositions was to try to convey the rhythm of the steam blast. This was clearly the intention of a *Characteristic Rondo* by S. Bryan, published probably in the early 1830s.[58] Its cover carried a picture of the famous viaduct over the Sankey valley on the Liverpool and Manchester Railway. The score itself is annotated to indicate the various stages in the journey from Manchester to Liverpool; the tempo is continuouously adjusted, according to assumed changes in speed. A crescendo is reached with the passing of the train through the Liverpool tunnel, echoing the striking combination of fear and fascination that such subterranean experiences brought to early railway travellers. In Jos Gung'l's *Railroad Steam Engine* galop (1840), a separate stave accommodated the rhythm of the steam blast, with a note suggesting how to imitate the noise.[59]

229. Jos Gung'l, *Railroad Steam Engine*, galop for the pianoforte, 1840: cover and part of the instructions in the score for imitating the sound of a steam engine.

Here, then, is another vivid reminder of the way in which the steam railway became fixed in popular minds – it was not just the sensations of sight and smell that fascinated people, but equally the sound. William Wilkes's *Quadrille* for the piano forte (c. 1840) carried a picture of the newly opened London and Birmingham Railway at the Wolverton viaduct;[60] here, the association between music and railway was somewhat cosmetic, appearing largely to be a case of a music publisher looking for a topical picture. Perhaps the best-known railway image to be depicted on a sheet music score is the moonlit scene of the Dee viaduct across the Vale of Llangollen, which featured on Charles d'Albert's *Express Galop* (c. 1855).[61] The piece offered a clear echo of the rhythm of the steam blast, much in the manner of earlier compositions. The train on the cover is obviously moving across the viaduct at speed, with its near-horizontal smoke trail. The contrast of dark and light leads the eye straight to the viaduct top with its train in flight.

As the railway became a more familiar part of the Victorian scene, so the manner of its representation in popular music altered. The growth of cheap excursion traffic, for example, brought a 'tender narrative' song by Vandervell and Vandervell. The music cover of this (and the subsequent examples in this chapter) was by the popular artist Alfred Concanen. It depicts a crowd of people fighting to get into a train marked 'Brighton'. The piece is undated, but is likely to be from the late 1840s or early 1850s, when excursion traffic, particularly to seaside towns like Brighton, had reached massive levels.[62] Subsequent musical offerings tended to focus on the personnel of the railway and the variety of social associations that railway travel drew. In turn, the music-hall style of song rather than the piano forte solo became the dominant medium. In G. P. Norman's *Great Semaphore Song: There's Danger on the Line* (c. 1855), the cover shows a railway guard in the middle of the tracks holding up a red lamp.[63] This was essentially a song that explored the way the railway journey could be cast as a metaphor for life, especially in terms of courtship and matrimony.[64] Similar romantic associations figured in G. W. Munt's *Johnny the Engine Driver* (c. 1867).[65] Here, the engineman was portrayed much in the manner of the soldier or sailor – a brave heart for the object of feminine affections. Among the more amusing of this genre of railway songs was a piece composed by Alfred Plumpton, *The Railway Guard, or the Mail Train to the North*.[66] It was dedicated to the Chairman and Directors of the London and North Western Railway, and dates from about 1866. The cover shows an LNWR guard on a station platform beside a second-class carriage in which sits a 'buxom wench'. The words of the song relate an all-too-common tale. The woman complains to the guard that she has been insulted by a gentleman in her compartment; on investigation, the guard discovers a basket of game-fowls beneath her seat, which have been pecking at her stockings. The moral of the tale, according to the last verse, was for all young men to be warned of the danger of riding in a train at night with a female all alone.

230 (opposite). Charles d'Albert, *The Express Galop*, c. 1855.

Following pages

231. G. P. Norman, *The Great Semaphore Song: There's Danger on the Line.*

232. Arthur Lloyd, *The Railway Guard*, c. 1866.

3/74

BRANDARD

CHARLES D'ALBERT.

THE GREAT SEMAPHORE SONG.

THERE'S DANGER ON THE LINE.

STANNARD & SON. IMP.T

WRITTEN & COMPOSED BY

G. P. NORMAN,

SUNG WITH THE GREATEST SUCCESS

BY

G. H. MACDERMOTT.

The first toy trains were in the hands of children almost
as soon as the first railways started running.[67]

The Victorians were acutely aware of the potential value of toys in improving and extending young minds. It has been suggested that Victorian fathers inaugurated an era of 'scientific' and 'philosophical' toys.[68] The magic lantern, a primitive kind of slide projector, was perhaps one of the most singular examples. Another was the model steam-engine, a true working replica of the life-size version. Some of these models were stationary, others mobile. Typically, they were made of brass, and the mobile versions were often known as 'dribblers' due to the trails of water left by their steam cylinders.[69] One key to the growth of the toy trade, as to the expansion in children's literature, was the improving standard of living of the Victorian middle classes. By the closing decades of the nineteenth century, the efficiency of the toy industry, both organizational and technical, meant that it became increasingly possible to produce toys for all but the poorest of families. Thus was born the era of the 'penny toy'.[70]

In France, firms were making toy trains in considerable numbers as early as 1835, the majority from sheet tin.[71] In England, it is not easy to establish the date of the first toy train, for very few survive. The Kirkstall Abbey Museum has a replica of a Liverpool and Manchester train, made from wood and dating from about 1840; it runs along a short track lined with trees and contains twelve passengers.[72] A toy train of roughly similar date in the Hove Museum, is made of metal.[73] By around 1870, there was a definable industry manufacturing model trains, ranging from 'delicate hand-painted trains from France, all the way to ponderous, brass, live steam locomotives mainly of English manufacture'.[74] In between were various items from Germany, including traditional carved wooden toys and tinplate toys from the factories around Nuremberg where sheet-metal stamping was first perfected in 1815.[75]

A notable feature of toy trains of the era from about 1870 to 1900 was their retrospective design. There appeared to be a curious reluctance to model anything that was at all contemporary.[76] A tinplate and cast alloy clockwork train manufactured by Britain's of London in the 1880s was in a style reminiscent of railways in their first decades of existence;[77] much the same was true of many German productions. Nor were they often very faithful reproductions of the real-world objects; not until around 1900 was there a clear shift in taste for 'realism over fantasy'. Then came the true scale railway model, led by firms like Bassett-Lowke in Britain and later imitated on the Continent by Carette, Marklin and Bing, all making trains specifically for the British market and following British prototypes.[78] Manufacturers also started to think of the toy train not just as an object in itself but as part of a system, a whole world in miniature. Train sets came to incorporate a whole range of accessories, including station buildings.[79]

The initial tendency towards retrospective designs, and sometimes rather naïve ones at that, was in part related to the way in which the first passenger-carrying railways in Britain caused such a public sensation, on the Continent as well as at home. A wonder of the age, the 'Liverpool–Manchester Railroad' was

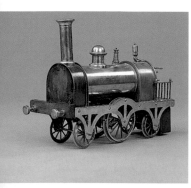

233. Working model steam engine in brass, British, c. 1870.

234. Toy engine in the form of an inkwell, British, c. 1856.

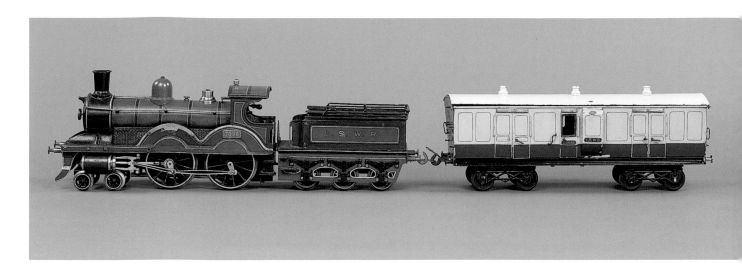

reproduced for many years, its popularity among artists and engravers reinforcing the trend. Eventually, the fading of this novelty and the progressive refinement of steam locomotive technology probably altered the focus towards toy trains as scale models. Improvements in casting and in sheet-metal stamping ultimately gave Edwardian schoolboys some of the finest miniature machinery ever seen.

The firm of A. W. Gamage of London became Britain's most famous retailer of toy trains; by 1906, their catalogue had some 150 types available.[80] These were nearly all German-made, and some were derived from German prototypes, but increasingly Gamages sought out accurate replicas of British railway systems. They were matched by the Northampton-based firm of W. J. Bassett-Lowke, whose catalogue in 1904 ran to 252 pages.[81] However, whereas Gamage's followed a marketing strategy that embraced scale models for adults as well as train sets for young children, Bassett-Lowke aimed at the adult enthusiast. Once again, however, the suppliers were German toy-makers, Marklin and Bing among them. Even in toy-shops in the English provinces, it was not British-made trains that adorned their windows, but products from the Continent.[82]

235. Toy train as a scale model, replica of a London and South Western Railway locomotive and van, German, 1902–6.

236. Toy train as a scale model, replica of a Caledonian railway 'Cardean' class locomotive, German, c. 1910.

WEST ENTRANCE, SUMMIT TUNNEL.

8

REPRESENTATIONS IN ART

Fully aware that we have jealous and fastidious critics to
deal with, both in the houses of parliament, & out of
them, I wish to remove, or at least to check, the tide
of prejudice against us, and display our powers,
capabilities & efforts.[1]

PART OF THE REMARKABLE FAME enjoyed by the Liverpool and Manchester Railway derived from its being drawn or painted by various artists whose work was then transformed into lithographs for public sale and consumption, a technology that was just coming into its own.[2] Over the first two decades of railway expansion, perhaps as many as two thousand different lithographs were made of railway lines or scenes – some as one-off items, others as loosely stitched or bound collections that sold for anything from a shilling to almost five pounds.[3] Such pictures became integral to the cultural production of the railway – in some cases, they were a direct means of promotion, part of the resolute efforts that many early railway companies were forced to make in the face of widespread opposition. The object was to try to create a public and accessible image, one that bred confidence in railway enterprise. However, artists themselves soon established an increasingly distinctive iconography of the railway, at once heroic in constructional scale, dramatic and sometimes highly radical in landscape form, and endlessly suggestive of the spirit of the age. The railway offered artists a particular opportunity for examining the interface between art and industrialization, a movement that had found primary inspiration in Coalbrookdale in Shropshire, especially in the paintings of de Loutherbourg.[4] Artists also sought to explore the experience of the railway against the background of the radical and sometimes disturbing transformations in thought and belief that characterized the Victorian age. Moreover, the pictures they drew or painted not only reflected the emerging patterns of social life, but became active in creating them. Some attempt has been made here to follow familiar canons of art-historical interpretation, but ultimately the purpose has been 'to specify the potential functions and effects of such images upon an historical and ideological field of social practices and meanings'.[5]

PICTORIAL PRODUCTION AND CONSUMPTION

Ackerman took the principles of the division of labour
established by the eighteenth-century print makers and
developed them to a pitch of great excellence.[6]

When the directors of the Liverpool and Manchester Railway saw the measure of the opposition to their enterprise, specifically in relation to local vested interests

237. A. F. Tait, west entrance to the Summit tunnel, Manchester and Leeds Railway, lithograph, 1845.

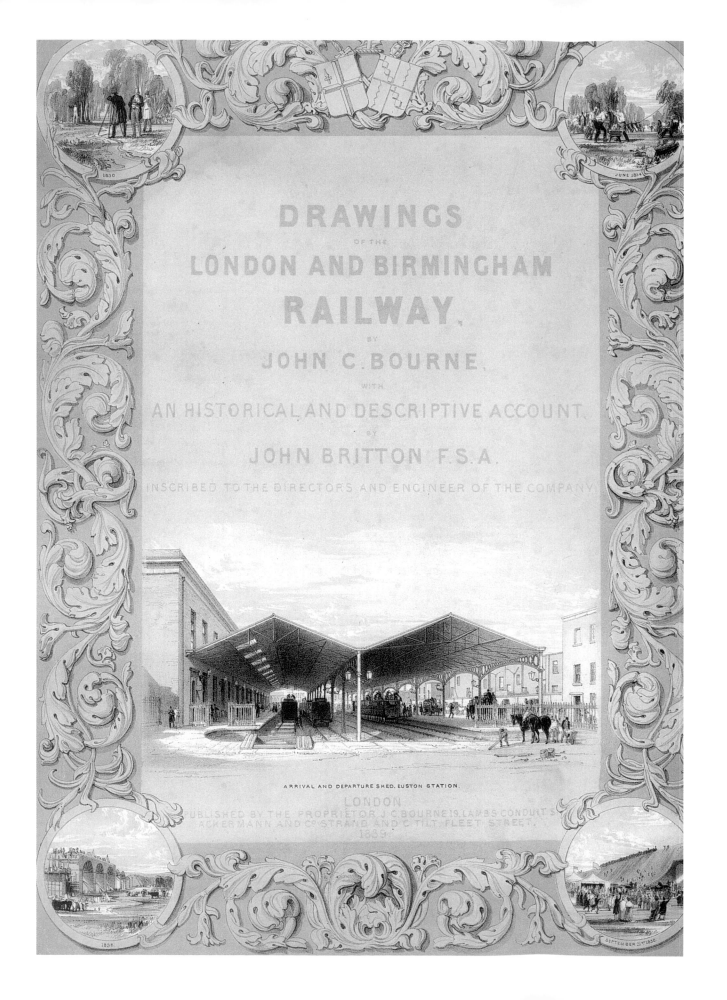

DRAWINGS
OF THE
LONDON AND BIRMINGHAM
RAILWAY,
BY
JOHN C. BOURNE,
WITH
AN HISTORICAL AND DESCRIPTIVE ACCOUNT,
BY
JOHN BRITTON F.S.A.
INSCRIBED TO THE DIRECTORS AND ENGINEER OF THE COMPANY.

ARRIVAL AND DEPARTURE SHED, EUSTON STATION.

LONDON.
PUBLISHED BY THE PROPRIETOR J. C. BOURNE 19, LAMBS CONDUIT S.
ACKERMANN AND Cᵒ STRAND AND C. TILT, FLEET STREET,
1839.

239. T. T. Bury, aquatint, 1831, of the skew bridge at Rainhill on the Liverpool and Manchester Railway.

and generally in relation to popular disbelief about the merits of railroad technology, they engaged the help of Rudolf Ackerman, one of the most distinguished lithographic publishers of the day. In effect, the company was embarking upon what today would be described as an exercise in corporate advertising. Ackerman commissioned a series of pictures from a young architect, T. T. Bury, later to become known for his collaboration with the younger Pugin.[7] The resulting studies proved a roaring commercial success. The original six prints grew to a collection of thirteen, and some were re-engraved. There were Spanish and Italian editions, while separate copies of the prints were also produced in France and Germany.[8] The company's extreme sensitivity to its public image was clearly apparent in the alterations that were made to a number of the early engravings: in one, a steam locomotive had been depicted inside the Edge Hill tunnel, whereas the railway's authorizing Act prohibited the use of steam propulsion there.[9] It was largely through the medium of the Bury prints that the Liverpool and Manchester Railway acquired such international renown. Moreover, contemporary with the Bury series, Ackerman also published the famous 'long prints' of the railway, the artist in this case being Isaac Shaw.[10] The company does not, however, appear to have been directly involved in the launch of the Shaw pictures, nor with a second series of prints that Shaw himself published (the series was planned to contain twenty scenes, but only eight were ever issued).[11] Some artists found their inspiration in depicting the Liverpool and Manchester Railway from what they already knew of the Stockton and Darlington Railway, opened in 1825. This must certainly have been the case with Calvert's picture of the line at Newton, for it was dated 1825, some time before construction had begun.[12] The scene was thus imaginary, but none the less significant for being so.

238 (opposite). J. C. Bourne, title page of folio, *Drawings of the London and Birmingham Railway*, 1839.

The public relations efforts of the Liverpool and Manchester Railway's directors were repeated, if in a more roundabout way, on the London and Birmingham Railway.[13] J. C. Bourne began recording construction scenes on the line in 1836.[14] His work came to the notice of the antiquarian John Britton, who was an enthusiastic railway supporter. The result was the publication of a series of 36 drawings to which the then secretaries of the line lent their support, allowing specimens to be exhibited at stations along it.[15] Bourne's folio of pictures, however, did not meet with the same commercial success as T. T. Bury's for the Liverpool and Manchester. This was true, too, of Bourne's later volume on the Great Western Railway.[16] For all the work's 'simplicity, boldness and drama',[17] it appeared at a time when confidence in railways was at a turning-point. By late 1846, the year of publication, railway investment was in a state of collapse.

Artists who depicted other lines and other companies often did so with the tacit support, if not the direct involvement, of their secretaries or directors. D. O. Hill's views of the Glasgow and Garnkirk line came about as the result of a request by a friend connected with the company.[18] A. F. Tait's views of the Manchester and Leeds Railway were dedicated to the officers of the railroad.[19] Tait's brother-in-law was station-master at Brighouse and it appears that this is where Tait may have stayed while executing his work. However, there is no evidence to indicate how the company's board received the pictures of the line, or whether it in any way supported their publication.[20] J. W. Carmichael, who made drawings of the Newcastle and Carlisle Railway, apparently did so at the express suggestion of the line's directors.[21] His work was published in the same year as Bourne's remarkable folio of the London–Birmingham line.[22] It appears to have been mainly in the 1830s that railway boards saw publication of prints of their ventures as valuable propaganda in the face of often fierce opposition from many quarters of society. The prints helped to educate a suspicious public in what was

then a novel and, for some, very frightening technology. By the 1840s, however, familiarity with the railway meant that propaganda of this sort became increasingly superfluous. There came a point, too, when the railway had *too* high a profile in the public consciousness, notably after the collapse of the Mania of 1844–7.

No figures exist of the number of copies sold of individual railway prints. Nor is there anything to indicate the size of the print runs of those that were sold in book form, or of the scale of their circulation.[23] The commercial success of T. T. Bury's Liverpool and Manchester views is indisputable, but this does not in itself tell us about the measure of their circulation or who bought them.[24] Freeling's *Grand Junction Railway Companion* (1838) incorporated a full-page advertisement for many of the Ackerman prints, including those by Bury and Shaw, which were available from a bookseller in Liverpool. However, his companion guide to the London and Birmingham Railway of almost the same date had no similar advertisement. A. F. Tait's prints of the Manchester–Leeds line appear to have been produced only for those who made advance subscriptions.[25] J. C. Bourne's folio of drawings of the London and Birmingham Railway had an impressive list of subscribers, including leading engineers, landowners and capitalists, but many patrons of the arts had no enthusiasm for the work.[26] Bourne's volumes would have had limited appeal simply by virtue of their relatively high cost, running to pounds rather than shillings. By contrast, the first edition of Bury's pictures of the Liverpool and Manchester line sold for 12*s*, and Henry Booth's slightly earlier, if inferior, set of eight views sold for 5*s* on plain paper and 7*s* 6*d* on India paper.[27]

241 (top). J. C. Bourne, *Oblique Wooden Bridge, Bath*, lithograph, 1846.

242. Richard Creed, Secretary of the London and Birmingham Railway, mezzotint by H. W. Phillips, 1848. He recognised the potential publicity value of J. C. Bourne's drawings of the line under construction.

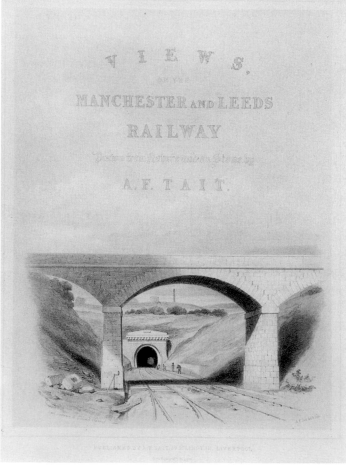

9

RAILROAD VIEWS, &c.
PUBLISHED BY
ACKERMANN & CO., LONDON,
AND SOLD BY
H. LACEY, 100, BOLD-STREET, LIVERPOOL.

TWELVE COLOURED VIEWS OF THE LIVERPOOL AND MANCHESTER RAILWAY.—In Two Parts, each containing Six Plates, from Drawings made on the Line by Mr. T. T. Bury, with descriptive particulars, and an additional Plate of Carriages. Elephant 4to. Price, each part, 12s.; or the two parts, bound together, with a View of the Intersection Bridge, which crosses the Line near the foot of the Sutton Inclined Plane, and two long sheets of Trains of Carriages, &c., showing the different ways of conveyance. Price, complete, £2 2s.

SIX VIEWS OF THE LONDON AND GREENWICH RAILWAY—Sketched on the spot by G. F. Bragg; and on stone by himself, in the improved method of two tints. Imperial 4to. Price, the set, 5s.; coloured, 9s.

FIVE COLOURED VIEWS OF THE DUBLIN AND KINGS-TOWN RAILWAY—From Drawings made on the spot by A. Nicholl, accompanied with description. Elephant 4to. Price 10s.

TWO COLOURED PLATES—Showing the different ways of conveyance on the Liverpool and Manchester Railroad, for passengers by the first and second class trains, luggage, cattle, and other live stock, merchandise, &c. Price 4s. 6d. each. The same in one sheet. on a reduced scale. Price 5s.

THE NEW GRAND ENTRANCE, LIME STREET, LIVERPOOL—Station at Edge Hill, and Lime-street station. On one sheet. Price, coloured, 5s.

VIEW OF THE INTERSECTION BRIDGE—On the line of the St. Helen's and Runcorn Gap Railway, crossing the Liverpool and Manchester line. Price, coloured, 4s. 6d.

GEOMETRICAL ELEVATION OF THE LONDON AND GREENWICH RAILWAY—Representing that portion crossing Corbett's Lane. Price, coloured, 6s.

VIEW OF THE GRAVESEND RAILROAD—As it was proposed passing through Greenwich Park. Price, coloured, 4s. 6d.

WESTMINSTER BRIDGE, DEPTFORD AND GREENWICH RAILWAY — As it will appear when viewed from the summit of the Duke of York's Column. Price, plain, 3s. 6d.; coloured, 10s. 6d.

BIRD'S EYE VIEW OF THE LONDON GRAND JUNCTION RAILWAY—From Skinner-street to Camden Town. Price, plain, 2s.; coloured, 4s.

THE ENTERPRISE STEAM OMNIBUS.—Price, in colours, 7s. 6d.

HANCOCK'S STEAM CARRIAGE.—Price, in colours, 5s.

THE THAMES TUNNEL.—Price, in colours, 5s.

THE CIVIL ENGINEER AND MECHANIST—Designed for the use of engineers, iron masters, manufacturers, and operative mechanics, &c. By C. J. Blunt and R. M. Stephenson. The working plans and general views of this work are laid down in original drawings of great practical accuracy and careful execution. Price, each part, with descriptive letter press, £1 1s. Parts I. to V. have appeared.

Leaving the subterranean darkness of the tunnel behind
. . . a long stretch of Railway, perfectly straight, opens to
our view . . . along which the majestic train of steedless
chariots passes with the rapidity of the wind.[28]

In the emerging iconography of railway art, one of the most striking themes was
the railway as straight line. It is often viewed in steeply recessional perspective, as
if offering a lesson in drawing space. Many artists chose to focus their pictures
in this way, the most powerful example perhaps being T. T. Bury's view of the
Liverpool and Manchester line as it crosses the boggy fen known as Chat Moss.[29]
Bury employed a similar treatment in some of his views of the London and
Birmingham line, published in 1837.[30] The picture of the line where it crosses the
canal at Camden Town provides an eye-level view along the lines of the track until
they converge at points on the horizon. A. F. Tait, when drawing scenes of the
Manchester and Leeds Railway, also focused on its sharp linearity – in this case
even where the physiography was such that some sections of the line could not be
straight.[31] Tait's view of Normanton station looks directly up the line of tracks
rather than at the station itself. Even in the Pennine Hills, as at Gawksholme
viaduct, the straight line of the permanent way dominates the picture. It is hard
now to imagine the sheer novelty and strangeness of the lines that the railway cut
across the landscape. Of course, the straight line had long been a feature of formal
gardens. It was also manifest sometimes in the enclosure roads constructed in the

243 (opposite). David Hill, Germiston embankment on the opening day of the Glasgow and Garnkirk Railway, 27 September 1831, lithograph, 1832.

244 (opposite, below left). A. F. Tait, title page of folio, *Views on the Manchester and Leeds Railway*, 1845.

245 (opposite, below right). Ackermann and Co., advertisement for railroad views, 1838. The highly successful 'Bury' prints head the list.

246. T. T. Bury, Liverpool and Manchester Railway traversing Chat Moss, aquatint, 1831.

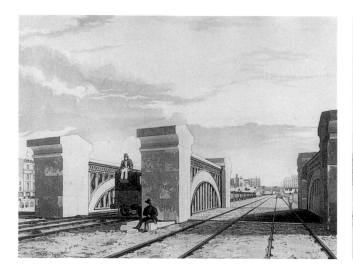

247. T. T. Bury, the rope-worked incline up from Euston to Camden Town, aquatint, 1837, a much lesser known picture of the London and Birmingham Railway.

248. A. F. Tait, view along the tracks through Normanton station on the Manchester and Leeds Railway, lithograph, 1845.

249 (right). A. F. Tait, *Gawksholme Viaduct and Bridge*, lithograph, 1845.

eighteenth century and early in the nineteenth. But to the population at large, working in fields and in factories, linearity in nature and in the cultural landscape was rare. It became a frequent feature of comment; artists, in their turn, both reflected and reinforced the phenomenon.

Where the railway intercepted an existing line of communication – turnpike, river or canal – the need to maintain linearity, or the sometimes intransigent stance of turnpike tustees, demanded that crossings were constructed in a manner that was described as 'askew', thereby creating an acute or obliquely angled bridge. Engineers had long known how to construct such bridges, but they became common only with the railway. Artists lost no time in drawing these unfamiliar structures. The first of many examples was Isaac Shaw's picture of Rainhill Bridge (1831), the point at which the Liverpool–Warrington turnpike crossed the railway.[32] Another was Bourne's arresting picture of the bridge at Box Moor on the London and Birmingham Railway.[33] In Henry Booth's series of prints of the Liverpool and Manchester Railway, the accompanying text incorporated a schedule of bridges along the line's course. This indicated the material of their construction, but also whether they were 'square' or 'askew', illustrating the fascination that such structures held.[34] The skew bridge quickly became part of the railway's iconography, alongside the sharp linearity of its landscape form.

250. Isaac Shaw, skew bridge at Rainhill on the Liverpool and Manchester Railway, etching, 1831.

The railway's linearity stemmed, of course, in significant part from its particular locomotive technology. This clearly goes some way towards enabling us to understand the fascination that observers, artists or otherwise, had with its parallel tracks and the way in which they converged on the horizon.[35] However, the linear form also bore witness to the novel power of compulsory land purchase that every railway Act conferred upon its promoters. Chat Moss, for example, was no empty landscape across which surveyors could mark out their sight lines. In some parts, it offered grazing and smallholdings which, without compulsory purchase, would have interfered seriously with the surveyor's sweeping pen. So the straight line of tracks across Chat Moss was not just a function of its prairie-like landscape; it reflected a fundamental change in land law, the railways' so-called 'invasion of the land'.[36] Even more, the recessional perspective was implicit recognition by artists of the astounding time–space transformation that the railway brought. Looking along the line of railway tracks brought home to observers the 'melting' of space, as many chose to describe it. Some, when watching the passage of trains, thought that they were actually growing physically in size. As Edward Stanley recorded in 1830:

> there is an optical deception worth noticing. A spectator observing their approach, when at extreme speed, can scarcely divest himself of the idea, that they are not enlarging and increasing in size rather than moving.

Stanley likened this to the enlargement of objects in a phantasmagoria:

> At first the image is barely discernible, but as it advances from the focal point it seems to increase beyond all limit. Thus an engine, as it draws near, appears to become rapidly magnified, and as if it would fill up the entire space between the banks, and absorb everything within its vortex. [37]

Contemporaries were unused to the dramatic time–space convergence that railway speed introduced. The recessional perspective of some railway prints offered a conception of space which was consistent with such time–space compression. It linked the near and the far in a way that was quite novel to the common eye. In this respect, it was no accident that J. M. W. Turner's famous painting *Rain, Steam, and Speed* (1845) employed just such a perspective, notwithstanding its coincident thermodynamic genius.[38] As one distinguished commentator has remarked, Turner's composition certainly bears some relation to the illustrations of T. T. Bury, even if the inspiration for his picture does not.[39]

The power of the linear form in some railway prints is thrown into sharper relief by the way in which a number of artists presented the railway as panorama, the train and its carriages running from left to right or right to left across the page. Shaw's 'long prints' follow this format, a choice made the more interesting because the artist also used the recessional view in some of his other pictures of the line. There are views of the Stockton and Darlington Railway and the Bodmin and Wadebridge line that repeat, in broad terms, the pattern of the 'long prints'.[40] All

251. C. Ingrey, *View of the Opening of the Bodmin and Wadebridge Railway* (30 September 1834), lithograph.

these pictures are fundamentally 'stills', offering no sense of the railway as a conqueror of time and space. In part, this is clearly related to the difficulties observers had in apprehending the phenomenon of railway speed. Artists were drawing according to a familiar pattern. When road-coaches, for example, seldom reached much more than ten or twelve miles an hour, it was easy for observers to form a sideways view of them. To try to do so with a railway train moving at thirty-five miles an hour was fruitless – it just became a fleeting impression. The Shaw 'long prints' gave a wealth of detail about the locomotives and their trains. However, they also presented a sanitized version of the railway – one not merely without the smoke, the fumes and the noise, but without any sense of the awesome energy and momentum of artificial locomotion.

A standard genre within lithography and its various precursor technologies was topographical imagery; it was thus entirely logical that artists and print-makers should also set the railway in this format. The view from the railway carriage, as much contemporary and later commentary makes plain, could be highly distinctive. New vistas were offered of landed seats. Early railway guide-

252. J. W. Carmichael, Corby viaduct on the Newcastle and Carlisle Railway, oil on canvas, 1836 (subsequently issued in print form).

books, taking their cue from the road-books and itineraries of John Cary and Daniel Paterson, gave railway travellers new and much more extended perspectives from which they could gain a vicarious experience of the life of the English landed élites. Meanwhile, from the vantage points of the high ground around railway lines, artists grafted the novel engineering works of the railway on to their topographical compositions. Livestock grazed peacefully beneath towering viaducts, while diminutive trains, emitting wispy lines of smoke, appeared to pass mostly unobserved by potential onlookers. J. W. Carmichael painted Corby viaduct on the Newcastle and Carlisle Railway very much in this manner,[41] and A. F. Tait's folio of views of the Manchester and Leeds Railway affords numerous examples of it.[42] Against the many eye-witness accounts of the passage of trains through the countryside, which invariably dwell upon the roar and smell of the fleeting locomotives,

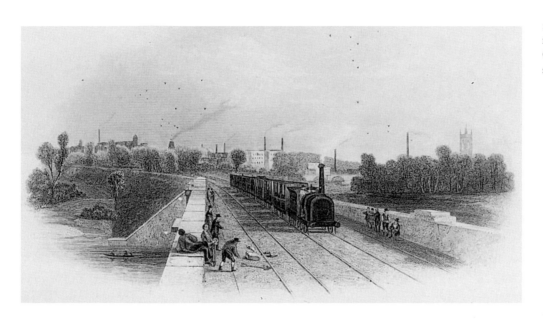

253. Thomas Roscoe, view near Warrington on the Grand Junction Railway, steel engraving, c. 1839.

these are clearly partly contrived images. However, some pictures revealed a creeping recognition of the spreading tentacles of industrialization of which the railway was obviously part. The smoking chimneys of the textile mills thus formed a counterpart to the smoking trails etched across the skies by passing steam locomotives. In Thomas Roscoe's account of the Grand Junction Railway, the chimney stacks of Warrington offered travellers on the line a measure of the town's wealth and consequence.[43]

Railway prints never really attained or approached the picture format represented by Turner's *Rain, Steam and Speed*, with all its symbolism of surging energy and movement. This was partly due to limitations in print technology, but it was also a clear reflection of the difficulties of perception that railway speed presented for observers. It is fair to claim, therefore, that Turner's painting revealed almost unique visionary powers for the time.[44] In France, it was not until 1873 that Edouard Manet addressed the same phenomenon in *The Railroad*, a picture that contained no locomotive at all, merely its product: steam.[45] Until then, no artist had managed to capture 'that strange and mysterious power which hides a volcano in its flanks', a 'monster in bronze carapace' with 'snout of fire which devours space'.[46] *Rain, Steam and Speed* can be usefully put into context alongside Turner's two parallel paintings, *The Fighting Temeraire* (1839) and *The Burning of the*

Houses of Parliament (1835).[47] On the one hand, all three pictures are associated with the River Thames. But each also symbolizes the march of technology, of renewal, of reform. *Rain, Steam and Speed* juxtaposes 'new railway bridge and old road bridge, speeding train and drifting boat, steam driven locomotive and horse drawn plough, direct track and meandering river'.[48] The *Temeraire* pictures a distinguished old battleship being towed to the breaker's yard by a steamer. The destruction of Parliament by fire was only a few years after the passage of the Reform Bill. All three paintings present a fascinating dialectic of destruction and renewal.[49] A number of commentators, however, have seen *Rain, Steam and Speed* as a train of death, symbolizing on one hand the close of Turner's life and on the other the potentially destructive power of railroad technology, akin to the cataclysms of nature.[50] This was a theme that Charles Dickens addressed in *Dombey and Son* (1848), notably in the account of Carker's suicide. And Turner's fellow painter, John Martin, depicted a train in his *Last Judgement* (1853). In the centre, the bridge that Satan built over Chaos, to last for all time, is collapsing; on the right, Armageddon is in progress and an arriving railway train, filled with troops, tumbles into the chasm beneath.[51] Martin was fascinated by the drama of industry and used its images in various paintings of the ancient world, including scenes from the Old Testament. He once travelled on the footplate of a Great Western engine in the company of the line's engineer, I. K. Brunel; reputedly, it reached ninety miles an hour, offering the painter a

> headlong dioramic scene . . . as streaking perspectives dashed up and over him from the twinkling vanishing point to the volleying immensity of embankments, cuttings, and bridges flashing by.[52]

The train in *The Last Judgement* has inscribed on its carriages the names of cities from around the world, powerfully symbolic of the railway's time–space trans-

formations.[53] Indeed, Martin thought of railway speed as almost infinite.[54] The painting was also, however, a disturbing reminder to Victorian observers of the way railroad accidents were commonplace in the first decades of operation, some with horrific outcomes for human life. In this respect, it was as well for those who viewed the steam railway with suspicion that most railway prints did not convey much sense of the steam locomotive's extraordinary power.

With the collapse of investment in railway enterprise from 1846–7, the railway print industry withered rapidly. Perhaps the last important production was a set of pictures of construction work on the Britannia Tubular Bridge across the

255. John Martin, *The Last Judgement*, oil on canvas, 1853.

256. J. O. Brown, Belah viaduct on the line of the North Eastern Railway between Barnard Castle and Kirkby Stephen, watercolour (n.d.). The all-metal structure was 1,040 feet long and 196 feet high.

257. Life in the railway compartment as satirised in *Punch*, 1861: a young boy suggests to his cousin that the guard may take them for 'a runaway couple'.

258. Cartoon in *Punch*, 1859: 'Lady: "I want One Ticket – First!" Clerk: "Single?" Lady: "Single! What does it matter to you, Sir, whether I'm Single or not? Impertinence!"'

259, 260 (opposite). Abraham Solomon, *First Class – the meeting* and *Second Class – the parting*, both oil on canvas, 1854. The painting of the first-class scene was altered from its original state in response to public criticism. Originally, the old gentleman was asleep, and the young man and woman in closer proximity in what was regarded as too compromising a setting. iSuch sensitivities further underline the social significance of the railway compartment.

Menai Straits in North Wales.[55] It was instead left to painters to continue to provide an opening upon the evolving railway world. Here the topographical genre retained a central place, as seen in J. O. Brown's dramatic picture of Belah viaduct of 1869. The steel girder structure appears almost to float across the ravine, its vertical scale enhanced by the relative flatness of the Pennine hillscape.

Alongside such pictures was a growing interest among artists in narratives of human life – either in often elaborately peopled station scenes, or else within the setting of the railway compartment.[56] The railway carriage was rapidly accommodated to offer a window on everyday living, perhaps no more so than in *Punch* which found it an almost perpetual source of satirical copy. The pictorial frame of the compartment became a medium for conveying Victorian society's emerging dispositions of class, including all the various social and moral narratives that they proferred. The station and the compartment scene reflected, in the words of one analyst, 'a culturally self-confident industrial middle-class . . . demanding realistic renditions of modern life'.[57]

PICTORIAL SUBJECT

The earliest known printed illustration of a locomotive appears to be the engraving of 'Catch me who can' on the back of tickets issued by Richard Trevithick for his exhibition off the Euston Road in 1808.[58]

If the ultimate interest of railway prints, as well as of paintings, rests on the specific subjects they sought to depict, the logical starting point has to be pictures of lines on their opening days. Here was the railroad as 'theatre': for Marxist commentators like Klingender, this involved the use of elaborate ceremonial and pageant to underscore the pre-existing social order, the hierarchy of social relations.[59] The opening of lines was transformed into a social spectacle that reflected and endorsed society's governing status quo. The social élites paraded in often elaborately decorated railway carriages in a manner not dissimilar to the way they processed to the opening of the Assizes.[60] The social theatre that accompanied the opening of the Liverpool and Manchester Railway was repeated in varying form as new lines of railway were opened. In David Hill's picture of the first day of the Glasgow and Garnkirk line on 27 September 1831, the parading train contrasts sharply with the remains of the thatched hovels that housed the navvies who had excavated the cutting through which it is passing (see page 176).[61] The Canterbury and Whitstable Railway's opening day, 3 May 1830, was captured by T. M. Baynes.[62]

The social polarities often presented by such opening ceremonial were frequently re-exposed in depictions of the class divisions that so dominated the early railways. These found most prominent expression in paintings rather than in prints and, in turn, within the pictorial format of the railway compartment. Abraham Solomon's pair of paintings, exhibited at the Royal Academy in 1854, perhaps best illustrated the genre: the first-class compartment opulent in its furnishings and in the style of its passengers, the second-class much more austere in both its occupants and fabric.[63] Other artists provided renditions of third-class and excursion travel, sometimes revealing carriage scenes that offered more detailed social narratives than Solomon's. In the pages of *Punch*, the focus of the satire was not so much the class divisions of rail travel *per se*, but the social proprieties and potential social indignities within their respective realms.

261. Primrose Hill tunnel on the London and Birmingham line, pen, ink and wash, 1848 (artist unknown).

Perhaps the commonest subject for railway prints was the detailed depiction of the civil engineering works required by the railway's permanent way. It was not just the skew bridges that attracted artists, but the entire spectrum of viaducts, cuttings, embankments and tunnel entrances. These feature in T. T. Bury's series on the Liverpool and Manchester Railway, and are especially prominent in his drawings of the London and Birmingham line which met more stringent engineering standards than many lines constructed before or after. They figure, too, in J. C. Bourne's record of construction of the same route. Inevitably, they feature in depictions of railway lines traversing major watersheds such as the Pennines, as in A. F. Tait's views of the Manchester and Leeds Railway. Lithography was an ideal medium to convey the line and symmetry of bridges, viaducts and tunnel entrances which, given the often heroic form that they took, became an almost immediate target for artists. Many artists contributed to what has been described as a 'triumphalist vision' of civil engineering structures. A famous Bury print of the viaduct over the Sankey Valley on the Liverpool–Manchester line, for example, is rendered more dramatic by the viewpoint from which the picture is composed.[64] Such compositions were obvious counterparts to the superlatives in which early railway guide-books described the various structures of the permanent way and the buildings that graced its termini. By the time that J. C. Bourne produced his drawings of the Great Western Railway in the mid 1840s, a distinctive iconography of the railway had emerged, centred on the railway's static structures as distinct from the trains that ran upon it. In many respects, Bourne provided the travelling public with pictures that they could not have seen from the trains themselves. The view from the carriage window may well have offered passengers previously unobserved vistas and allowed scenery to be enjoyed in 'longer draughts', but many could not have appreciated the precise features of the structures of the lines as they travelled. The speed of the train caused features to coalesce – they became lost in the velocity of railway 'flight', in its machine ensemble.[65]

One kind of railway engineering work, however, was not just a reminder of the onward march of technology. The commentaries that accompanied many bound collections of prints often remark on the fascination of the geology through which lines passed. J. C. Bourne's volume on the Great Western Railway has page after page of geological description. Edwin Butterworth, in the account that accompanied A. F. Tait's views of the Manchester and Leeds Railway, stated how many of the cuttings afforded

> a rich treat to the geologist, exhibiting numerous beautiful sections of strata, consisting of alternate beds of rock, shale, sandstone, and coal, in which the parallelism and thickness of each is preserved.[66]

Henry Booth, in describing the Edge Hill tunnel on the Liverpool and Manchester Railway, observed how it was 'cut through various strata of red rock, blue shale and clay'; unfortunately, the geologist would have been disappointed when passing through the tunnel owing to the fact that its whole surface was lime-washed to reflect the gas illumination.[67] Modern commentaries on railway prints have likewise remarked upon the range of geological reports in their accompanying texts. Yet neither old commentary nor new explores the obvious connections with the newly emergent science of geology which, with the publication of Lyell's *Principles of Geology* of 1830–33, saw the increasing eclipse of Catastrophism and its replacement by Uniformitarianism.[68] Newly excavated railway cuttings in the 1830s and 1840s became instantaneous field sites for budding geologists, amateur and professional alike. As the navvies picked, shovelled and blasted their way through all kinds of sedimentary strata up and down the country, geologists flocked to the sites to confirm Lyell's account of the uniformity of the fossil record and all its implications for the Biblical account of creation and hence for Christian belief. The artistry of Bury and Bourne was not just a celebration of engineering

262. T. T. Bury, *Viaduct across the Sankey Valley / Bahnleitung über das Sankey Thal*, 1831. This triumphalist representation of the bridge on the Liverpool and Manchester Railway was widely reproduced: this version of the Bury prints of the line comes from the German edition, *Das grösste Wunderwerk unserer Zeit, oder die Eisenbahn für Dampfwägen zwischen Liverpool und Manchester in England*, Nuremberg, 1831.

263. J. C. Bourne, the
western entrance to Long
tunnel, Fox's Wood, on the
Great Western main line
near Bristol, lithograph,
1846.

genius, but a vivid reminder of a scientific revolution. Thomas Roscoe's guide to
the London and Birmingham Railway, published the same year as Bourne's
drawings of it, recorded how the stratigraphic sections exposed in deep cuttings
and tunnels had been 'numerously visited' by geologists.[69] Blisworth, especially,
abounded with fossil shells, wonderfully preserved.[70] It was no accident that it
featured in so many railway prints (see page 15).

The railways' invasion of land – their destruction of the order and tranquillity
of the countryside – was a central basis for much of the opposition they attracted.
But beyond this was a deeper and more disturbing issue which centred upon ideas
about Nature. The drawings of Bury and Bourne make no mistake about the way
railways were rewriting Nature's signature. Bourne's documentary construction
scenes on the London and Birmingham make the point unambiguously. This transformation of Nature was a perilous task, and the accompanying calamities to both
life and project made it yet starker. For some, it amounted to the death of Nature
in its Biblical sense and the triumph of man over the natural order, the birth of a
'second nature'. As ideas about biological evolution unfolded, charting the ascent
of man, such a view inevitably grew in significance, bringing fascination for some
and deep anxiety for others. The text accompanying David Hill's picture of the
Glasgow–Garnkirk line near Proven Mill Bridge comments on the 'artificial valley'
through which the line was carried.[71] In A. F. Tait's depiction of the Summit tunnel
on the Manchester and Leeds Railway (page 214), the shades of triumphalism in
engineering are clear, as is the geological cleft created by its hundred-foot-deep
entrance. But perhaps the most conspicuous element in this composition was a representative navvy ascending the rock side adjacent to the tunnel mouth, as powerful a symbol of the eclipse of the Creation story as one could imagine. The text,
written by Edwin Butterworth, describes the experience of travelling through this
tunnel:

. . . the rapidity of the flight, the screech of the warning signal from the engine, the overhanging column of mingled smoke and steam, the rush of air, together with the lurid glare and innumerable sparks thrown by the flambeaux which the train carries, and others borne by persons stationed in the tunnel, conspire, with the feeling that we are passing through the body of a huge mountain, to excite and awe our mind . . .[72]

Here, it seems, was a descent into Hell; but it proved quite otherwise as the train broke out of the tunnel into daylight on the other side. This was the kind of sensation that John Martin's satanic canvases embodied, with their compelling flights into the underworld, the terror of the sublime. Such cross-referencing between antiquity and the machine age was frequent in this period; Martin used quasi-geological structures, for example, for supernatural effect.[73] He was also fully aware of the inadequacy of the Flood to explain the geological record, and brought prehistory to life with illustrations like the *Iguanadon*.[74] Here was art evoking a link between science, technology and the wider world. Tait's view of the Summit Tunnel may have had little of the apocalyptic drama of Martin's paintings, but its associations were similar, as the text testifies. Tait's print of Whiteley's Viaduct offers a dramatic representation of the way the railway established a 'machine ensemble' between man and nature[75] – the canal winding round the interlocking spurs of the Pennine Hills in complete harmony with Nature's design, and the permanent way of the railroad striding confidently across the valley apparently dismissive of hill and dale, mimicking in pictorial form the almost exactly contemporary description by Dickens of the railroad's war with rude nature.[76] After the viaduct came the 'Charleston Curves'. Here, the line was forced away from its chosen route by tunnelling difficulties which took years to overcome.[77] But such trials simply added to the impact of the railway's triumph over the natural world.

264. A. F. Tait, Whiteley's viaduct, Charleston curves, on the Manchester and Leeds Railway, lithograph, 1845.

265. J. C. Bourne, sketches for drawings of the London and Birmingham Railway, with the emphasis on human and animal labour.

266, 267. J. C. Bourne, the working shaft (left) and great ventilation shaft (right) in Kilsby tunnel in 1837, lithographs, 1839. The working shaft shows navvies being lowered in a basket.

One major artist alone appeared interested in the actual business of railway construction. In his folio volume on the London and Birmingham Railway, J. C. Bourne offered a remarkable documentary of the line in its making. His prints are fundamentally depictions of human labour – 'it is the navvies who energize the scene'[78] – and reflect the remarkable reliance of railway building upon human and animal muscle power. The initial sketches that have survived of Bourne's final drawings underline the point further.[79] However, his documentary goes further than this. He depicts, for example, steam- and horse-worked pumping engines, sheerlegs and other ingenious contrivances for manipulating heavy loads. So his prints are also testament to the 'Grand Construction',[80] a record of human engineering genius and, in particular, the genius of Robert Stephenson, the line's engineer. Bourne's most powerful prints are undeniably the dramatic pictures of the inside of Kilsby Tunnel. In that depicting the scene beneath one of the working shafts, it is clearly the huge size of the engineering concept that is most striking, rather than the labour of the navvy. In his highly detailed drawing of the building of the stationary engine-house at Camden, the navvy comes into his own. Not only is the viewer's attention arrested by the scale of such organized labour, but equally significant is Bourne's narrative of construction tasks, showing 'the posture of navvies, men working with tools, with their bare hands, men talking, supervising, resting'.[81] The brutal society of the navvy is nowhere present in this picture; the overwhelming sense is of an assiduous and disciplined workforce. Plain, too, in both prints is the dramatic scale of the forces and elements that the navvies were creating. Bourne's creation of a detailed narrative of construction tasks is seen again in a view of the building of the retaining wall near Park Street in Camden, the scene immortalized by Dickens in *Dombey and Son*. A careful study of the picture reveals exactly how engineers and foremen accomplished their work. The same detail appears in the view of the construction works at the cutting at Tring,

Hertfordshire, with horse-operated gins spaced at equal intervals along each embankment (page 52).

Bourne's scenes of construction were, of course, documentary records of temporary subjects, fleeting events. This was not the case with railway stations or depots, which were more permanent manifestations of the railway phenomenon. The variety of architectural styles offered artists ready copy, and print-makers rarely failed to include station edifices in their portfolios of particular lines. It is essential to remember, however, the novelty of the station *per se* as a constituent of the urban mosaic. It became a new concourse for urban activity, akin in some ways

270. A. F. Tait, *Victoria Station, Hunt's Bank, Manchester*, lithograph, 1845, showing the station interior.

271. A. F. Tait, *Victoria Street, Hunt's Bank, Manchester*, lithograph, 1845, showing Victoria station, terminus of the Manchester and Leeds Railway.

to the medieval marketplace or the town square. Artists depicted stations both outside and in. A. F. Tait's series of prints of the Manchester and Leeds Railway contains a remarkably elegant view of the station at Hunt's Bank in Manchester. To a twentieth-century eye, it may be so familiar a view as to pass notice, but to the populace of the 1840s such configurations of buildings and space were largely unknown. Beyond the Euston Arch in London was a similar kind of concourse, even though the grand portico tended to attract artists more. But concourses within stations, particularly at terminals, were important subjects when the business of taking a train was an extreme novelty. There was also the bustle and confusion, the excitement and expectation that accompanies departure or arrival. In Tait's picture of the interior of Victoria station in Manchester, a group of railway servants on the right are using their body weight to shunt a carriage, a vivid reminder of how light railway vehicles were in the early days of operation. Bourne drew a similar picture of the Great Western station at Bristol, complete with broad-gauge trains under an elaborate timber roof.

It was left to painters, however, later in the century, to convey the measure of railway stations as hives of human activity, a subject that found its apotheosis in W. P. Frith's *The Railway Station* (1863), sold by the artist for the staggering sum of £4,500.[82] This famous painting afforded a fascinating social narrative of quite a complex form. Frith spent a year working on it, and each figure was separately modelled.[83] Comparable scenes included those by L. J. Cranstone, *Waiting at the Station* (1850), and by F. B. Barwell, *Parting Words* (1859), set at Fenchurch Street. Some pictures reveal a coalescence of subject types, as in George Earl's scene at King's Cross of 1893, where animals are as common as people. Some station scenes, however, were focused less upon the bustle and excitement of the crowd than on the emotions of individuals who were parting. The railway platform became a stage-set for displaying the pain of leaving loved ones, of soldiers going off to join their troops, of young women setting out for a life in service. Frank Holl contributed 'sympathetic' but 'unsentimental' pictures of the poor for the *The Graphic* magazine.[84] The Scottish painter Erskine Nicol depicted Irish emigrants as they waited on platforms for the trains that would remove them from the poverty

272. W. P. Frith, *The Railway Station*, oil on canvas, 1863: unmistakably a depiction of the Great Western Railway's Paddington station.

273. Erskine Nicol, *Irish Emigrants Waiting for a Train*, oil on canvas, 1864.

274. George Earl, *Going North, King's Cross Station*, oil on canvas, 1893.

275 (opposite, top). Bicester station, Oxfordshire, on the London and North Western Railway, late nineteenth century. A son and daughter-in-law and their eight children say farewell to the remainder of the family as they prepare to leave for Australia.

276 (opposite). Navvies during construction of the Great Central line from the Midlands to London, 1890s. This was the final chapter in the constructional narrative of the Victorian railway.

and destitution that faced so many of their countrymen. Despite the fact that much Irish railway development was planned by government commissioners, in stark contrast to mainland Britain, it did little to help the country's desperate economic plight after the Famine of the 1840s.

In the closing decades of the Victorian era, photography increasingly came to be the dominant medium of recording and advertising the railway. The construction of the last main line into London, the Great Central, in the 1890s, was captured in a remarkable photographic record.[85] Even the Midland Railway's London extension of the late 1860s was recorded in a series of often hazy prints.[86] Black-and-white photography gave much less scope for artistry – the almost tangible energy of steam locomotion in Turner's *Rain, Steam and Speed* could barely be approached by early film, and nor, of course, could the rainbow liveries of Victorian trains. In a curious sense, the monochrome photograph registered the commonplaceness of the railway by the end of the century – its ramifications had become so broad that artistry like that of J. C. Bourne and T. T. Bury had become largely superfluous.

Epilogue

... like Silbury Hill or Offa's Dyke, the towering
embankments of the great chalk defiles at Tring and
Sonning will remain to prompt future archaeologists to
ponder upon the wonders of the Age of Steam.[1]

THE VICTORIAN RAILWAY AS 'ALL THE WORLD'

IN CRITICAL SOCIAL THEORY, the phrase 'Los Angeles is all the world' symbolizes
the way in which American culture has become a world culture over the course
of the twentieth century.[2] By the late nineteenth century, one might equally well
have claimed that the Victorian railway was 'all the world'. It was not merely that
it loomed large in all the complex machinery of Britain's empire, but that Victorian
iron foundries, steel mills and engineering shops furnished permanent way and
rolling stock for railways across all continents. British contractors carried their
expertise across the seas, sometimes never to return. Frequently it was British
investment finance that underpinned overseas railway projects, particularly in the
decades up to 1914.

In India under the British Raj, railway construction began as early as the
1850s. Within ten years, some 2,500 miles had been laid, and by 1900 the sub-
continent boasted a network longer than that in Britain.[3] Its railway practice was,
in many respects, indistinguishable from Britain's, and successive Governors-
General were wholly unambiguous in their enthusiasm for extending the railway
project there.[4] The outcome was that railways and the Raj became 'inseparably
intertwined', which was perhaps no more clearly displayed than in the way writers
such as Rudyard Kipling, E. M. Forster and Paul Scott used them as a central focus
in many of their works.[5] On continental Europe, Britain also had a critical part in
railway building. As early as 1840, Robert Stephenson's company supplied locomotives for railways in Austria, Belgium, France and several of the German states.[6]
Joseph Locke, one of George Stephenson's assistant engineers on the Liverpool and
Manchester Railway, was responsible for setting out the line from Paris to Rouen
in the early 1840s.[7] The building contract for this line was undertaken by the
English entrepreneur Thomas Brassey, along with some 5,000 English navvies
who, true to legend, terrorized all respectable Frenchmen.[8] As the period of grand
construction in Britain came to a close, contractors like Brassey directed their
attention to other parts of Europe and, later, the Americas, Asia and Australia.[9] In
association, a rising proportion of British pig-iron output was exported for railways in the making abroad.[10] In December 1847, such was the demand that
Wolverhampton iron-masters were reputedly converting calcined ore into rails and
delivering them to Liverpool within just two days.[11] Over the entire Victorian age,
35 million tons of iron and steel rails went overseas.[12]

277. A standard class
XB 'Pacific' locomotive
in service on the Bombay,
Baroda and Central India
Railway, early 1930s. The
locomotive was built in
Glasgow to the Indian
railways 5 ft 6 in gauge.

Among British locomotive-building companies, the story by the close of the century was little different. At the North British Locomotive Company's works outside Glasgow, narrow-gauge steam engines were constructed for use not in Britain but in countries abroad. In many areas across the world, topographical and cost considerations made narrow-gauge rather than standard-gauge tracks the preferred mode of railway building. The Company's list of customers thus reads like a geographical lexicon: they were found in Western Australia, North West Bengal, Santiago, Manila, Costa Rica, the Cape, Egypt, Uganda, Ceylon and Java, not to mention destinations closer to home such as Donegal in Ireland.[13] And when Britain was not suppplying railway stock to overseas concerns, it was investing in them. By 1913, some £306 million of a total of £3,760 million invested by Britons in public companies overseas was to be found in railway securities in the colonies and the dominions.[14]

THE VICTORIAN RAILWAY AS EXHIBITION

A future generation denied the spectacle of a steam
locomotive in full cry will suffer a loss as great as we
have suffered who have never seen a full-rigged ship
with all her canvas set.[15]

Steam locomotion finally disappeared from Britain's railways in the late 1960s. Its demise was prolonged, and set Britain apart from the Continent where electric traction had been developed earlier and on a much larger scale. Somewhat perversely to many commentators at the time, the Railway Executive, after nationalization in 1948, clung to steam traction as the way forward.[16] It represented a tried and tested form, and comprehensive re-equipment would have been very costly. But there was also a psychological difficulty in Britain in dissociating the railway from steam power.[17] The railway may have been 'England's gift to the world',[18] but by the mid twentieth century British railway practice had become anachronistic. Even when the reins of modernization were firmly grasped, after about 1960, investment decisions were taken that, in retrospect, proved highly unsatisfactory. While European railway systems were moving more and more towards full-scale electrification, Britain's policy was dominated by diesel traction but without any standardization of equipment.[19] Only with the Millennium approaching did British railway managers seem to have fully accepted the merits of electric traction, to the great cost of taxpayer and traveller alike.

The deep association of the railway with steam power has been manifested in other ways. Britain leads the world in the scale and number of its preserved railways – lines that have been resurrected from disuse, with tracks re-laid, stations refurbished and, above all, steam traction reinstated.[20] There are now 65 standard-gauge preserved railways, along with 63 miniature steam centres and museums.[21] By 1991, they reputedly accounted for 3 per cent of the market for all commercial leisure attractions.[22] Initially based on volunteer labour and organization, many of these lines have now become fully fledged companies. They have tapped into and helped cement a nostalgia movement tied to what has been described as 'the cultural logic of late capitalism'.[23] The past is being rediscovered, re-exposed, packaged and commoditized as part of the continuing process of capital accumula-

tion.[24] Preserved railways have become, alongside theme and safari parks, land-scapes of consumption. The 'puffing billies', with their carriages and relics from a bygone era, are a reminder of what, for some, was a surer and more disciplined age.[25] Arguably, preserved railways rediscover the curious blend of romantic freedom and classic order that the Victorian railway came to symbolize.[26] However, we continually need to be reminded that these lines are only the railway 'as exhibition'.[27] They form not an exhibition of the Victorian railway, but the railway conceived and grasped *as though it were an exhibition*.

The continuing fascination with the steam railway is likewise apparent in the realm of toy trains. Despite intermittent turmoil in the British toy trade, almost every model-shop window up and down the country displays toy trains from yesteryear. The craze for scale model trains, which the Liverpool firm of Hornby helped to start in the early 1900s and then progressively popularized, remains for all to see. It is less a province for boys than it once was, but its appeal for adult men seems undiminished.

When the Conservative administration under Margaret Thatcher was formed in 1979, it had the free market as one of its guiding ideological stars. The state monolith that then constituted Britain's railways (British Rail) seemed an obvious target for the declared campaign to 'roll back the frontiers of the state', and a private railway system, along Victorian lines, seemed once more on the horizon. However, for more than a decade, the nationalized railway system remained much as it was, albeit struggling with a history of low investment. Recession and the existence of other, easier targets for privatization were the principal reasons for its relative isolation on the political agenda. By the time of John Major's premiership in the early 1990s, various blueprints for a privatized system were being formulated. One that was said to have particularly appealed to the new Prime Minister was a territorial division much along the lines of the Victorian railway or, at the very least, its inter-war successor, comprising the so-called 'Big Four'.[28] In the end, a very different scheme of privatization was adopted, one that split the railway into a vast array of product divisions, including a separate national track authority and a whole array of train-operating companies whose franchises were constructed around routes as much as around territories.

Theorists of the workings of capital in the late twentieth century have styled this kind of organizational regime as 'post-Fordist'.[29] It represents moves towards a system of 'flexible accumulation'. The newly configured British railway system was intended to be more in tune with market demand, with fewer half-empty trains, less rolling stock standing idle in sidings and a greater sensitivity to customer preference. Above all, the system was intended to profit its investors, in contrast to the nationalized system that it replaced, with its apparently insatiable need for state subsidy.

To the casual observer, it might seem that Britain in the late 1990s witnessed the re-birth of the Victorian railway, particularly in respect of its ethos of corporate private capital. A number of the new operating companies took their names straight from the Victorian age – Great Western Trains principal among them – and many have sought identity in distinctive liveries. To the more critical observer, however, the idea that the Victorian railway was re-born is a myth. The new British railway system is heavily regulated by the state; more paradoxically, it remains heavily subsidized by the Exchequer. The fissiparous labyrinth that now constitutes its organizational form would probably astound the staff of the old Railway Clearing House. Complaints of poor time-keeping and overcrowded trains have become commonplace; in their wake, lawyers have been having a field-day as the different railway divisions seek compensation from each other for contractual failures.

By far the more potent symbol of the residual power of the Victorian railway in the contemporary imagination has to be *Thomas the Tank Engine*. The stories written by the Reverend Wilber Awdry for his son Christopher have attained a cultural significance that nobody in the 1940s, when he began writing, could

279. Thomas the Tank Engine, illustration from the original edition of Wilber Awdry's children's story, 1946.

possibly have expected. Thomas, the blue-painted tank engine with the cheeky smoke-box-door smile, has become a cultural icon – reproduced in model form, on wall-posters, on wallpaper, as window curtains and in all manner of other ways.[30] The preface to the story of Thomas the Tank Engine (incidentally, the second and not the first of Awdry's creations), contained what was in hindsight a prophetic observation: 'Dear Christopher, Here is your friend Thomas the Tank Engine. He wanted to come out of his station-yard and see the world.'[31] Fifty years on, Thomas has indeed seen the world. He has been transformed into a piece of world merchandizing, somewhat to his creator's unease.[32] Japanese children are reputedly mesmerized by Thomas and all his memorabilia. Even in Britain, the passion for him seems undimmed, especially among the very young – he can be found outside supermarkets offering stationary rides, and at fun fairs and theme parks offering mobile ones. Inevitably, Awdry's stories have had their critics, in much the way that Enid Blyton's became a focus for vigorous debate among structuralist commentators in the 1970s. But none of this has altered their underlying appeal. They touch upon basic human emotions. For some, the fact that these are displayed by steam engines is seen as beside the point; it is arguably the inscription of human characteristics upon machine phenomena that is a fundamental key to their success. When Fanny Kemble sought to humanize Stephenson's 'Rocket' in that first train journey in 1830,[33] she was displaying what appears to be a gut instinct. When Awdry wrote his first story in 1945, he was unwittingly continuing a tradition of social and educational reproduction begun at the dawn of the railway age. Whatever the measure of Thomas's transformation as a commodity icon in the capitalist culture of the late twentieth century, he stands with all his fellow engine characters in Awdry's stories as a vivid reminder of the force of the railway in the Victorian imagination.

Notes

PROLOGUE

1 *Mechanics' Magazine* 2 (1824), p. 362.

2 B. R. Mitchell, *Abstract of British Historical Statistics* (Cambridge, 1962), p. 225. These figures exclude Ireland.

3 H. J. Dyos and D. H. Aldcroft, *British Transport: an economic survey from the seventeenth century to the twentieth* (Leicester, 1969), p. 129.

4 M. Robbins, *The Railway Age in Britain and its impact on the world* (London, 1962; Harmondsworth, repr. 1965), p. 38.

5 *Ibid.*, p. 31.

6 See H. G. Lewin, *The Railway Mania and its aftermath, 1845–52* (London, 1936).

7 An encyclopaedic account of the development of the railway system can be found in E. F. Carter, *An Historical Geography of the Railways of the British Isles* (London, 1959); see also J. Simmons, *The Railway in England and Wales, 1830–1914* (Leicester, 1978; Newton Abbot, 1986); D. Turnock, *An Historical Geography of Railways in Great Britain and Ireland* (Aldershot, 1998); H. Pollins, *Britain's Railways: an industrial history* (London, 1971); T. R. Gourvish, 'Railways, 1830–70: the formative years', in M. J. Freeman and D. H. Aldcroft, eds., *Transport in Victorian Britain* (Manchester, 1988), pp. 57–91.

8 H. J. Dyos and D. H. Aldcroft, *op. cit.*, p. 129.

9 See M. Freeman and D. Aldcroft, *The Atlas of British Railway History* (Beckenham, 1985), p. 22.

10 H. J. Dyos and D. H. Aldcroft, *op. cit.*, pp. 133–4.

11 See E. F. Carter, *op. cit.*; J. Simmons, *op. cit.*; D. Turnock, *op. cit.*; see also P. J. Cain, 'Railways, 1870–1914: the maturity of the private system', in M. J. Freeman and D. H. Aldcroft, eds., *op. cit.*, pp. 92–133.

12 B. R. Mitchell, *op. cit.*, p. 226.

13 Some of these feats are dealt with in M. Freeman and D. Aldcroft, *The Atlas of British Railway History, op. cit.*

14 D. St John Thomas, *The Country Railway* (Newton Abbot, 1976), p. 44.

15 H. Belloc, *On Nothing and Kindred Subjects* (London, 1908), pp. 71–2.

16 W. G. Hoskins, *The Making of the English Landscape* (London, 1955; Harmondsworth, repr. 1970), p. 265. Since Hoskins wrote, the railway preservation movement has ensured that some

of these vistas have survived the inexorable march of economic rationalization (see Epilogue).

INTRODUCTION

1 T. Roscoe, *Home and Country Scenes on each side of the line of the London and Birmingham and Grand Junction Railways* (London, n.d.), p. 34 (Yale Center for British Art, Rare Books Collection, DA625 R).

2 See, for example, P. Mathias, *The First Industrial Nation: an economic history of Britain, 1700–1914* (London, 1969), p. 3.

3 D. Cannadine, 'British History: Past, Present, and Future', *Past and Present* 116 (1987), p. 183.

4 See W. D. Rubinstein, *Capitalism, Culture, and Decline in Britain, 1750–1990* (London, 1993), p. 24.

5 See A. J. Meyer, *The Persistence of the Old Regime* (London, 1981), p. 10.

6 P. Hudson, *The Industrial Revolution* (London, 1992), p. 1.

7 *Ibid.*, p. 237, quoting J. A. Schumpeter.

8 See J. Langton, 'Urban growth and economic change from the seventeenth century to 1841', in P. Clarke, ed., *The Urban History of Britain, 2, 1540–1840* (Cambridge, forthcoming 1999).

9 A. Desmond and J. Moore, *Darwin* (London, 1991; repr., 1992), p. xv.

10 *Illustrated London News* 1 (1842), p. 116.

11 *Ibid.*, p. 129.

12 *Ibid.*, p. 225.

13 *Ibid.*, p. 231.

14 *Ibid.*, p. 225 ff.

15 J. F. C. Harrison, *Early Victorian Britain, 1832–51* (first published as *The Early Victorians, 1832–51*, London, 1971; repr. 1979), p. 34.

16 For commentary on Malthus, a useful starting point is D. Winch, *Malthus* (Oxford, 1987); also M. Turner, ed., *Malthus and his Time* (London, 1986).

17 J. F. C. Harrison, *op. cit.*, p. 30.

18 See A. Desmond and J. Moore, *op. cit.*, p. 283.

19 W. L. Burn, *The Age of Equipoise; a study of the mid-Victorian generation* (London, 1964), p. 66.

20 F. M. L. Thompson, *The Rise of Respectable Society: a social history of Victorian Britain, 1830–1900* (London, 1988), p. 13.

21 *Ibid.*, p. 22.

22 *Ibid.*, p. 26.

23 *Ibid.*, pp. 22–3.

24 *Ibid.*, pp. 23–5.

25 P. Hudson, *op. cit.*, p. 1.

26 F. M. L. Thompson, *op. cit.*, p. 23.

27 *Ibid.*, p. 16.

28 R. J. Morris, *Class and Class Consciousness in the Industrial Revolution* (London, 1979), p. 9; a vital commentary on the issue of class remains A. Briggs, 'The language of class in Early Nineteenth-Century England', in A. Briggs and J. Saville, eds., *Essays in Labour History* (London, 1960).

29 See R. J. Morris, *op. cit.*, pp. 37 ff.

30 *Ibid.*, p. 57. The theory of social hegemony has been explored by A. Gramsci, *Selections from Prison Notebooks*; repr. ed. and trans. Q. Hoare and G. Nowell Smith, London, 1971).

31 R. J. Morris, *op. cit.*, p. 59.

32 The Poor Law and the New Poor Law are discussed at some length in J. F. C. Harrison, *op. cit.* and in F. M. L. Thompson, *op. cit.*

33 F. M. L. Thompson, *op. cit.*, p. 355.

34 *Illustrated London News* 1 (1842), p. 97.

35 Essential background is provided in T. M. Greene, *Geology in the Nineteenth Century: changing views of a changing world* (Ithaca, 1982).

36 See A. Desmond and J. Moore, *op. cit.*, chapters 8–13.

37 *Ibid.*, p. 249.

38 *Ibid.*, p. 208.

39 D. R. Dean, '"Through Science to Despair": Geology and the Victorians', in J. Paradis and T. Postlewait, eds., *Victorian Science and Victorian Values: literary perspectives* (New Brunswick, 1985), p. 115.

40 *Ibid.*, p. 121.

41 H. Jennings, *Pandaemonium: the coming of the machine as seen by contemporary observers* (London, 1985; repr. 1995).

42 *Ibid.*, p. 212.

43 The various eye-witness accounts of travelling on the Liverpool–Manchester railroad make plain the shock, the terror, the sheer novelty and exhilaration of the first passengers. One of the best descriptions appeared in *Buck's Gazette*, reproduced in John Herepath's *The Railway Magazine and Annals of Science*, 1 (1836), pp. 111 ff.

44 See F. Klingender, *Art and the Industrial Revolution* (London, 1947; ed. and rev. A. Elton, London, 1968), p. 106.

45 The thesis of Uniformitarianism held that the processes active in the earth's formation were the same in the past as in

the present. This was in contrast to Catastrophism, which claimed that the earth's history had been characterized by a succession of cataclysmic events in which all existing life forms were wiped out to be replaced by new. The terms were popularized in the 1830s.

46 The London and Birmingham Railway cut through a remarkable sequence of strata, beginning with the London clays and extending as far as the Coal Measures; see T. Roscoe, *The London and Birmingham Railway* (London, 1839), p. 31. Charles Darwin's friend, Hugh Strickland, was mown down by a train near Retford in 1853 while 'geologizing his way through the railway cuttings'; A. Desmond and J. Moore, *op. cit.*, p. 397.

47 See *Chambers Encyclopaedia* VI (London, 1963), p. 230; also T. M. Greene, *op. cit.*

48 One of the most powerful evocations of this transformation was penned by William Wordsworth in the face of the construction of the Kendal and Windermere Railway; see W. Wordsworth, *Guide to the Lakes* (5th edn., London, 1835), Appendix II.

49 The railways' invasion of land forms part of a remarkable recent study on railways and the law; R. W. Kostal, *Law and English Railway Capitalism, 1825–1875* (Oxford, 1994).

50 B. Disraeli, *Sybil, or The Two Nations* (1845; repr. Harmondsworth, 1954), p. 105.

51 See S. A. Broadbridge, 'The sources of railway share capital', in M. C. Reed, ed., *Railways in the Victorian Economy: studies in finance and growth* (Newton Abbot, 1969), pp. 207–9.

52 L. T. C. Rolt, *Lines of Character: a steam age evocation* (2nd edn., London, 1974), p. 19.

53 W. Wordsworth, *op. cit.*, p. 166.

54 On Darwin and railways, see A. Desmond and J. Moore, *op. cit.*, pp. 396–7, 421.

55 Some indication of the role of the early railway police can be found in T. Roscoe, *op. cit.*, pp. 118–19.

56 This facet is treated in F. C. Mather, 'The railways, the electric telegraph, and public order during the Chartist period, 1837–8', *History*, XXXVIII (1953), pp. 40–53.

57 *Illustrated London News*, I (1842), p. 232.

58 A. Desmond and J. Moore, *op. cit.*, p. 301.

59 For one particularly significant recent manifestation of this, see J. Simmons and G. Biddle, *The Oxford Companion to British railway history from 1603 to the 1990s* (Oxford, 1997).

60 See G. Ottley, *A Bibliography of British Railway History* (2nd edn., Leicester, 1988).

61 Examples are David and Charles and the Oxford Publishing Company.

62 See M. C. Reed, *op. cit.*

63 See G. R. Hawke, *Railways and Economic Growth in England and Wales, 1840–1870* (Oxford, 1970); an older view can be found in W. H. B. Court, *A Concise Economic History of Britain from 1750 to recent times* (Cambridge, 1954), pp. 165 ff, in which the level of economic activity in Britain in the mid nineteenth century is considered to have been 'unintelligible without reference to the railways' (p. 165).

64 See the survey of railway history in T. Gourvish, 'What kind of railway history did we get? Forty years of research', *Journal of Transport History* 14 (1993), pp. 111–25.

65 One of the best contributions (if only partially concerned with Britain and specifically with stations) has to be J. Richards and J. M. MacKenzie, *The Railway Station: a social history* (Oxford, 1986); much less successful is J. Simmons, *The Victorian Railway* (London, 1991), which never proceeds far beyond anthology. One of the most notable contributions was written almost three decades ago, namely H. Perkin, *The Age of the Railway* (London, 1970). Another remarkable and even earlier treatment of the railway is contained in F. D. Klingender, *Art and the Industrial Revolution* (rev. edn., London, 1972); Klingender's contribution has a currency within much contemporary debate that is almost uncanny.

66 See, for example, F. Whishaw, *The Railways of Great Britain and Ireland* (London, 1840); F. S. Williams, *Our Iron Roads: their history, construction and social influences* (London, 1852).

67 H. Jennings, *op. cit*, p. xxxv.

68 *Ibid.*, p. xxxvi.

69 See L. J. Jordanova and R. Porter, eds., *Images of the Earth: essays in the history of the environmental sciences* (2nd edn., London, 1997), p. 2, Introduction.

70 H. Jennings, *op. cit*, p. xxxv.

71 A good introduction is M. Robbins, *The Railway Age* (London, 1962), but see also H. J. Dyos and D. H. Aldcroft, *British Transport: an economic survey from the seventeenth to the twentieth* (Leicester, 1969); M. Freeman and D. Aldcroft, *An Atlas of British Railway History* (London, 1985).

72 The term 'second' nature is sometimes also used to describe the phenomenon. The 'production' of nature is generally used in Marxist commentary; see

N. Smith, *Uneven Development* (Oxford, 1984), pp. 32 ff.

73 See A. Briggs, *Victorian Things* (London, 1988).

74 M. Arnold, *Culture and Anarchy* (London, 1869), pp. 49–53.

75 One of the earliest records of this phrase comes in the Liverpool *Railway Companion* (London, 1833), pp. 16–17 (Bodleian MS Gough Add. Lancs 8ᵛᵒ 56 (6)). It can also be found in the *Mechanics' Magazine*, 33 (1840), p. 518, by which time it appears to have achieved a measure of common currency.

76 As early as 1840, one railway correspondent observed how 'want of punctuality' was the greatest sin of railway managers; *ibid.*

77 This term is especially identified with the writing of Raymond Williams; see, for example, R. Williams, *The Long Revolution* (repr. Harmondsworth, 1965).

78 See *Hilda Lessways* (1911) and *A Man from the North* (1898).

79 J. Betjeman, *Summoned by Bells* (London, 1960), pp. 53 ff.

80 See, for example, R. J. Irving, *The North Eastern Railway Company, 1870–1914: an economic history* (Leicester, 1976).

81 See Mrs Marcet (Jane Haldimand), *Willy's Travels on the Railroad: intended for young children* (London, 1847), p. 6 (Bodleian, Opie Collection A748).

82 See exhibition poster, Bodleian, John Johnson Collection, Railways Box 4; also *The Railway Companion* (London, 1833), p. 47 (Bodleian MS, Gough Add. Lancs 8ᵛᵒ 56 (6)).

83 J. Francis, *A History of the English Railway; its social relations and revelations, 1820–1845*, II (London, 1851), pp. 140–1.

84 *Ibid.*, p. 143.

1 DEATH OF THE OLD ORDER?

1 H. Perkin, *The Age of the Railway* (London, 1970), pp. 80–81.

2 *Ibid.*, p. 65.

3 See, for example, P. S. Bagwell, *The Transport Revolution from 1770* (2nd edn., London, 1988).

4 For fuller discussion of these issues, see M. J. Freeman, introduction, in D. Aldcroft and M. Freeman, eds., *Transport in the Industrial Revolution* (Manchester, 1983), pp. 1–4.

5 J. C. D. Clark, *English Society, 1688–1832* (Cambridge, 1985). For a comprehensive review of Clark's work, see J. Innes, 'Jonathan Clark, Social History and England's "Ancien Regime"', *Past and Present* (1987), pp. 165–200.

6 M. J. Freeman, *op. cit.*, pp. 3–4.

7 J. C. D. Clark, *op. cit.*, pp. 67–9.

8 Pickfords and Russells offered two leading examples: see G. L. Turnbull, *Traffic and Transport: an economic history of Pickfords* (London, 1979), and D. Gerhold, *Road Transport before the Railways: Russell's London flying waggons* (Cambridge, 1993).

9 See J. Armstrong and P. S. Bagwell, 'Coastal Shipping', in D. Aldcroft and M. Freeman, eds., *op. cit.*, p. 165.

10 The joint stock company was quite a common means of financing canals but, as Duckham has commented, 'canals were a form of self-help which sprang from local initiatives and relied in the main on local resources'; see B. F. Duckham, 'Canals and river navigations', in D. Aldcroft and M. Freeman, eds., *op. cit.*, p. 114.

11 See H. J. Dyos and D. H. Aldcroft, *British Transport: an economic survey from the seventeenth century to the twentieth* (Leicester, 1971), p. 117.

12 See M. J. Freeman, Introduction, in M. J. Freeman and D. H. Aldcroft, eds., *Transport in Victorian Britain* (Manchester, 1988), p. 8; also T. R. Gourvish, 'Railways 1830–70; the formative years', in M. J. Freeman and D. H. Aldcroft, eds., *op. cit.*, p. 83.

13 See T. R. Gourvish, *op. cit.*

14 R. W. Kostal, *Law and English Railway Capitalism, 1825–1875* (Oxford, 1994), p. 183.

15 J. C. D. Clark, *op. cit.*, p. 69.

16 *Ibid.*, p. 70.

17 See F. M. L. Thompson, *The Rise of Respectable Society: a social history of Victorian Britain, 1830–1900* (London, 1988), p. 28.

18 For relevant theoretical discussion, see D. Harvey, *The Urbanization of Capital: studies in the history and theory of capitalist urbanization* (Oxford, 1985), pp. 2 ff.

19 C. Barman, *Early British Railways* (London, 1950), p. 26.

20 Quoted in W. E. Houghton, *The Victorian Frame of Mind, 1830–1870* (New Haven, 1957), p. 4.

21 Quoted in E. Royston Pike, *Human Documents of the Victorian Golden Age* (London, 1963), p. 41.

22 William Pickering, Railroad Eclogues (London, 1846), p. 23, in Bodleian MS 46.1361.

23 G. Rees, *Early Railway Prints: a social history of the railways from 1825 to 1850* (Oxford, 1980), p. 25.

24 See F. D. Klingender, *Art and the Industrial Revolution* (rev. edn., London, 1968), p. 128.

25 See *Blackwood's Edinburgh Magazine*, XXVIII (1830), p. 824.

26 See F. M. L. Thompson, *op. cit.*, p. 13.

27 F. D. Klingender, *op. cit.*, p. 128.

28 *Blackwood's Edinburgh Magazine*, XXVIII (1830), p. 828.

29 See H. Jennings, *Pandaemonium: the coming of the machine as seen by contemporary observers* (London, 1985; repr. 1995), p. 179.

30 W. E. Houghton, *op. cit.*, p. 77.

31 F. D. Klingender, *op. cit.*, pp. 123–4.

32 See the account in R. E. Carlson, *The Liverpool and Manchester Railway Project, 1821–1831* (1969), pp. 71–2.

33 W. Pickering, *op. cit.*, p. 6.

34 G. Eliot, *Middlemarch* (1871–2; repr. Harmondsworth, 1994), p. 597.

35 *Ibid.*, p. 604.

36 R. W. Kostal, *op. cit.*, p. 144.

37 *Ibid.*, p. 152.

38 *Ibid.*, p. 145.

39 See chapter three.

40 Quoted in R. W. Kostal. *op. cit.*, p. 173.

41 *Ibid.*, pp. 178–9.

42 Bodleian MS 46.1361, *op. cit.*, p. 45.

43 *Ibid.*, p. 144.

44 See C. Barman, *op. cit.*, p. 27.

45 T. Roscoe, *The London and Birmingham Railway* (London, 1839), p. 13.

46 D. Cannadine, *Aspects of Aristocracy: grandeur and decline in Modern Britain* (New Haven, 1994), p. 56.

47 *Ibid.*, p. 15.

48 *Ibid.*, pp. 72–3.

49 See J. Francis, *A History of the English Railway; its social relations and revelations, 1820–1845*, I (London, 1851), p. 174.

50 See E. P. Thompson, *Customs in Common* (London, 1991), p. 73.

51 See, for instance, R. E. Carlson, *op. cit.*, pp. 72, 146.

52 *Ibid.*, p. 128.

53 *Ibid.*, p. 128 ff.

54 H. J. Dyos and D. H. Aldcroft, *op. cit.*, p. 117.

55 See D. Cannadine, *op. cit.*, pp. 58 ff.

56 *Ibid.*, p. 58.

57 *Ibid.*, p. 59.

58 See F. M. L. Thompson, *op. cit.*, pp. 13–22; also A. J. Meyer, *The Persistence of the Old Regime* (London, 1981), pp. 10 ff.

59 Quoted in A. J. Meyer, *op. cit.*, p. 12.

60 *Ibid.*, p. 12.

61 L. T. C. Rolt, *Victorian Engineering* (London, 1970), p. 54.

62 See S. and B. Webb, *The Manor and the Borough*, 2 vols. (London, 1908).

63 See S. and B. Webb, *The Parish and the County* (London, 1906).

64 See K. D. M. Snell, *Annals of the Labouring Poor: social change and agrarian England, 1660–1900* (Cambridge, 1985).

65 This is most often associated with the French geographer, Paul Vidal de la Blache: see his *Principes de Géographie Humaine* (Paris, 1923); also A. Buttimer, 'Charism and Context: the challenge of La Géographie Humaine', in D. Ley and M. Samuels, eds., *Humanistic Geography: prospects and problems* (London, 1978), pp. 58–76.

66 See D. Underdown, *Revel, Riot and Rebellion: popular politics and culture in England, 1603–1660* (Oxford, 1985), especially chap. 4; also D. Underdown, 'The Chalk and Cheese: contrasts among the English Clubmen', *Past and Present*, 85 (1979), pp. 25–48.

67 *Ibid.*

68 See G. R. Hawke, *Railways and Economic Growth in England and Wales, 1840–70* (Oxford, 1970), pp. 324–6.

69 T. Hardy, *Tess of the D'Urbervilles* (1891; repr. Harmondsworth, 1994), p. 40.

70 *Ibid.*, p. 41

71 T. Hardy, *The Woodlanders* (1889; repr. Harmondsworth, 1981), p. 63.

72 T. Hardy, *Tess of the D'Urbervilles*, *op. cit.*, p. 239.

73 *Ibid.*, p. 240.

74 T. Hughes, *Tom Brown's Schooldays* (London, 1856), p. 17.

75 *Ibid.*, p. 16.

76 Quoted in W. E. Houghton, *op. cit.*, p. 79.

77 Quoted in E. Royston Pike, *op. cit.*, p. 41.

78 F. S. Williams, *Our Iron Roads: their history, construction and social influences* (London, 1852), p. 285.

79 See P. White and R. Woods, eds., *The Geographical Impact of Migration* (London, 1980), pp. 34 ff.

80 E. Royston Pike, *op. cit.*, p. 156.

81 See R. W. Kostal, *op. cit.*, pp. 222 ff.

82 *Ibid.*, p. 229.

83 *Ibid.*, p. 230.

84 *Ibid.*, p. 248.

85 *Ibid.*, p. 251.

86 Christian Anderson, 'A Poet's View of a Railroad', in *Railway Readings* (1847), Bodleian MS 2705. f.422.

87 *Ballad on the Western Railroad*, Bodleian MS, John Johnson collection, Railways Box 1.

88 W. Pickering, *op. cit.*, p. 22.

89 Christian Anderson, *op. cit.*

90 Quoted in J. Warburg, *The Industrial Muse* (Oxford, 1958), p. 79.

91 T. Roscoe, *The Book of the Grand Junction Railway* (London, 1839), p. 43.

92 See H. Jennings, *op. cit.*, p. 212.

93 Quoted in J. Warburg, *op. cit.*, p. 52.

94 W. Cronon, *Nature's Metropolis: Chicago and the Great West* (London, 1991), p. 72.

95 *The Railway Companion, describing an excursion along the Liverpool line . . .* (London, 1833), p. 28 (Bodleian MS Gough Add. Lancs 8° 56(6)).

96 Quoted in W. M. Ackworth, *The Railways of England* (5th edn., London, 1900), p. 78.

97 T. Roscoe, *op. cit.*, p. 44.

98 W. Schivelbusch, *The Railway Journey: the industrialisation of time and space in the 19th century* (New York, 1977), pp. 53–4.

99 *Ibid.*, p. 54.

100 Quoted in *The Railway Magazine and Annals of Science*, I (1836), p. 112.

101 Bodleian MS, John Johnson Collection, Railways Box 4.

102 S. Carr, ed., *The Poetry of Railways* (London, 1978), p. 24.

103 F. S. Williams, *op. cit.*, p. 222.

104 G. Head, *A Home Tour through the Manufacturing Districts of England in the summer of 1835* (London, 1836), p. 420.

105 F. B. Head, *Stokers and Pokers; or The London & North Western Railway* (London, 1850), pp. 97–8.

106 F. S. Williams, *op. cit.*, p. 235.

107 T. Roscoe, *op. cit.*, p. 53.

108 W. L. Burn has commented on the extraordinary popularity of John Martin's paintings, reflective of the grandiose conceptions of the period: W. L. Burn, *The Age of Equipoise: a study of the mid-Victorian generation* (London, 1964), p. 61.

109 W. Feaver, *The Art of John Martin* (Oxford, 1975), p. 143.

110 See M. D. Paley, *The Apocalyptic Sublime* (New Haven, 1986), pp. 148–50; also W. Feaver, *op. cit.*, pp. 189 ff.

111 F. Klingender, *op. cit.*, p. 109.

112 *The Railway Companion* (London, 1833) (Bodleian MS Gough Add. Lancs 8° 56(6)), *op. cit.*

113 Quoted in F. S. Williams, *op. cit.*, p. 27.

114 Quoted in W. E. Houghton, *op. cit.*, p. 41.

115 For discussions of the concept of the *production* of nature, see N. Smith, *Uneven Development: nature, capital and the production of space* (Oxford, 1984).

116 Quoted in C. Barman, *op. cit.*, p. 25.

117 See J. Francis, *A History of the English Railway: its social relations and revelations, 1820–1845*, I (London, 1851), p. 131.

118 Quoted in G. Rees, *op. cit.*, p. 46.

119 Quoted in W. M. Ackworth, *op. cit.*, p. 77.

120 G. Head, *op. cit.*, p. 23.

121 C. Dickens, *Dombey and Son* (1848; repr. Oxford, 1982), p. 236.

122 *Ibid.*, pp. 236–7.

123 *Illustrated London News*, II (1843), pp. 76–7.

124 Bodleian MS 46.1361, *op. cit.*, p. 9.

125 S. Carr, *op. cit.*, p. 14.

126 C. Dickens, *op. cit.*, p. 185.

127 P. S. Bagwell, *op. cit.*, p. 125.

128 See G. Rees, *op. cit.*, p. 14.

129 S. Kern, *The Culture of Time and Space, 1880–1918* (Cambridge, Mass., 1983), p. 37.

130 See M. Gold, 'A history of nature', in D. Massey and J. Allen, eds., *Geography Matters* (Cambridge, 1984), pp. 12–33; also N. Smith, *op. cit.*

131 W. E. Houghton, *op. cit.*, p. 40.

132 C. Dickens, 'Mugby Junction', in *Christmas Stories*, II (London, 1866), p. 139.

133 *Ibid.*, p. 131.

134 *Ibid.*, p. 139.

135 H. House, *The Dickens World* (London, 1941), p. 143.

136 *Ibid.*, p. 144.

137 *The Railway Magazine and Annals of Science*, I, new series, no. 3 (1836), p. 112.

138 L. Faucher, *Manchester in 1844: its present condition and future prospects* (Manchester, 1844), p. 18.

139 See H. Jennings, *op. cit.*, pp. 173–4.

140 W. E. Houghton, *op. cit.*, p. 54.

141 Quoted in *ibid.*, p. 68.

142 See P. S. Bagwell, *op. cit.*, pp. 126–7.

143 J. Simmons, *The Victorian Railway* (London, 1991), p. 287.

144 *Ibid.*, p. 288.

145 A. Trollope, *Barchester Towers* (1856; repr. Oxford, 1996), p. 37.

146 E. T. MacDermot, *History of the Great Western Railway*, I, 1833–1863 (edn. rev. C. R. Clinker, London, 1964), p. 12.

147 *Ibid.*

148 Bodleian MS Gough Add. Lancs 8° 56(6), *op. cit.*, p. 46.

149 A. Freeling, *The Railway Companion from London to Birmingham* (London, n.d.), pp. 34 ff; the date is almost certainly 1838.

150 See C. Barman, *An Introduction to Railway Architecture* (London, 1950), p. 27.

151 See H. House, *op. cit.*, p. 139.

152 See E. A. Pratt, *A History of Inland Transport and Communication in England* (London, 1912), p. 245.

153 See *The Railway Magazine*, January 1836, p. 293.

154 W. E. Houghton, *op. cit.*, p. 66.

155 Quoted in *ibid.*, p. 66.

156 *Ibid.*, p. 64.

157 C. Dickens, *Dombey and Son*, *op. cit.*, p. 53.

158 *Ibid.*, pp. 184–5.

159 *Ibid.*, p. 184.

160 See M. T. Greene, *Geology in the Nineteenth Century: changing views of a changing world* (Ithaca, 1982).

161 D. R. Dean, 'Through Science to Despair: Geology and the Victorians', in J. Paradis and T. Postlewait, eds., *Victorian Science and Victorian Values: literary perspectives* (New Brunswick, 1985), p. 114.

162 *A Handbook for Travellers along the London and Birmingham Railway* (London, 1839), p. 46 ff. (Bodleian MS Gough Adds. Eng. rlys 16° 102).

163 *Ibid.*, p. 113.

164 T. Roscoe, *The London and Birmingham Railway* (London, 1839) p. 31.

165 E. T. Cook and A. D. O. Wedderburn, eds., *The Works of John Ruskin*, 36 (London, 1903–), p. 62.

166 M. T. Greene has even referred to the period as forming geology's 'heroic age'; see *op. cit.*, p. 70.

167 See F. Burkhardt and S. Smith, eds., *The Correspondence of Charles Darwin*, 2, 1837–43 (Cambridge, 1986), pp. 72–3.

168 See C. Barman, *Early British Railways*, *op. cit.*, p. 24.

169 T. Roscoe, The London and Birmingham Railway, *op. cit.*, p. 74.

170 See the account quoted in M. Robbins, *The Railway Age in Britain and its impact on the world* (London, 1962; repr. Harmondsworth, 1965), p. 70.

171 See F. Burkhardt and S. Smith, eds., *op. cit.*, 3, 1844–46 (Cambridge, 1987), p. 224.

172 See D. R. Dean, *op. cit.*, p. 121.

2 THE 'MARCH OF INTELLECT'

1 E. J. Hobsbawm, *Industry and Empire* (London, 1969), pp. 110–11; Michael Robbins has also remarked how 'railway' became a sort of cant word for 'modern', just as 'atomic' was used after 1945 to impute to objects the quality of being up to date; M. Robbins, *The Railway Age in Britain and its impact on the world* (London, 1962; repr. Harmondsworth, 1965), p. 55.

2 W. Schivelbusch, *The Railway Journey: the industrialization of time and space in the 19th Century* (New York, 1977), p. 10.

3 See W. Cronon, *Nature's Metropolis: Chicago and the Great West* (London, 1991), p. 80.

4 *Ibid.*, p. 24.

5 H. Booth, *Views of Liverpool and Manchester Railway* (Liverpool, 1830), p. 47

6 See H. Jennings, *Pandemonium: the coming of the machine as seen by contemporary observers* (1985; repr. London, 1995), p. 179.

7 *The Railway Companion, describing an excursion along the Liverpool line . . . etc.* (London, 1833), p. 23 (Bodleian MS Gough Add. Lancs 8° 56 (6)).

8 *Ibid.*, pp. 23–4.

9 *Blackwood's Edinburgh Magazine*, XXVIII (1830), p. 825.

10 W. Schivelbusch, *op. cit.*, pp. 23–4.

11 G. Head, *A Home Tour through the*

Manufacturing Districts of England (London, 1836), p. 313.

12 *Chambers's Encyclopaedia*, 13 (London, 1959), pp. 498–9.

13 *Ibid.*, p. 499.

14 E. T. MacDermot, *History of the Great Western Railway*, I: *1833–1863* (rev. edn. C. R. Clinker, London, 1964), pp. 324–5.

15 *Ibid.*, pp. 326–7.

16 J. Richards and J. MacKenzie, *The Railway Station: a social history* (Oxford, 1986), p. 304.

17 F. S. Williams, *Our Iron Roads: their history, construction and social influences* (London, 1852), pp. 320–21.

18 Quoted in S. Kern, *The Culture of Time and Space, 1880–1918* (Cambridge, Mass., 1983), p. 68.

19 *Ibid.*

20 C. Dickens, *Hard Times* (1854; repr. Harmondsworth, 1969), p. 233.

21 See D. Harvey, *The Condition of Postmodernity: an enquiry into the origins of cultural change* (Oxford, 1989), pp. 240 ff.

22 *Punch*, XXXIII (1857), p. 132.

23 Quoted in R. Williams, *Culture and Society, 1780–1950* (1958; repr. Harmondsworth, 1961), p. 86.

24 See E. T. MacDermot. *History of the Great Western Railway*, II: *1863–1921* (rev. edn. C. R. Clinker, London, 1964), pp. 105 ff.

25 See F. S. Williams, *op. cit.*, pp. 262 ff; also E. T. MacDermot, II, pp. 103 ff.

26 See F. S. Williams, *op. cit.*, pp. 262–3.

27 E. T. MacDermot, II, *op. cit.*, p. 113.

28 *Ibid.*

29 F. S. Williams, *op. cit.*, p. 263.

30 See E. T. MacDermot, II, *op. cit.*, pp. 112 ff.

31 See J. Copeland, *Roads and their Traffic, 1750–1850* (Newton Abbot, 1968), pp. 163 ff.

32 E. T. MacDermot, I, *op. cit.*, p. 16.

33 *Ibid.*, p. 20.

34 *Ibid.*, pp. 35 ff.

35 On the lines to Chelmsford and Cambridge; W. M. Ackworth, *The Railways of England* (5th edn., London, 1900), p. 413.

36 F. S. Williams, *op. cit.*, p. 193.

37 E. T. MacDermot, I, *op. cit.*, p. 17.

38 *Ibid.*

39 *Ibid.*, pp. 100–1.

40 *Ibid.*, p. 104.

41 *Ibid.*, pp. 104 ff.

42 M. Robbins, *op. cit.*, p. 28.

43 W. M. Ackworth, *op. cit.*, p. 262.

44 E. T. MacDermot, I, *op. cit.*, p. 104.

45 L. T. C. Rolt, *Victorian Engineering* (London, 1970), p. 42.

46 *Penny Cyclopaedia of the Society for the Diffusion of Useful Knowledge*, XIX (1841), p. 256.

47 *Ibid.*, p. 103.

48 F. S. Williams, *op. cit.*, p. 247.

49 L. T. C. Rolt, *op. cit.*, p. 158.

50 E. T. Macdermot, I, *op. cit.*, p. 347.

51 *Ibid.*, p. 411.

52 R. A. Williams, *The London and South Western Railway*, I, *The Formative Years* (Newton Abbot, 1968), pp. 40, 244.

53 *Ibid.*, p. 263.

54 F. Whishaw, *The Railways of Great Britain and Ireland* (London, 1840), appendix, p. xiii.

55 F. S. Williams, *op. cit.*, p. 254.

56 'The Arriving Train', in S. Carr, ed., *The Poetry of Railways* (London, 1978), p. 59.

57 G. Head, *op. cit.*, p. 203.

58 H. Booth, *op. cit.*, p. 92.

59 J. Francis, *A History of the English Railway; its social relations and revelations, 1820–1845*, II (London, 1851), p. 143.

60 Quoted in W. E. Houghton, *The Victorian Frame of Mind, 1830–1870* (Newhaven, 1957), p. 39.

61 *Household Words*, 8 (1853–4), p. 412.

62 *A Handbook for Travellers along the London and Birmingham Railway* (London, 1839), p. 9 (Bodleian MS, Gough Adds. Eng. rlys 16° 102).

63 *Ibid.*, p. 10.

64 *Ibid.*, p. 39.

65 *Ibid.*, p. 46.

66 *Ibid.*, p. 65.

67 F. S. Williams, *op. cit.*, p. 218.

68 *Ibid.*

69 Quoted in W. E. Houghton, *op. cit.*, p. 40.

70 See R. Williams, *op. cit.*, p. 86.

71 C. Dickens, *op. cit.*, p. 52.

72 W. E. Houghton, *op. cit.*, p. 38.

73 T. Roscoe, *The London and Birmingham Railway* (London, 1839), p. 165.

74 See H. Jennings, *op. cit.*, p. 209.

75 *Punch*, XI (1845) p. 163.

76 See H. Booth, *op. cit.*, p. 94.

77 See M. Robbins, *op. cit.*, p. 23.

78 *Ibid.*, p. 25.

79 E. J. Hobsbawm, *op. cit.*, p. 110.

80 *Osbourne's Guide to the Grand Junction or Birmingham. Liverpool and Manchester Railway* (2nd edn., Birmingham, November 1838), pp. 66–7.

81 See J. Simmons, *The Victorian Railway* (London, 1991), p. 183.

82 J. Richards and J. MacKenzie, *op. cit.*, p. 96.

83 G. Royde Smith, *The History of Bradshaw* (London, 1939), p. 47.

84 Angus B. Reach, *The Comic Bradshaw: or, Bubbles from the Boiler* (London, 1848).

85 *Ibid.*, pp. 21–2.

86 *Punch*, XXX (1856), p. 202.

87 *Punch*, XVIII (1850), p. 167.

88 *Punch*, XX (1851), p. 225.

89 F. Klingender, *Art and the Industrial Revolution* (London, 1947; rev. edn., London, 1972), p. 95.

90 A. Desmond, *Huxley: From Devil's Disciple to Evolution's High Priest* (Harmondsworth, 1998), p. 14.

91 *The Penny Magazine of the Society for the Diffusion of Useful Knowledge*, I (1832), pp. 262–3.

92 *The Penny Cyclopaedia of the Society for the Diffusion of Useful Knowledge*, I: *A–Andes* (1833).

93 *Ibid.*, XIX (1841), pp. 245–67.

94 *Ibid.*, p. 253.

95 T. Roscoe, *op. cit.*, pp. 62–3.

96 *The Penny Cyclopaedia*, *op. cit.*, p. 249.

97 *Mechanics' Magazine*, 2 (1824), p. 362.

98 *The Penny Cyclopaedia*, *op. cit.*, p. 254.

99 L. Faucher, *Manchester in 1844: its present condition and future prospects* (Manchester, 1844), p. 21.

100 *Mechanics' Magazine*, 1 (1823).

101 *Ibid.*, preface.

102 *Ibid.*, 2 (1824), p. 278.

103 *Ibid.*, 25 (1836), p. 292.

104 See the case of the Brighton Railway Bill; *ibid.*, pp. 326 ff.

105 *Ibid.*, 26 (1837), pp. 407 ff.

106 *Ibid.*, p. 442.

107 *Ibid.*, 33 (1840), p. 518.

108 See F. Klingender, *op. cit.*, p. 127; also *The Railway Companion*, *op. cit.*, p. 47.

109 F. Klingender, *op. cit.*, p. 132.

110 *Ibid.*, p. 123.

111 C. Dickens, *Dombey and Son* (1846–8; repr. Oxford, 1974), p. 185.

112 *Ibid.*, p. 184.

113 J. Richards and J. MacKenzie, *op. cit.*, p. 20.

114 See, as a starting-point, C. Barman, *An Introduction to Railway Architecture* (London, 1950).

115 *Punch*, XIV (1848), p. 219.

116 J. Richards and J. MacKenzie, *op. cit.*, p. 20.

117 Quoted in *ibid.*, p. 20.

118 See W. Feaver, *The Art of John Martin* (Oxford, 1975), p. 144; also M. D. Paley, *The Apocalyptic Sublime* (New Haven, 1986). Brunel's association with John Martin extended to offering the painter a ride on the footplate of a Great Western locomotive in 1841 as part of speed trials on the line (see the fuller discussion in chapter eight).

119 See F. Klingender, *op. cit.*, p. 109; W. Feaver, *op. cit.*, p. 144.

120 According to C. Barman, *op. cit.*, p. 41.

121 *Ibid.*, p. 30.

122 *Ibid.*, p. 36.

123 *Punch*, XII (1847), p. 59.

124 One of the first major references to it is in D. Harvey, *The Limits to Capital* (Oxford, 1982), pp. 377 ff.

125 K. Marx. *Grundrisse: foundations of the critique of political economy* (1857–8;

repr. Harmondsworth, 1973).

126 Christian Anderson, 'A poet's view of a railroad', p. 8, in *Railway Readings* (1847) (Bodleian MS 2705 f. 422).

127 *The Railway Companion, op. cit.*, pp. 16–17.

128 H. Booth, *op. cit.*, p. 89.

129 S. Smiles, *The Life of George Stephenson* (1857; repr. London, 1903), p. vii.

130 See J. Sutherland, introduction to A. Trollope, *Barchester Towers* (repr. Oxford, 1996), pp. xv–xvi.

131 W. Schivelbusch, *op. cit.*, p. 37; 'eotechnical' refers to those relationships that have existed in the landscape since earliest times.

132 E. J. Hobsbawm, *op. cit*, p. 110.

133 W. Schivelbusch, *op. cit.*, p. 38.

134 This feature is discussed further in W. Schivelbusch, *op. cit.*, p. 39.

135 F. S. Williams, *op. cit.*, p. 212.

136 W. M. Ackworth, *op. cit.*, p. 58.

137 Quoted in W. Schivelbusch, *op. cit.*, p. 39.

138 See, for instance, the numerous uses in the handbook for travellers on the London and Birmingham Railway (Bodleian MS, Gough Adds. Eng. rlys 16° 102, *op. cit.*).

139 Bodleian MS, 2705 f. 422, *op. cit.*, p. 8.

140 *Household Words*, 16 (1857–8), p. 314.

141 See J. F. C. Harrison, *Early Victorian Britain, 1832–1851* (first published as *The Early Victorians, 1832–51*, London, 1971; repr. London, 1979), p. 80 ff.

142 See H. House, *The Dickens World* (2nd edn., Oxford, 1942), p. 135.

143 See D. Harvey, *The Condition of Postmodernity, op. cit.*, pp. 46–9.

144 F. S. Williams, *op. cit.*, p. 285.

145 A copy is at the Yale Center for British Art, Rare Books Collection, DA625 R6 (undated).

146 *Ibid.* (London and Birmingham section), p. 45.

147 B. Disraeli, *Sybil or The Two Nations* (1845; repr. Harmondsworth, 1954), p. 88.

148 W. Schivelbusch, *op. cit.*, p. 35.

149 *Household Words*, 19 (1858–9), pp. 137–9.

150 F. S. Williams, *op. cit.*, p. 284.

151 G. Eliot, *Adam Bede* (1859; repr. London, 1980), p. 557.

152 W. M. Ackworth, *op. cit.*, p. 30.

153 *Ibid.*, p. 31.

154 W. Pickering, *Railroad Eclogues*, (London, 1846), p. 29 (Bodleian MS, 46. 1361).

155 J. F. C. Houghton. *op. cit.*, p. 7.

156 *Ibid.*, p. 61.

157 Quoted in S. Kern, *op. cit.*, p. 125.

158 *Punch*, XLVII (1864), pp. 217, 241.

159 F. Burckhardt and S. Smith, eds., *The Correspondence of Charles Darwin*, 2, 1837–1843 (Cambridge, 1986), p. 94.

160 *Ibid.*, p. 165.

161 See S. Kern, *op. cit.*, p. 111.

162 *Ibid.*, p. 110.

163 W. Schivelbusch, *op. cit.*, pp. 130–1.

164 *Ibid.*, p. 131.

165 L. T. C. Rolt, *Red for Danger* (rev. edn., London, 1966), p. 21.

166 See W. Schivelbusch, *op. cit.*, p. 130.

167 *Illustrated London News*, liii (1868), p. 189.

168 *Ibid.*, VII (1845), p. 150.

169 See L. T. C. Rolt, *op. cit.*, p. 31.

170 *Punch*, XXIII (1852), p. 157.

171 *Ibid.*, XVI (1851), p. 139.

172 F. S. Williams, *op. cit.*, p. 369.

173 W. Pickering, *op. cit.*, p. 20.

174 S. Phillips, 'The Literature of the Rail', *The Times*, 9 August 1851.

175 See J. Sutherland, *op. cit.*, pp. xxi–xxii.

176 F. B. Head, *Stokers and Pokers; or The London & North-Western Railway* (London, 1850), p. 96.

177 R. Williams, *The Long Revolution* (Harmondsworth, 1965), p. 189.

178 J. Richards and J. MacKenzie, *op. cit.*, p. 299.

179 J. Simmons, *op. cit.*, p. 247.

180 *The Railway Anecdote Book* (London, 1852) (Bodleian MS, 270 a.2).

181 *Ibid.*, p. 10.

182 *Ibid.*, p. 24.

183 J. Richards and J. MacKenzie, *op. cit.*, p. 300.

184 *Ibid.*, p. 298.

185 S. Phillips, *op. cit.*

186 Quoted in J. Richards and J. MacKenzie, *op. cit.*, p. 298.

187 R. Williams, *op. cit.*, p. 72.

188 S. Phillips, *op. cit.*

189 A. Desmond and J. Moore, *Darwin* (Harmondsworth, 1992), p. 477.

190 S. Phillips, *op. cit.*

3 CAPITAL

1 K. Marx, *Capital* II (1887; repr., Harmondsworth, 1978), p. 228.

2 Railway Clearing House, *List of Alterations in, and additions to, the general classification of goods* (London, 1869).

3 T. Richards, *The Commodity Culture of Victorian England: Advertizing and spectacle, 1851–1914* (Stanford, 1990), p. 3.

4 See M. J. Freeman, introduction, in M. J. Freeman and D. H. Aldcroft, eds., *Transport in Victorian Britain* (Manchester, 1988), pp. 32 ff.

5 K. Marx, *Capital* II, *op. cit.*, p. 249.

6 K. Marx, *Capital* III (1887; repr., Harmondsworth, 1981), p. 538.

7 K. Marx, *Capital* I (1867; repr., Harmondsworth, 1976), p. 363.

8 Quoted in D. Harvey, *The Limits to Capital* (Oxford, 1982), p. 377.

9 See F. S. Williams, *Our Iron Roads: their history, construction and social influences* (London, 1852), Appendix A, abstract of the proceedings of the committee of the House of Commons on the Liverpool and Manchester Railroad Bill.

10 *Ibid.*; see also R. E. Carlson, *The Liverpool and Manchester Railway Project, 1821–1831* (Newton Abbot, 1969), p. 128.

11 L. Faucher, *Manchester in 1844: its present condition and future prospects* (Manchester, 1844), pp. 151–2.

12 H. Booth, *Views of Liverpool and Manchester Railway* (Liverpool, 1830), p. 88.

13 *Ibid.*, p. 89.

14 *British Parliamentary Papers* [hereafter abbreviated to *BPP*], Appendix to the Fifth Report of the Select Committee on Railways, XI (1844), p. 32.

15 G. Rees, *Early Railway Prints: a social history of the railways from 1825 to 1850* (Oxford, 1980), p. 64.

16 *BPP*, Appendix to the Fifth Report of the Select Committee on Railways, *op. cit*.

17 R. W. Kostal, *Law and English Railway Capitalism, 1825–1875* (Oxford, 1994), p. 115.

18 *Ibid.*, pp. 110–11.

19 *Ibid.*, p. 114.

20 *Ibid.*, p. 126.

21 H. M. Ross, *British Railways: their organization and management* (London, 1904), p. 215.

22 R. W. Kostal, *op. cit.*, p. 150.

23 D. Cannadine, *Aspects of Aristocracy: grandeur and decline in Modern Britain* (New Haven, 1994), p. 57.

24 R. W. Kostal, *op. cit.*, pp. 164–5.

25 *Ibid.*, p. 172.

26 K. Marx, *Capital* II, *op. cit.*, pp. 260–61.

27 K. Marx, *Capital* III, *op. cit.*, p. 534.

28 R. Williams, *Keywords: a vocabulary of culture and society* (London, 1983), p. 50.

29 *Railway reform – its expediency and practicability considered* (1844), p. 4 (Bodleian MS 44.1640).

30 *Ibid.*, p. 71.

31 *A letter to the Rt. Hon. W. E. Gladstone on railway legislation* (1844), pp. 1–2 (Bodleian MS 44.1640).

32 P. S. Bagwell, *The Transport Revolution from 1770* (London, 1974), pp. 173 ff.

33 *Railway reform, op. cit.*, p. 4 (Bodleian MS 44.1640).

34 F. Engels, *The Condition of the Working Class in England* (1844; repr., London, 1969).

35 *Punch*, V (1843), p. 48.

36 R. W. Kostal, *op. cit.*, p. 6.

37 For further discussion, see E. J. Hobsbawm, *Industry and Empire* (Harmondsworth, 1969), p. 112.

38 F. Whishaw, *The Railways of Great Britain and Ireland* (London, 1840).

39 William Pickering, *Railroad Eclogues* (London, 1846), p. 12 (Bodleian MS 46. 1361).

40 *The Railway Almanac, Directory, Yearbook of Statistics and Digest of Railway Law for 1846* (London, 1846), p. 15 (Bodleian MS (Alm.) 247917 e. 175).

41 K. Marx, *Capital* III, *op. cit.*, p. 534.

42 Quoted in M. C. Reed, 'Railways and the growth of the capital market', in M. C. Reed, ed., *Railways in the Victorian Economy – studies in finance and growth* (Newton Abbot, 1969), p. 175.

43 P. S. Bagwell, *op. cit.*, p. 96.

44 See M. C. Reed, *op. cit.*, p. 174.

45 P. S. Bagwell, *op. cit.*, p. 96.

46 See M. C. Reed, *op. cit.*, p. 175.

47 *London Mercantile Journal*, 1 March 1836, quoted in M. C. Reed, *op. cit.*, p. 177.

48 *Ibid.*, pp. 179 ff.

49 *Ibid.*, p. 162

50 Quoted in M. C. Reed, *op. cit.*, p. 180.

51 *Ibid.*, pp. 165–6.

52 R. W. Kostal, *op. cit.*, p. 56.

53 M. C. Reed, *op. cit.*, p. 166.

54 R. W. Kostal, *op. cit.*, p. 36.

55 *Illustrated London News*, VII (1845), pp. 353, 361–2.

56 W. Wordsworth, *Guide to the Lakes* (5th edn., London, 1835), pp. 162–6.

57 M. C. Reed, *op. cit.*, p. 168.

58 See D. Morier Evans, *The Commercial Crisis, 1847–1848* (London, 1849), p. 2.

59 See P. S. Bagwell, *op. cit.*, p. 94.

60 *Ibid.*, p. 93.

61 T. R. Gourvish, 'Railways, 1830–70: the formative years', in M. J. Freeman and D. H. Aldcroft, eds., *Transport in Victorian Britain* (Manchester, 1988), p. 60.

62 M. C. Reed, *op. cit.*, p. 171.

63 *Ibid.*, pp. 179–80.

64 Frederic Harrison, 'A few words about the nineteenth century' (1882), quoted in W. E. Houghton, *The Victorian Frame of Mind 1830–1870* (New Haven, 1957), p. 39.

65 See P. Jackson, *Maps of Meaning* (London, 1989), p. 33.

66 See R. Williams, *Marxism and Literature* (Oxford, 1977).

67 J. Simmons, *The Victorian Railway* (London, 1991), p. 244.

68 J. Francis, *A History of the English Railway; its social relations and revelations, 1820–1845*, II (London, 1851), p. 149.

69 *Ibid.*, p. 243.

70 M. C. Reed, *op. cit.*, p. 171.

71 J. Simmons, *op. cit.*, p. 243; after 1839, it was re-titled *Herepath's Journal*.

72 *Railway Almanac*, *op. cit.* (Bodleian MS (Alm.) 247917 e. 175).

73 F. S. Williams, *op. cit.*, p. 44.

74 J. Simmons, *op. cit.*, p. 211.

75 *Ibid.*

76 *Punch*, IX (1845), p. 161.

77 Quoted in F. S. Williams, *op. cit.*, p. 46.

78 F. S. Williams, *op. cit.*, p. 47.

79 *Punch*, IX (1845), p. 177.

80 See F. S. Williams, *op. cit.*, p. 54.

81 *Railroad Eclogues*, *op. cit.*, p. 12 (Bodleian MS 46. 1361).

82 P. S. Bagwell, *op. cit.*, p. 94.

83 *Ibid.*, p. 95.

84 *Punch*, IX (1845), p. 183.

85 *The Railway Meeting: a satire dedicated to pillaged and plundered shareholders of Great Britain by a Lancashire victim* (London, 1856), p. 30 (Bodleian MS 280 s.377).

86 *Ibid.*, p. 23.

87 *Ibid.*, p. 33.

88 *Ibid.*

89 *Ibid.*, p. 52.

90 *Illustrated London News*, VIII (1846), p. 242.

91 R. W. Kostal, *op. cit.*, p. 12.

92 *Ibid.*, p. 45.

93 *Ibid.*, p. 34.

94 *Ibid.*, chapter 2, gives a full account of the legal aftermath of the Railway Mania.

95 *Ibid.*, pp. 53, 109.

96 *Ibid.*, p. 102.

97 *Ibid.*, pp. 11 ff.

98 C. Dickens, *Household Words*, 18 (1858), p. 506.

99 P. S. Bagwell, *op. cit.*, p. 98.

100 K. Marx, *Capital* III, *op. cit.*, p. 538.

101 *Ibid.*, p. 534.

102 *Ibid.*, p. 535.

103 *Ibid.*, p. 536.

104 See the report in *Illustrated London News*, XII (1848), p. 405.

105 C. Rowcroft, 'Currency and Railways', pp. 18 ff (Yale University, Beinecke Rare Book Library, NZ 846r).

106 F. Engels, *op. cit.*, p. 226.

107 *Punch*, XVI (1848), pp. 214–15.

108 See *Household Words*, 8 (1853–4), p. 412.

109 For more details of amalgamation, see M. Freeman and D. Aldcroft, *The Atlas of British Railway History* (London, 1985), p. 22.

110 P. S. Bagwell, *op. cit.*, p. 103.

111 See R. A. Williams, *The London and South Western Railway, I: the formative years* (Newton Abbot, 1968), pp. 141 ff.

112 P. J. Cain, 'Railways 1870–1914: the maturity of the private system', in M. J. Freeman and D. H. Aldcroft, eds., *op. cit.*, p. 103.

113 W. M. Ackworth, *The Railways of England* (5th edn., London, 1900), p. 58.

114 P. J. Cain, *op. cit.*, pp. 103, 128.

115 *Ibid.*, p. 104.

116 D. Harvey, *op. cit.*, p. 140.

117 P. J. Cain, *op. cit.*, p. 104.

118 See R. W. Kostal, *op. cit.*, pp. 183 ff.

119 For further details, see the commentary in P. J. Cain, *op. cit.*, pp. 106 ff; also M. J. Freeman, introduction, in M. J. Freeman and D. H. Aldcroft, eds., *op. cit.*, pp. 34 ff.

120 P. J. Cain, *op. cit.*, p. 108.

121 H. J. Dyos and D. H. Aldcroft, *British Transport: an economic survey from the seventeenth century to the twentieth* (Leicester, 1969), p. 175.

122 See P. S. Bagwell, *The Railway Clearing House in the British Economy, 1842–1922* (London, 1968), p. 85.

123 H. J. Dyos and D. H. Aldcroft, *op. cit.*, p. 151.

124 See T. R. Gourvish, *Railways 1830–1870: the formative years*, in M. J. Freeman and D. H. Aldcroft, eds., *op. cit.*, p. 83; also T. R. Gourvish, 'The railways and the development of managerial enterprise in Britain, 1850–1939', in K. Kobayashi and H. Morikawa, eds., *Development of Managerial Enterprise* (Tokyo, 1986).

125 See P. J. Cain, *op. cit.*, pp. 113–14.

126 R. J. Irving, *The North Eastern Railway Company, 1870–1914; an economic history* (Leicester, 1976), p. 138.

127 See G. R. Hawke, *Railways and Economic Growth in England and Wales 1840–1870* (Oxford, 1970), pp. 325–6.

128 R. J. Morris, *Class and Class Consciousness in the Industrial Revolution, 1780–1850* (London, 1979), p. 10.

129 J. Simmons, *op. cit.*, p. 359.

130 See J. Copeland, *Roads and their Traffic, 1750–1850* (Newton Abbot, 1968), p. 64.

131 B. Trinder, *The Making of the Industrial Landscape*, (London, 1982), p. 150.

132 W. M. Ackworth, *op. cit.*, p. 43.

133 For a comprehensive guide to train accommodation about this time, see F. Whishaw, *op. cit.*

134 See W. M. Ackworth, *op. cit.*, p. 43; also F. Whishaw, *op. cit.*, p. 248.

135 F. Whishaw, *op. cit.*, p. 92.

136 E. T. MacDermot, *History of the Great Western Railway*, I: *1833–63* (2nd edn., Newton Abbot, 1964), pp. 332–3.

137 See F. Whishaw, *op. cit.*

138 See J. Simmons, *op. cit.*, p. 359.

139 F. Whishaw, *op. cit.*, p. 248.

140 *Ibid.*, pp. 98, 429.

141 See E. T. MacDermot, *op. cit.*, p. 335.

142 *Ibid.*, p. 334.

143 *Ibid.*, p. 335.

144 S. C. Brees, *Railway Practice* (4th ser., London, 1847), p. cviii.

145 *Ibid.*, p. cxi.

146 W. M. Ackworth, *op. cit.*, p. 40.

147 Quoted in A. Clayre, *Nature and Industrialization: an anthology* (Oxford, 1977), p. 88.

148 E. T. MacDermot, *op. cit.*, p. 436.

149 See W. M. Ackworth, *op. cit,*, p. 41.
150 F. S. Williams, *op. cit.*, p. 215.
151 *Ibid.*, p. 43.
152 F. Whishaw, *op. cit.*, p. 248.
153 E. T. MacDermot, *op. cit.*, p. 338.
154 *Ibid.*, p. 348.
155 A. Clayre, *op. cit.*, p. 89.
156 G. R. Hawke, *Railways and economic Growth in England and Wales, 1840–1870* (Oxford, 1970), pp. 37–8.
157 *Ibid.*, p. 38.
158 A. Delgado, *The Annual Outing* (London, 1977), p. 28.
159 J. K. Walton, *The English Seaside Resort: a social history, 1750–1914* (Leicester, 1983), p. 26.
160 W. Wordsworth, *op. cit.*, p. 154.
161 *Hampshire Advertizer*, 23 March 1844.
162 *Ibid.*, 11 May 1844.
163 *Ibid.*, 21 September 1850.
164 R. A. Williams, *op. cit.*, p. 224.
165 See D. A. Reid, 'The "iron roads" and "the happiness of the working classes": the early development and social significance of the railway excursion', *Journal of Transport History*, 17 (1996), pp. 57–73.
166 J. K. Walton, *op. cit.*, p. 29.
167 H. Perkin, *The Age of the Railway* (London, 1970), p. 101.
168 *Illustrated London News*, XVII (1850), pp. 237–8.
169 H. Perkin, *op. cit.*, p. 99.
170 A. Delgado, *op. cit.*, p. 124.
171 H. Perkin, *op. cit.*, p. 96–7.
172 A. Delgado, *op. cit.*, p. 43.
173 *Punch*, XIX (1850), p. 159.
174 A. Bennett, *A Man from the North* (1898; repr., London, 1994), p. 72.
175 H. Perkin, *op. cit.*, p. 214.
176 See D. A. Reid, *op. cit.*, pp. 57, 70.
177 W. M. Ackworth, writing in 1900, *op. cit.*, p. 460.
178 C. E. Lee, *Passenger Class Distinctions* (London, 1946), p. 41.
179 *Ibid.*, p. 43.
180 *Ibid.*
181 W. M. Ackworth, *op. cit.*, p. 205.
182 C. E. Lee, *op. cit.*, p. 46.
183 *Ibid.*, p. 45.
184 *Ibid.*, p. 56.
185 P. S. Bagwell, *op. cit.*, p. 134.
186 C. E. Lee, *op. cit.*, p. 56.
187 P. S. Bagwell, *op. cit.*, p. 134.

4 URBANIZATION

1 J. R. Kellett, *The Impact of Railways on Victorian Cities* (London, 1969), p. xv.
2 D. Harvey, *The Urbanization of Capital: studies in the history and theory of capitalist urbanization* (Oxford, 1985), p. 40.
3 *Ibid.*, p. 37.
4 R. Lawton, 'Population and Society, 1730–1900', in R. A. Dodgshon and R. A. Butlin, eds., *An Historical Geography of England and Wales* (London, 1978), p. 348.
5 D. Harvey, *The Urbanization of Capital*, *op. cit.*, p. 138.
6 See D. Harvey, *Consciousness and the Urban Experience: studies in the history and theory of capitalist urbanization* (Oxford, 1985), pp. 28–9.
7 D. Harvey, *The Urbanization of Capital*, *op. cit.*, p. 139.
8 J. R. Kellett, *op. cit.*, p. 2.
9 *Ibid.*
10 L. Faucher, *Manchester in 1844: its present condition and future prospects* (Manchester 1844), p. 18.
11 *Ibid.*, p. 15.
12 J. R. Kellett, *op. cit.*, p. 173.
13 *Ibid.*, p. 172.
14 *Ibid.*, p. 174.
15 *Ibid.*, p. 326.
16 *Ibid.*, p. 290.
17 *Ibid.*, p. 326.
18 B. Trinder, *The Making of the Industrial Landscape* (London, 1982), p. 229.
19 F. Engels, *The Condition of the Working Class in England* (1844; repr., London, 1969), p. 84.
20 J. R. Kellett, *op. cit.*, pp. 339–40.
21 *Ibid.*, p. 331.
22 *Ibid.*, p. 333.
23 See A. S. Wohl, 'Unfit for human habitation', in H. J. Dyos and M. Wolff, eds., *The Victorian City: images and realities*, II (London, 1973), p. 605.
24 *The Times*, 2 March 1861.
25 J. R. Kellett, *op. cit.*, p. 332.
26 *British Parliamentary Papers* [hereafter BPP], Report of the Commissioners appointed to investigate the various projects for establishing Railway Termini within or in the immediate vicinity of the Metropolis, XVII (1846); Three Reports of Lords Committees on Metropolitan Railway Communication, VIII (1863).
27 R. A. Williams, *The London and South Western Railway, I: The formative years* (Newton Abbot, 1968), p. 159.
28 H. C. Binford, 'Land tenure, social structure and railway impact in North Lambeth', *Journal of Transport History*, NS II (1974), p. 131.
29 See H. J. Dyos, 'Railways and housing in Victorian London', *Journal of Transport History*, II (1955), part I, pp. 11–21; part II, pp. 90–100.
30 *Ibid.*, p. 15.
31 *Punch*, XLVI (1864), p. 49.
32 *Ibid.*, XLV (1863), p. 62.
33 *Ibid.*, XLIV (1863), p. 128.
34 *Illustrated London News*, XLII (1863), p. 342.
35 *Ibid.*, XLI (1862), p. 705.
36 *Ibid.*, XLV (1864), p. 661.
37 *Ibid.*, XLIX (1866), p. 232.
38 See Bodleian, John Johnson Collection, Railways Box 23.
39 *The Working Man*, quoted in H. J. Dyos, 'Railways and housing', *op. cit.*, p. 12.
40 *Illustrated London News*, XLIX (1866), p. 146.
41 H. J. Dyos, 'Railways and housing', *op. cit.*, p. 13.
42 *Ibid.*, p. 14.
43 H. J. Dyos, 'Some social costs of railway building in London', *Journal of Transport History*, III (1957), appendix.
44 See, for example, H. C. Binford, *op. cit.*, p. 143.
45 H. J. Dyos, 'Railways and housing', *op. cit.*, p. 18.
46 *Ibid.*
47 *Illustrated London News*, XLII (1863), p. 57.
48 *Ibid.*, XLI (1862), p. 294.
49 *Ibid.*, XLII (1863), p. 74.
50 *Ibid.*, XLV (1864), p. 99.
51 See H. J. Dyos and D. H. Aldcroft, *British Transport: an economic survey from the seventeenth to the twentieth centuries* (Leicester, 1969), p. 218.
52 *Punch*, XI (1846), p. 133.
53 *Ibid.*, XLVI (1864), p. 227.
54 Adeline, in A. Bennett, *A Man from the North* (1898; repr., London, 1994), p. 44.
55 A. Bennett, *Hilda Lessways* (1911; repr., London, 1975), pp. 114–15.
56 A. Bennett, *Anna of the Five Towns* (1902; repr., London, 1936), p. 109.
57 *Ibid.*, pp. 109–10.
58 D. Harvey, *Consciousness and the Urban Experience*, *op. cit.*, p. 13.
59 J. Richards and J. MacKenzie, *The Railway Station: a social history* (Oxford, 1986), p. 166.
60 G. and W. Grossmith, *The Diary of a Nobody* (1892; repr. Harmondsworth, 1995).
61 J. Stevenson, *British Society, 1914–45* (Harmondsworth, 1984), p. 25.
62 *The Builder*, VI (1848), p. 500.
63 A. Bennett, *Hilda Lessways*, *op. cit.*, p. 108.
64 A. Bennett, *A Man from the North*, *op. cit.*, p. 44.
65 *Ibid.*, p. 46.
66 *Ibid.*, p. 45.
67 *Ibid.*, p. 46.
68 H. J. Dyos and D. A. Reeder, 'Slums and suburbs', in H. J. Dyos and M. Wolff, eds., *op. cit.*, I, p. 360.
69 *Ibid.*, p. 359.
70 A. Bennett, *A Man from the North*, *op. cit.*, p. 44.
71 H. J. Dyos and D. A. Reeder, *op. cit.*, p. 359.
72 D. Harvey, *Consciousness and the Urban Experience*, *op. cit.*, p. 9.
73 G. Simmel (1971), quoted in *ibid.*

74 A. A. Jackson, *Semi-detached London: suburban development, life and transport* (London, 1973), p. 173.

75 K. Chorley, *Manchester Made Them* (London, 1950), p. 115.

76 D. Harvey, *Consciousnes and the Urban Experience, op. cit.*, p. 9.

77 A. A. Jackson, *op. cit.*, pp. 21–2.

78 H. J. Dyos and D. A. Reeder, 'Slums and suburbs', in H. J. Dyos and M. Wolff, eds., *op. cit.*, I, p. 369.

79 *The Builder*, VI (1848), pp. 500–1.

80 A. Bennett, *Hilda Lessways, op. cit.*, p. 107.

81 H. J. Dyos, *Victorian Suburb: a study of the growth of Camberwell* (Leicester, 1961), p. 24.

82 H. Perkin, *The Age of the Railway* (London, 1970), p. 270.

83 H. J. Dyos, 'Railways and Housing', *op. cit.*, p. 91.

84 J. R. Kellett, *op. cit.*, p. 372.

85 *Illustrated London News*, XXXVI (1860), p. 32.

86 *Punch*, XXXV (1858), p. 132.

87 H. J. Dyos, *Victorian Suburb, op. cit.*

88 J. R. Kellett, *op. cit.*, p. 372.

89 *Ibid.*, p. 373.

90 A. A. Jackson, *Semi-detached London, op. cit.*, p. 202.

91 *Ibid.*, p. 374.

92 J. R. Kellett, *op. cit.*, p. 376.

93 J. Richards and J. MacKenzie, *op. cit.*, p. 167.

94 J. R. Kellett, *op. cit.*, p. 379.

95 *Ibid.*, p. 382.

96 See *Illustrated London News*, XLVI (1865), p. 371.

97 J. Simmons, *The Victorian Railway* (London, 1991), p. 329.

98 37 & 38 Victoria. c. 109.

99 A. A. Jackson, *London's Metropolitan Railway* (London, 1986), pp. 140–2.

100 *The Economist*, 25 July 1885, p. 912.

101 A. A. Jackson, *Semi-detached London, op. cit.*, p. 224.

102 A. A. Jackson, *London's Metropolitan Railway, op. cit.*, pp. 238 ff.

103 A. A. Jackson, *Semi-detached London, op. cit.*, p. 225.

104 J. Simmons, 'The Power of the Railway', in H. J. Dyos and M. Wolff, eds., *op. cit.*, I, p. 299.

105 *Ibid.*, p. 289.

106 *Ibid.*, p. 299.

107 See J. Richards and J. MacKenzie, *op. cit.*, pp. 167–8.

108 D. Harvey, *The Limits to Capital* (Oxford, 1982), p. 376.

109 W. Schivelbusch, *The Railway Journey: the industrialization of time and space in the 19th century* (New York, 1986), p. 189.

110 *Ibid.*, p. 190.

111 T. Richards, *The Commodity Culture of Victorian England: Advertizing and Spectacle, 1851–1914* (Stanford, 1990), p. 4.

112 A. J. Cronin, *Hatter's Castle* (London, 1931), p. 183.

113 W. Schivelbusch, *op. cit.*, p. 192.

114 K. Marx, *Capital* II (1887; repr. Harmondsworth, 1978), p. 228.

115 See T. Richards, *op. cit.*, p. 5.

116 *Ibid.*, p. 194.

117 W. M. Ackworth, *The Railways of England* (5th edn., London, 1900), p. 152.

118 Quoted in H. J. Dyos and D. H. Aldcroft, *op. cit.*, p. 215.

119 Bodleian, John Johnson Collection, Railways Box 6.

120 *Ibid.*, Railways Box 8.

121 F. S. Williams, *Our Iron Roads* (London, 1852), p. 217.

122 *Ibid.*, p. 218.

123 E. A. Pratt, *A History of Inland Transport and Communication in England* (London, 1912), p. 391.

124 W. M. Ackworth, *op. cit.*, p. 113.

125 See E. A. Pratt, *op. cit.*, p. 392.

126 *Ibid.*, p. 393.

127 *Ibid.*, p. 394.

128 See J. Medcalf, 'Railway Goods Depots: IV – King's Cross Goods Station', *Railway Magazine*, VI (1900), pp. 314, 316.

129 *Ibid.*, pp. 316–7.

130 *Ibid.*, p. 316.

131 See D. T. Timms, 'Railway Goods Depots: I – Nine Elms, London and South Western Railway', *Railway Magazine*, VI (1900), p. 76.

132 R. A. Williams, *op. cit.*, pp. 36, 160.

133 J. Richards and J. MacKenzie, *op. cit.*, p. 199.

134 W. M. Ackworth, *op. cit.*, p. 125.

135 *Ibid.*, p. 111.

136 E. A. Pratt, *op. cit.*, p. 389; W. M. Ackworth, *op. cit.*, pp. 111 ff.

137 W. M. Ackworth, *op. cit.*, pp. 112–13.

138 *Ibid.*, p. 108.

139 *Ibid.*, pp. 108–9.

140 *Ibid.*, p. 109.

141 E. A. Pratt, *op. cit.*, p. 389.

142 W. M. Ackworth, *op. cit.*, p. 113.

143 See, for example, G. L. Turnbull, *Traffic and Transport: an economic history of Pickfords* (London, 1979), p. 136.

144 E. A. Pratt, *op. cit.*, p. 389.

145 H. J. Dyos and D. H. Aldcroft, *op. cit.*, p. 214.

146 See G. L. Turnbull, *op. cit.*; F. S. Williams, *op. cit.*, p. 217–8.

147 T. C. Barker, 'Urban Transport', in M. J. Freeman and D. H. Aldcroft, *Transport in Victorian Britain* (Manchester, 1988), pp. 136–7.

148 See F. M. L. Thompson, *Victorian England: the horse-drawn society* (London, 1976).

149 F. M. L. Thompson, 'Nineteenth-century horse sense', *Economic History Review*, XXIX (1976), p. 80.

150 See the commentary in D. Harvey, *The Urbanization of Capital, op. cit.*, p. 35.

151 See P. J. Atkins, 'The growth of London's railway milk trade, c. 1845–1914', *Journal of Transport History*, IV (1978), p. 208.

152 *Ibid.*, p. 209.

153 *Ibid.*, p. 222.

154 *Ibid.*, p. 209.

155 *Ibid.*, p. 224.

156 J. Richards and J. MacKenzie, *op. cit.*, p. 194.

5 TERRITORY

1 Gilbert Thomas, 'Nostalgia' (n.d.), in B. Morgan, ed., *The Railway Lover's Companion* (London, 1963), p. 547.

2 D. Harvey, *The Limits to Capital* (Oxford, 1982), p. 398.

3 M. Robbins, *The Railway Age in Britain and its impact on the world* (Harmondsworth, 1965), p. 104.

4 See, for example, G. Revill, 'Working the system: journeys through corporate culture in the "railway age"', *Environment and Planning, D: Society and Space*, 12 (1994), pp. 705–25.

5 These issues are fully discussed in chapter 6, and see P. W. Kingsford, *Victorian Railwaymen: the emergence and growth of railway labour, 1830–1870* (London, 1970); also F. McKenna, *The Railway Workers, 1840–1870* (London, 1980).

6 M. Robbins, *op. cit.*, p. 105.

7 G. Revill, *op. cit.*, p. 713.

8 See also C. Hamilton Ellis, *The Trains We Loved* (London, 1947).

9 See P. W. B. Semmens, *Bill Hoole: engineman extraordinary* (London, 1966), pp. 23–4.

10 Gilbert Thomas, in B. Morgan, *op. cit.*, p. 548.

11 J. Betjeman, *Summoned by Bells* (London, 1960), p. 57.

12 See E. A. Pratt, *A History of Inland Transport and Communication in England* (London, 1912), p. 270.

13 J. Francis, *A History of the English Railway; its social relations and revelations, 1820–1845*, II (London, 1851), p. 163.

14 E. A. Pratt, *op. cit.*, p. 266.

15 *Ibid.*

16 *Ibid.*, p. 273.

17 *Ibid.*, p. 285.

18 H. J. Dyos and D. H. Aldcroft, *British Transport: an economic survey from the seventeenth to the twentieth* (Leicester, 1971), p. 129.

19 *Ibid.*, p. 289.

20 See R. J. Irving, *The North Eastern Railway Company, 1870–1914: an economic history* (Leicester, 1976), p. 15.

21 E. A. Pratt, *op. cit.*, p. 289.

22 See the discussions in J. Langton, 'The industrial revolution and the regional geography of England', and M. Freeman, 'The industrial revolution and the regional geography of England: a comment', *Transactions of the Institute of British Geographers*, 9 (1984), pp. 145–67, 507–12.

23 Pro-forma letter from the office of the North Eastern Railway's commercial agent, York, 1908 (Bodleian, John Johnson Collection, Railways Box 8).

24 See P. J. Cain, 'Railways, 1870–1914: the maturity of the private system', in M. J. Freeman and D. H. Aldcroft, eds., *Transport in Victorian Britain* (Manchester, 1988), p. 114; also R. J. Irving, *op. cit.*, pp. 130 ff.

25 E. A. Pratt, *op. cit.*, p. 288.

26 W. M. Ackworth, *The Railways of England* (5th edn., London, 1900), p. 152.

27 *Ibid.*

28 *Ibid.*, p. 153.

29 Quoted in S. Kern, *The Culture of Time and Space, 1880–1918* (Cambridge, Mass., 1983), p. 213.

30 E. A. Pratt, *op. cit.*, p. 289.

31 See J. Simmons, 'South Western v. Great Western Railway competition in Devon and Cornwall', *Journal of Transport History*, IV (1959), p. 18.

32 R. A. Williams, *The London and South Western Railway: the formative years*, I (Newton Abbot, 1968), pp. 18, 48.

33 See E. T. MacDermot, *History of the Great Western Railway, I: 1833–1863; II: 1863–1921* (rev. edn., C. R. Clinker, Newton Abbot, 1964), I, chapter one.

34 R. A. Williams, *op. cit.*, p. 52.

35 *Ibid.*, pp. 101 ff.

36 E. T. MacDermot, *op. cit.*

37 See *ibid.*, I, pp. 100 ff; II, pp. 68 ff.

38 *Ibid.*, II, p. 85.

39 W. M. Ackworth, *op. cit.*, p. 250.

40 H. J. Dyos and D. H. Aldcroft, *op. cit.*, p. 160.

41 H. M. Ross, *British Railways: their organization and management* (London, 1904), pp. 28–9.

42 *Ibid.*, p. 30; see also P. S. Bagwell, *The Railway Clearing House in the British Economy, 1842–1922* (London, 1968).

43 H. M. Ross, *op. cit.*, p. 31.

44 *Ibid.*, pp. 32 ff.

45 *Ibid.*, pp. 34 ff.

46 *Ibid.*, p. 35.

47 W. M. Ackworth, *op. cit.*, p. 192.

48 *Ibid.*, p. 193.

49 *Ibid.*

50 *British Parliamentary Papers* [hereafter *BPP*], Royal Commission on Railways, Minutes of Evidence, XXXVIII (1867), Q. 12377.

51 See G. R. Hawke, *Railways and Economic Growth in England and Wales,*

52 *1840–1870* (Oxford, 1970), pp. 163 ff.

52 *BPP*, Royal Commission on Coal, XVIII (1871), Report of Committee E, pp. 139–40.

53 G. R. Hawke, *op. cit.*, p. 182.

54 All data on South Wales coal-flows derives from *BPP*, Royal Commision on Coal, *op. cit.*

55 P. J. Cain, *op. cit.*, p. 97.

56 *BPP*, Royal Commission on Coal (1871), *op. cit.*, Appendix to report of Committee E, p. 91.

57 G. R. Hawke, *op. cit.*, p. 323.

58 See W. Albert, *The Turnpike Road System in England, 1663–1840* (Cambridge, 1972), pp. 168 ff and Appendix 1.

59 See H. J. Dyos and D. H. Aldcroft, *op. cit.*, p. 165.

60 G. R. Hawke, *op. cit.*, pp. 85–6.

61 See J. Langton, *Geographical Change and Industrial Revolution: coal-mining in south-west Lancashire, 1590–1799* (Cambridge, 1979).

62 See M. Freeman, 'Transport', in J. Langton and R. J. Morris, *Atlas of Industrializing Britain, 1780–1914* (London, 1986), pp. 86–7.

63 See the detailed discussion in G. R. Hawke, *op. cit.*, pp. 317 ff.

64 *BPP*, Report from the Select Committee on Railways – Part I, XIII (1881), p. 430.

65 *Ibid.*, pp. 81, 89.

66 *Ibid.*, p. 332.

67 *Ibid.*, p. 333.

68 *Ibid.*, p. 336.

69 See page 43.

70 *BPP*, Report from the Select Committee on Railways (1881), *op. cit.*, pp. 380 ff.

71 *Ibid.*, p. 453.

72 *Ibid.*, p. 447.

73 *Ibid.*, p. 444.

74 G. R. Hawke, *op. cit.*, pp. 334–5.

75 *Ibid.*, p. 324.

76 *Ibid.*, p. 323.

77 *Ibid.*, pp. 325–6.

78 *Ibid.*, pp. 326–7.

79 *BPP*, Royal Commission on Railways, *op. cit.*, Q. 11409.

80 H. M. Ross, *op. cit.*, p. 186.

81 G. R. Hawke, *op. cit.*, p. 334.

82 *Ibid.*, p. 162.

83 H. M. Ross, *op. cit.*, p. 186.

84 G. R. Hawke, *op. cit.*, p. 358.

85 See H. M. Ross, *op. cit.*, p. 199.

86 54 & 55 Victoria CCXIV–CCXXII; 55 & 56 Victoria XXXIX–LXIV.

87 See H. M. Ross, *op. cit.*, p. 200.

88 G. R. Hawke, *op. cit.*, p. 323.

89 *Ibid.*, p. 330; see also *BPP*, Report from Select Committee on Railways (1881), *op. cit.*, p. 408.

90 *Ibid.*, p. 471.

91 H. J. Dyos and D. H. Aldcroft, *op. cit.*, p. 142.

92 See H. E. C. Newham, *Hull as a Coal Port* (Hull, 1913).

93 H. J. Dyos and D. H. Aldcroft, *op. cit.*, p. 142.

94 E. M. Patterson, *The County Donegal Railways* (London, 1972), p. 184.

95 T. W. Freeman, *Ireland: a general and regional geography* (3rd edn., London, 1965), p. 240.

96 See J. I. C. Boyd, *The Festiniog Railway: a history* (Oxford, 1975).

97 See S. R. Garrett, *The Kent and East Sussex Railway* (Oxford, 1987).

98 See W. J. K. Davies, *Light railways; their rise and decline* (London, 1964).

6 LABOUR

1 Thomas Roscoe, describing the construction of the Newton excavation in about 1836 on the Grand Junction Railway linking Birmingham and Warrington, in T. Roscoe, *The Book of the Grand Junction Railway* (London, 1839), p. 43.

2 *British Parliamentary Papers* [hereafter *BPP*], Report from the Select Committee on Railway Labourers, XIII (1846), Minutes of Evidence, 19 June 1846.

3 J. F. C. Harrison, *Early Victorian Britain, 1832–1851* (first published as *The Early Victorians, 1832–1851*, London, 1971; repr. London, 1979), p. 63.

4 See, for example, Leicester Museums, *The Last Main Line* (2nd edn., Leicester, 1972).

5 T. Coleman, *The Railway Navvies: a history of the men who made the railways* (London, 1965), p. 200

6 C. Barman, *Early British Railways* (London, 1950), pp. 19–20.

7 See D. Brooke, 'Railway navvies on the Pennines', *Journal of Transport History*, III (1975), p. 42.

8 J. F. C. Harrison, *op. cit.*, p. 65.

9 *Ibid.*

10 F. S. Williams, *Our Iron Roads: their history, construction and social influences* (London, 1852), p. 137.

11 J. Francis, *A History of the English Railway; its social relations and revelations, 1820–1845*, II (London, 1851), p. 69.

12 *BPP*, Report from the Select Committee on Railway Labourers, *op. cit.*

13 See J. F. C. Harrison, *op. cit.*, chapter three; also B. Trinder, *The Making of the Industrial Landscape* (London, 1982), chapter six.

14 See, for example, D. Brooke, *op.. cit.*, pp. 41–53.

15 *BPP*, Report from the Select Committee on Railway Labourers, *op. cit.*, p. 427.

16 *Ibid.*, Minutes of Evidence, 19 May 1846.

17 *Ibid.*, p. 431.

18 *Ibid.*, Minutes of Evidence, 26 May 1846.

19 *Ibid.*, 19 June 1846.

20 *Ibid.*, 22 May 1846.

21 *Ibid.*, 26 May 1846.

22 T. Coleman, *op. cit.*, p. 56.

23 *Ibid.*, p. 57.

24 *Ibid.*, p. 61.

25 *Ibid.*, p. 62.

26 See the account in T. Coleman, *op. cit.*, pp. 192 ff.

27 Quoted in *ibid.*, pp. 195–6.

28 *Ibid.*, p. 196.

29 See Leicester Museums, *The Last Main Line, op. cit.*

30 *Ibid.*, p. 201.

31 C. Dickens, *Dombey and Son* (1846–8; repr., Oxford, 1982), p. 185.

32 *Ibid.*, p. 15.

33 *Ibid.*, pp. 233–4.

34 J. Richards and J. M. MacKenzie, *The Railway Station: a social history* (Oxford, 1986), p. 224.

35 P. W. Kingsford, *Victorian Railwaymen: the emergence and growth of railway labour, 1830–1870* (London, 1970), p. xii.

36 F. McKenna, *The Railway Workers, 1840–1970* (London, 1980), p. 28.

37 See E. Royston Pike, *Human Documents of the Victorian Golden Age (1850–1875)* (London, 1967), p. 187.

38 *Chambers's Journal of Popular Literature, Science and Arts*, 18 April 1891, p. 252.

39 P. W. Kingsford, *op. cit.*, p. 90.

40 *Ibid.*, p. 98.

41 E. T. MacDermot, *History of the Great Western Railway* (rev. edn., C. R. Clinker, London, 1964), I: *1833–1863*, p. 358.

42 F. McKenna, *op. cit.*, p. 27.

43 P. W. Kingsford, *op, cit.*, p. 149.

44 *Chambers's Journal, op. cit.*, 18 April 1891, p. 251.

45 E. A. Pratt, *A History of Inland Transport and Communication in England* (London, 1912), p. 423.

46 See page 73.

47 P. W. Kingsford, *op. cit.*, p. 135.

48 *Chambers's Journal, op. cit.*, 3 January 1891, p. 15.

49 *Ibid.*, 19 September 1891, p. 607.

50 F. McKenna, *op. cit.*, p. 156.

51 F. B. Head, *Stokers and Pokers; or The London & North-Western Railway* (London, 1850), p. 98.

52 E. T. MacDermot, *op. cit.*, p. 358.

53 P. W. Kingsford, *op. cit.*, p. 13.

54 3 & 4 Victoria c. 97; 5 & 6 Victoria c. 55.

55 See A. T. Story, 'Engine Drivers and Their Work', Part I, *Strand*, VIII (1894), p. 170.

56 F. McKenna, *op. cit.*, p. 31.

57 T. Roscoe, *The London and Birmingham Railway* (London, 1839), p. 119.

58 *Ibid.*, pp. 118–9.

59 E. T. MacDermot, *op. cit.*, p. 355.

60 F. McKenna. *op. cit.*, pp. 237, 31.

61 F. S. Williams, quoted in J. Richards and J. MacKenzie, *op. cit.*, p. 233.

62 J. Richards and J. MacKenzie, *op. cit.*, p. 225.

63 Railway Clerks' Association, *The Life of the Railway Clerk* (London, 1911), p. 6.

64 E. T. MacDermot, *op. cit.*, p. 358.

65 F. McKenna. *op. cit.*, p. 86.

66 *Ibid.*, pp. 40–1.

67 *Ibid.*, p. 233.

68 See A. T. Story, *op. cit.*, p. 172.

69 See A. T. Story, 'Engine Drivers and Their Work', Part II, *op. cit.*, p. 280.

70 F. McKenna, *op, cit.*, p. 178.

71 P. W. Kingsford, *op. cit.*, p. 82

72 E. A. Pratt, *op. cit.*, p. 417.

73 *Ibid.*, p. 418.

74 *Ibid.*, p. 420.

75 *Ibid.*, pp. 420 ff.

76 P. W. Kingsford, *op. cit.*, p. 73.

77 *Ibid.*, pp. 73–4.

78 E. T. MacDermot, *op. cit.*, p. 77.

79 P. W. Kingsford, *op. cit.*, p. 75.

80 F. McKenna, *op. cit.*, p. 50.

81 P. W. Kingsford, *op. cit.*, p. 75.

82 E. A. Pratt, *op. cit.*, p. 432.

83 See *Railway Signal, or Lights along the line*, XII, 3 (1894), reverse cover.

84 *Ibid.*, pp. 161–2.

85 P. W. Kingsford, *op. cit.*, p. 153.

86 *Ibid.*, pp. 153 ff.

87 *Ibid.*, p. 156.

88 *Ibid.*, pp. 158 ff.

89 *Ibid.*, Appendix I.

90 Bodleian MS, John Johnson Collection, Railways Box 6.

91 See E. A. Pratt, *op. cit.*, p. 438.

92 *Chambers's Journal, op. cit.*, 26 March 1892, p. 198.

93 P. W. Kingsford, *op. cit.*, p. 160.

94 *The Railway Clearing House, its objects, works & results* (London, 1877).

95 *Ibid.*, p. 34.

96 E. A. Pratt, *op. cit.*, p. 439.

97 F. M. L. Thompson, *The Rise of Respectable Society: a social history of Victorian Britain, 1830–1900* (London, 1988), p. 20.

98 P. W. Kingsford, *op. cit.*, pp. 166 ff.

99 *Ibid.*, p. 167.

100 General Railway Workers' Union, General Secretary's Report to the AGM, 1895, p. 7 (Bodleian, John Johnson Collection, Railways Box 23).

101 K. Marx, *Capital* I (1867; repr., Harmondsworth, 1976), p. 364.

102 *Ibid.*, p. 363.

103 See P. S. Bagwell, 'Early attempts at National Organization of the Railwaymen', *Journal of Transport History*, III (1957), p. 96.

104 General Railway Workers' Union, General Secretary's Report to the AGM, 1895, *op. cit.*, pp. 8, 13.

105 *Ibid.*, p. 7.

106 *Railway Service Gazette*, 9 March 1872, p. 8, quoted in F. McKenna, *op. cit.*, p. 103.

107 P. W. Kingsford, *op. cit.*, p. 115.

108 See L. T. C. Rolt, *Red for Danger: a history of railway accidents and railway safety precautions* (rev. edn., London, 1966), pp. 149–50.

109 F. McKenna, *op. cit.*, pp. 161–2.

110 See P. S. Bagwell, 'Early attempts at National Organization', *op. cit.*, p. 97.

111 See 'Railway Servants', II, *Leisure Hour* (1883), p. 658 (Bodleian, John Johnson Collection, Railways Box 23).

112 *Ibid.*, p. 659.

113 See BPP, Report from the Select Committee on Railway Servants' Hours of Labour, XVI (1890–91).

114 See 'Railway Servants', II, *Leisure Hour* (1883), *op. cit.*, p. 659.

115 F. McKenna, *op. cit.*, pp. 197–8.

116 See A. T. Story. 'Engine Drivers and Their Work', Part II, *op. cit.*, p. 282.

117 P. W. Kingsford, *op. cit.*, p. 56.

118 See G. Revill, 'Working the system: journeys through corporate culture in the "railway age"', *Environment and Planning, D: Society and Space*, 12 (1994), pp. 714–5.

119 *Ibid.*, p. 706.

7 EDUCATION AND SOCIAL REPRODUCTION

1 T. Mitchell, *Colonizing Egypt* (Berkeley, 1991), p. 69, discussing the adoption of the Lancaster system of schooling.

2 See J. Hurt, *Education in Evolution: Church, State, Society and Popular Education, 1800–1870* (London, 1971), p. 22; also F. M. L. Thompson, *The Rise of Respectable Society: a social history of Victorian Britain, 1830–1900* (London, 1988), pp. 144–5.

3 See J. Hurt, *op. cit.*, pp. 15 ff.

4 *Ibid.*, p. 12.

5 *Ibid.*, p. 13.

6 Mrs Marcet (Jane Haldimand), *Willy's travels on the railroad: intended for young children* (London, 1847), p. 3 (Bodleian, Opie Collection [hereafter Opie] A748).

7 The classic example must be 'Dan Dare', futuristic stories about a pilot that featured regularly in the *Eagle* comic.

8 *Cousin Chatterbox's Railway Alphabet* (London, n.d., but c. 1845).

9 *The Railway ABC* (London, n.d., but c. 1865) (Opie BB105).

10 Contained in *Pussy's Picture Book* (London, n.d., but inscribed 1879) (Opie M990).

11 *Cousin Chatterbox's Railway Alphabet, op. cit.*

12 See J. Simmons, *The Victorian Railway* (London, 1991), pp. 175–6.

13 F. Whishaw, *Analysis of Railways* (London, 1837), p. 286.

14 J. Simmons, *op. cit.*, p. 176.

15 See, for example, *Things out-of-doors* (London, n.d.), pp. 44–5 (Opie BB265).

16 J. Simmons, *op. cit.*, p. 176.

17 *Things out-of-doors, op. cit.*

18 *Ibid.*

19 *Master Punch's Comic Alphabet* (Mark's edition, London, n.d., but c. 1842) (Opie G9).

20 *The New London Alphabet in Rhyme* (London, n.d., but early 1850s) (Opie H105).

21 See W. Newman, *Rhymes and pictures about bread, tea, sugar, coals, cotton, gold, containing The History of the quartern loaf* (London, 1860), p. 9 (Opie BB90).

22 *Ibid.*

23 Religious Tract Society, *Railways* (London, n.d.) (Opie L276).

24 *Ibid.*, p. 10.

25 *Ibid,*, pp. 17–18.

26 *Ibid.*, pp. 21 ff.

27 See *The Railway Signal: a Journal of Evangelistic and Temperance Work on all Railways*, XII, 3 (1894), reverse cover.

28 Mrs Marcet, *op. cit.*, p. 6.

29 R. M. Ballantyne, *The Iron Horse or life on the line* (London, n.d., but c. 1871), p. 231 (Opie AA 639).

30 *Three Useful Giants: wind, water and steam, and what they do for us* (London, n.d.) (Opie BB126).

31 W. Martin, *The Young Student's Holiday Book; being lessons on architecture, mechanics, natural history, physics, manufacturing of pottery etc.* (7th edn., London, n.d., but c. 1870), p. 101 (Opie BB230).

32 E. Hale, *Stories of Inventions told by inventors and their friends* (London, 1887), p. 215 (Opie B201).

33 *Ibid.*, p. 221.

34 P. Parley (pseud. for George Mogridge), *Sergeant Bell and his raree show* (London, 1842), p. 311 (Opie H102).

35 R. Routledge, *Discoveries and Inventions of the Nineteenth Century* (London, 1876), pp. 72–3 (Opie BB250).

36 *The Train Scrap Book* (London, n.d., but c. 1900), chapter 4 (Opie BB131).

37 *The Birth Day Present* (London, n.d., but c. 1850–9) (Opie M83).

38 Walter Crane, *Annie and Jack in London* (London, n.d., but c. 1867–8), p. 1 (Opie M163).

39 Laura B. Valentine, ed., *Aunt Louisa's holiday guest* (London, c. 1870) (Opie M650).

40 C. Goodfellow, *A Collector's Guide to Games and Puzzles* (New Jersey, 1991), p. 6.

41 Bodleian MS, John Johnson Collection, Board Games. This particular example is undated, but an identical version in the Science Museum, London, appears to date from 1840; see A. and P. Smithson, *The Euston Arch and the Growth of the London, Midland and Scottish Railway* (London, 1968), final plate.

42 Yale Center for British Art, Rare Books Collection, uncatalogued MS. For the 1794 version, see C. Goodfellow, *op. cit.*, pp. 20–21 (NB the captions on these pages are reversed).

43 See C. Goodfellow, *op. cit.*, p. 9; also I. and R. Opie and B. Alderson, *The Treasures of Childhood* (London, 1989), p. 162.

44 Yale Center for British Art, Rare Books Collection: DA625 R6 (the volume is undated, but is probably c. 1840).

45 I. and R. Opie and B. Alderson, *op. cit.*, p. 162.

46 Yale Center for British Art, Rare Books Collection: GV1199/C58.

47 Bodleian MS, John Johnson Collection, Board Games.

48 *Ibid.*

49 See O. S. Nock, *The Railway Races to the North* (London, 1976).

50 L. Hannas, *The English Jig-saw Puzzle, 1760–1890* (London, 1972), p. 108.

51 See chapter one.

52 L. Hannas, *op. cit.*

53 C. Goodfellow, *op. cit.*, p. 115.

54 L. Hannas, *op. cit.*, p. 141.

55 *Ibid.*, p. 140.

56 *Ibid.*, p. 54.

57 Elton Collection, Ironbridge Gorge Museum Trust [hereafter Elton] AE 185. 510.

58 See Elton AE 185. 518; the piece is undated, but the use of the term 'Rail-Way' on the title page strongly suggests a date at the start of the railway era.

59 I am grateful to Warder Cadbury for the loan of this score and for first drawing it to my attention.

60 Elton AE 185. 520. Many of these musical offerings lack dates; unless specified otherwise, I have taken the dates suggested in the catalogue of the British Library.

61 Elton AE 185. 524.

62 Elton AE 185. 512.

63 Elton AE 185. 511.

64 According to Martha Vicinus, it was American missionaries who brought to England the familiar metaphor of the railway to heaven or hell; see M. Vicinus, *The Industrial Muse* (London, 1974), pp. 38–9.

65 Elton AE 185. 510.

66 Elton AE 185. 516.

67 P. Carlson, *Toy Trains* (London, 1986), p. 8.

68 L. Gordon, *Peepshow into Paradise: a history of children's toys* (London, 1953), p. 51.

69 See P. Carlson, *op. cit.*, p. 9.

70 See D. Pressland, *The Book of Penny Toys* (London, 1991); see also G. Craig, *Gordon Craig's Book of Penny Toys* (London, 1899) and M. Dearmer, *The Book of Penny Toys* (London, 1899).

71 See P. Carlson, *op. cit.*, p. 13.

72 See L. Gordon, *op. cit.*, pp. 184–5.

73 *Ibid.*, p. 185.

74 A. Levy, *A Century of Model Trains* (2nd edn., London, 1975), p. 7.

75 L. Gordon, *op. cit.*, p. 181.

76 P. Carlson, *op. cit.*, p. 15.

77 D. Pressland, *Great Book of Tin Toys* (London, 1995), p. 86.

78 *Ibid.*, p. 103.

79 See P. Carlson, *op. cit.*, p. 27.

80 *Ibid.*, p. 56.

81 *Ibid.*, p. 59.

82 *Ibid.*, p. 71.

8 REPRESENTATIONS IN ART

1 John Britton on the proposed publication of Bourne's drawings of the London and Birmingham Railway, quoted in F. D. Klingender, *Art and the Industrial Revolution* (1947; rev. edn., London, 1972), p. 135.

2 The best review of railway prints is probably G. Rees, *Early Railway Prints: a social history of the railways from 1825 to 1850* (Oxford, 1980); but see also C. Hamilton Ellis, *Railway Art* (London, 1977).

3 G. Rees, *op. cit.*, pp. 15 ff.

4 See F. D. Klingender, *op. cit.*, pp. 80 ff.

5 See C. Arscott, G. Pollock, and J. Wolff., 'The partial view: the visual representation of the early nineteenth-century city', in J. Wolff and J. Seed, eds., *The Culture of Capital* (Manchester, 1988), p. 228.

6 F. D. Klingender, *op. cit.*, p. 130.

7 *Ibid.*, pp. 129 ff.

8 See T. T. Bury, *Six Coloured Views on the Liverpool and Manchester Railway* (facsimile edn., Oldham, 1976), p. ix.

9 See F. Klingender, *op. cit.*, p. 132; also T. T. Bury, *op. cit.*, p. ix.

10 I. Shaw, *Travelling on the Liverpool and Manchester Railway* (Liverpool, 1831).

11 I. Shaw, *Views of the Most Interesting Scenery on the Line of the Liverpool and Manchester Railway* (Liverpool, 1831).

12 See M. Darby, *Early Railway Prints* (London, 1974), p. 9.

13 F. D. Klingender, *op. cit.*, pp. 133 ff.

14 Some of his original sketches can be found in the Elton Collection, Ironbridge Gorge Museum Trust.

15 J. C. Bourne, *Drawings of the London and Birmingham Railway* (London, 1839).

16 J. C. Bourne, *The History and Description of the Great Western Railway* (London, 1846).

17 F. D. Klingender, *op. cit.*, p. 138.

18 D. O. Hill, *Views of the Opening of the Glasgow and Garnkirk Railway* (Edinburgh, 1832), p. 3.

19 A. F. Tait, *Views on the Manchester and Leeds Railway* (Liverpool, 1845); see also facsimile edn. (Newcastle, 1971).

20 See W. H. Cadbury, *Arthur Fitzwilliam Tait: Artist in the Adirondacks* (Newark, 1986), p. 17.

21 S. Daniels, 'Images of the railway in nineteenth century paintings and prints', in *Trainspotting: images of the railway in art* (Nottingham Castle Museum, 1985), p. 7.

22 J. W. Carmichael, *Views of the Newcastle and Carlisle Railway* (Newcastle, 1836–8).

23 See G. Rees, *op. cit.*, p. 16.

24 Klingender remarked that the number of Bury prints still available when he was writing in 1947 suggested that great numbers must have been issued, but this claim must be tenuous; F. D. Klingender, *op. cit.*, p. 13.

25 W. H. Cadbury, *op. cit.*, p. 17.

26 F. D. Klingender, *op. cit.*, p. 137.

27 H. Booth, *Eight Views illustrating the Liverpool and Manchester Railway and the Engines and Carriages employed upon it* (Liverpool, 1830).

28 *A handbook for Travellers along the London and Birmingham Railway* (London, 1839), pp. 89–90 (Bodleian MS Gough Adds. Eng. rlys 16° 102).

29 T. T. Bury, *Six Coloured Views on the Liverpool and Manchester Railway* (London, 1831).

30 T. T. Bury, *The London and Birmingham Railroad* (London, 1837).

31 A. F. Tait, *op. cit.*

32 I. Shaw, *Views of the Most Interesting Scenery on the Line of the Liverpool and Manchester Railway, op. cit.*

33 J. C. Bourne, *Drawings, op. cit.*

34 H. Booth, *op. cit.*, p. 98.

35 See chapter two.

36 R. W. Kostal, *Law and English Railway Capitalism, 1825–1875* (Oxford, 1994).

37 *Blackwood's Edinburgh Magazine*, XXVIII (1830), p. 824.

38 See S. Daniels, *op. cit.*, p. 8; also S. Daniels, *Fields of Vision: landscape imagery and national identity in England and the United States* (Cambridge, 1993), chapter four.

39 J. Gage, *Turner: Rain, Steam and Speed* (New York, 1972), p. 14.

40 See the lithograph by J. Bousefield of the Stockton and Darlington, reproduced in G. Rees, *op. cit.*

41 See J. W. Carmichael, *op. cit.*

42 A. F. Tait, *op. cit.*

43 T. Roscoe, *The Book of the Grand Junction Railway* (London, 1839).

44 C. Hamilton Ellis, *op. cit.*, p. 18.

45 See P. Gay, *Art and Act: on causes in history – Manet, Gropius, Mondrian* (London, 1976), p. 104.

46 Couture, quoted in P. Gay, *op. cit.*, p. 104.

47 See S. Daniels, *Fields of Vision, op. cit.*, chapter four.

48 *Ibid.*, pp. 127-8.

49 *Ibid.*, p. 132.

50 See J. Gage, *op. cit.*, p. 33.

51 See W. Feaver, *The Art of John Martin* (Oxford, 1975); also M. D. Paley, *The Apocalyptic Sublime* (London, 1986), p. 150.

52 W. Feaver, *op. cit.*, p. 145.

53 M. D. Paley, *op. cit.*, p. 150.

54 W. Feaver, *op. cit.*, p. 145.

55 See G. Rees, *op. cit.*, pp. 118-121. A. F. Tait produced a series of drawings of the London and North Western Railway in the late 1840s, presumably intending publication in the fashion of his series on the Manchester and Leeds Railway, but they were never published; see W. H. Cadbury, *op. cit.*, p. 19.

56 See C. Hamilton Ellis, *op. cit.*, pp. 77 ff.; also S. Daniels, 'Images of the railway', *op. cit.*, pp. 9 ff.

57 S. Daniels, 'Images of the railway', *op. cit.*, p. 9.

58 F. D. Klingender, *op. cit.*, p. 124.

59 *Ibid.*, pp. 127-8.

60 See D. Hay, 'Property, authority and the criminal law', in D. Hay et al., *Albion's Fatal Tree: crime and society in Eighteenth-Century England* (London, 1975), pp. 26 ff.

61 D. O. Hill, *op. cit.*

62 See G. Rees, *op. cit.*, p. 33.

63 See C. Hamilton Ellis, *op. cit.*, p. 80.

64 S. Daniels, 'Images of the railway', *op. cit.*, p. 12.

65 W. Schivelbusch, *The Railway Journey: the industrialization of time and space in the 19th century* (New York, 1977), p. 4.

66 A. F. Tait, *op. cit.*, p. 26.

67 H. Booth, *op. cit.*, p. 49.

68 See T. M. Greene, *Geology in the Nineteenth Century: changing views of a changing world* (Ithaca, 1982).

69 T. Roscoe, *The London and Birmingham Railway* (London, 1839) p. 31.

70 *Ibid.*, p. 92.

71 D. O. Hill, *op. cit.*, p. 3.

72 A. F. Tait, *op. cit.*, p. 16.

73 See M. Pointon, 'Geology and landscape painting in nineteenth-century England', in L. J. Jordanova and R. Porter, eds., *Images of the Earth: essays in the history of the environmental sciences* (2nd edn., London, 1997), p. 98.

74 See W. Feaver, *op. cit.*, p. 147.

75 W. Schivelbusch, *op. cit.*, p. 4.

76 See chapter one.

77 A. F. Tait, *op. cit.*, p. 20.

78 S. Daniels, 'Images of the railway', *op. cit.*, p. 13.

79 Some of these can be found in the Elton Collection.

80 C. Hamilton Ellis, *op. cit.*, p. 25.

81 S. Daniels, 'Images of the railway', *op. cit.*, p. 14.

82 C. Hamilton Ellis, *op. cit.*, p. 81.

83 See C. Wood, *Victorian Panorama: paintings of Victorian Life* (London, 1976), pp. 207 ff.

84 C. Hamilton Ellis, *op. cit.*, p. 84.

85 See the collection in the Leicester Museum taken by S. W. A Newton. Some of the pictures are reproduced in *The Last Main Line: an illustrated history of the building of the Great Central Railway* (Leicester Museums, 2nd edn., Leicester, 1968).

86 See the examples in M. Freeman and D. Aldcroft, *The Atlas of British Railway History* (London, 1985).

EPILOGUE

1 L. T. C. Rolt, *Lines of Character: a steam age evocation* (2nd edn., London, 1974) p. 12.

2 See E. Soja, *Post-modern Geographies: the reassertion of space in critical social theory* (London, 1989), pp. 222-3.

3 See M. Robbins, *The Railway Age in Britain and its impact on the world* (Harmondsworth, 1965), p. 113.

4 *Ibid.*, pp. 113–14; also J. Richards and J. MacKenzie, *The Railway Station: a social history* (Oxford, 1986), p. 212.

5 J. Richards and J. MacKenzie, *op. cit.*, p. 354.

6 *Ibid.*, p. 187.

7 M. Robbins, *op. cit.*, pp. 28-9.

8 B. R. Mitchell, 'The coming of the railway and United Kingdom economic growth', in M. C. Reed, ed., *Railways in the Victorian Economy: studies in finance and growth* (Newton Abbot, 1969), p. 21

9 M. Robbins, *op. cit.*, p. 107.

10 B. R. Mitchell, *op. cit.*, p. 21.

11 *Illustrated London News*, XI (1847), p. 376.

12 H. Perkin, *The Age of the Railway* (London, 1970), p. 194.

13 North British Locomotive Company, *Catalogue of Narrow Gauge Locomotives* (Glasgow, 1912; repr. Newton Abbot, 1970).

14 *Chambers's Encyclopaedia*, 11 (London, 1963), pp. 491-2.

15 L. T. C. Rolt, *op. cit.*, p. 10.

16 See P. S. Bagwell, *The Transport Revolution from 1770* (London, 1974), p. 318.

Picture Credits

17 See D. H. Aldcroft, *Studies in British Transport History, 1870–1970* (Newton Abbot, 1974), pp. 243–62.

18 G. M. Trevelyan, quoted in M. Whitelaw, 'Preview', in B. Morgan, ed., *The Railway-Lover's Companion* (London, 1963), p. 61.

19 T. R. Gourvish, *British Railways, 1948–73: a business history* (Cambridge, 1986), p. 275.

20 See W. Awdry and C. Cooke, eds., *A Guide to the Steam Railways of Great Britain* (rev. edn., London, 1984).

21 R. Sykes, A. Austin, M. Fuller, T. Kinoshita and A. Shrimpton, 'Steam attraction: railways in Britain's national heritage', *Journal of Transport History*, 18 (1997), p. 159.

22 *Ibid.*, p. 157.

23 F. Jameson, 'Postmodernism, or the cultural logic of late capitalism', *New Left Review*, 146 (1984), pp. 53–92; *idem.*, *Postmodernism, or the cultural logic of late capitalism* (Durham, N.C., 1991); see also D. Harvey, *The Condition of Postmodernity: an enquiry into the origins of cultural change* (Oxford, 1989), chapter three.

24 See R. Hewison, *The Heritage industry: Britain in a climate of decline* (London, 1987).

25 See R. Sykes, et al., *op. cit.*, p. 166.

26 L. T. C. Rolt, *op. cit.*, p. 11.

27 The phrase is borrowed from Heidegger; see T. Mitchell, *Colonizing Egypt* (Los Angeles, 1988), pp. 10–13.

28 The Great Western, the Southern, the London and North Eastern and the London, Midland Scottish.

29 See D. Harvey, *op. cit.*, chapters seven to eleven.

30 See R. Sykes, *op. cit.*, p. 169.

31 W. Awdry, *Thomas the Tank Engine* (London, 1946), p. 3.

32 See *The Times*, 22 March 1997, obituary of Wilber Awdry.

33 See chapter one.

Any errors or omissions in this list are inadvertent and will be corrected in subsequent editions if notification is given in writing to the publisher. References are to plate numbers.

Abingdon Museum: 202

Adirondack Museum: 40

W. Awdry, *Thomas the Tank Engine* (London, 1946): 279

Birmingham Central Library Services: 5, 10, 11, 12, 13, 21, 22, 23, 61, 64, 65, 68, 72, 92, 99, 100, 109, 110, 126, 128, 129, 135, 141, 142, 143, 144, 145, 146, 147, 149, 154, 156, 158, 162, 163, 193, 205

Birmingham Museums and Art Gallery: 130

Bodleian Library, University of Oxford

    Bod 2 Delta 310: 1, 124
    Bod 247917 d.3: 262
    Bod 2799 b.5: 16
    Bod 48.1517: 71
    Bod Arch. AA c.2: 30
    Bod Arch. AA f.15 (7): 79
    Bod Dir. 232318 f.6: 174
    Bod Maps C17:4 (65): 173
    Bod N. 1330 d.11: 209, 210
    Bod Per. 1861 e.73: 82
    Bod Per. 18811 d.271: 58, 59
    Bod Per. 247917 e.29: 106
    Vet. A6 d.697: 17

    Gough Adds.: Eng. rlys. a 1: 49
    Eng. rlys. 16° 15: 245
    Eng. rlys. 16° 56: 178
    Eng. rlys. 16° 100: 2
    fol c.4: 60
    Gen. Top. 4° 8: 3
    Gen. Top. 8° 435: 177

    John Johnson Collection:
    Artifacts (Games): 226
    Board Games: 227
    Johnson e. 2608: 103
    Railways Box 4: 36, 44, 83, 111, 155, 180
    Railways Box 6: 159
    Railways Box 7: 78
    Railways Box 8: 152, 167, 168, 175, 176
    Railways Box 10: 94
    Railways Box 11: 4, 28, 48, 56, 102, 107, 119, 127
    Railways Box 13: 157
    Railways Box 23: 213
    Railways Box 24: 37
    Railways Box 27: 112, 181, 212
    Railways Folder II: 189, 238, 266, 267, 268

    Opie Collection: B2a: 219
    BB 90: 221
    BB 105: 216
    BB 131: 218, 223
    G 9: 220

    M 650: 225
    M 672: 222
    uncatalogued: 217

Bucknall Collection / Ian Allan Picture Library: 187

Michael Freeman: 182, 183

Greenwich Libraries: 201

Hornsey Historical Society: 151

Ironbridge Gorge Museum Trust, Elton Collection: 19, 24, 26, 33, 43, 50, 51, 54, 57, 67, 69, 75, 85, 88, 90, 93, 95, 113, 122, 161, 169, 188, 190, 192, 198, 230, 231, 232, 242, 251, 261, 265, 272

The Laing Art Gallery, Newcastle-upon-Tyne: 89

Leicestershire Museums, Arts and Record Service: 166, 195, 196, 276

London Toy and Model Museum: 233, 234, 235, 236

London Transport Museum: 134

Manchester Central Libraries, Local Studies Unit: 139, 140

Mid-Hants Railway plc: 278

National Gallery, London: 254

National Railway Museum / Science and Society Picture Library: 6, 7, 27, 29, 38, 45, 52, 62, 73, 74, 97, 104, 105, 120, 123, 131, 132, 160, 165, 170, 171, 179, 184, 185, 186, 197, 199, 204, 211, 214, 215, 274, 277

Newport Museum and Art Gallery: 70

Oxfordshire County Council: 164, 200, 275

Principal and Fellows of Regent's Park College, Oxford: 194

Private collection: 8, 18, 32, 34, 41, 42, 55, 91, 125, 133, 136, 137, 153, 208, 229, 247, 250

Provost and Fellows of Worcester College, Oxford: 31, 66, 76, 80, 84, 98, 101, 108, 114, 115, 116, 117, 118, 150, 148, 172, 257, 258

Sheffield Galleries and Museums Trust / Bridgeman Art Library: 273

Southampton City Art Gallery / Bridgeman Art Library: 259, 260

Swindon Museum and Art Gallery: 208

Tate Gallery, London © 1998: 47, 255

University of Oxford School of Geography: 15, 46, 77

University of Oxford Social Studies Library: 14

Courtesy of the Trustees of the Victoria and Albert Museum: 228

Wolverton and District Archaeological Society: 206, 207

Yale Center for British Art, Paul Mellon Collection: 9, 20, 25, 35, 39, 53, 63, 81, 86, 87, 96, 121, 138, 191, 203, 224, 237, 239, 240, 241, 243, 244, 246, 248, 249, 252, 253, 256, 263, 264, 269, 270, 271

Index